from paddy to studs

Recent Titles in Contributions in Ethnic Studies
Series Editor: Leonard W. Doob

Operation Wetback: The Mass Deportation of Mexican Undocumented
Workers in 1954
Juan Ramon Garcia

The Navajo Nation
Peter Iverson

An Unacknowledged Harmony: Philo-Semitism and the Survival of European
Jewry
Alan Edelstein

America's Ethnic Politics
Joseph S. Roucek and Bernard Eisenberg, editors

Minorities and the Military: A Cross-National Study in World Perspective
Warren L. Young

The Emergence of Ethnicity: Cultural Groups and Social Conflict in Israel
Eliezer Ben-Rafael

Minority Aging: Sociological and Social Psychological Issues
Ron C. Manuel, editor

From Colonia to Community: The History of Puerto Ricans in New York
City, 1917–1948
Virginia E. Sánchez Korrol

Human Rights, Ethnicity, and Discrimination
Vernon Van Dyke

Year of Crisis, Year of Hope: Russian Jewry and the Pogroms of 1881–1882
Stephen M. Berk

A War of Words: Chicano Protest in the 1960s and 1970s
John C. Hammerback, Richard J. Jensen, and Jose Angel Gutierrez

Hibernia America: The Irish and Regional Cultures
Dennis Clark

from paddy to studs

Irish-American Communities
in the Turn of the Century Era,
1880 to 1920

Edited by timothy j. meagher

CONTRIBUTIONS IN ETHNIC STUDIES, NUMBER 13

GREENWOOD PRESS
New York • Westport, Connecticut • London

Library of Congress Cataloging-in-Publication Data
Main entry under title:

From Paddy to Studs.

(Contributions in ethnic studies, ISSN 0196-7088; no. 13)
Bibliography: p.
Includes index.
1. Irish Americans—History—Addresses, essays, lectures. 2. Irish Americans—
Social conditions—Addresses, essays, lectures. 3. United States—Social conditions—
1865–1918—Addresses, essays, lectures.
I. Meagher, Timothy J. II. Series.
E184.I6F76   1986   973'.049162   85-27304
ISBN 0-313-24670-X (lib. bdg. : alk. paper)

Library of Congress Catalog Card Number: 85-27304
ISBN: 0-313-24670-X
ISSN: 0196-7088

First published in 1986

Greenwood Press, Inc.
88 Post Road West, Westport, Connecticut 06881

Printed in the United States of America

The paper used in this book complies with the Permanent Paper Standard issued by the
National Information Standards Organization (Z39.48-1984).

10   9   8   7   6   5   4   3   2   1

To Mary Christine Towey, Margaret Costello,
Charles McDermott, and Louise McDermott Saulsbury

contents

Tables   ix

Acknowledgments   xi

Series Foreword   xiii

1. Introduction
   Timothy J. Meagher   1

2. "Man Overboard": Change and Stability in Post Famine Ireland
   Kevin O'Neill   27

3. "They Do Not Differ Greatly": The Pattern of Community Development among the Irish in Late Nineteenth Century Lowell, Massachusetts
   Brian C. Mitchell   53

4. Irish, American, Catholic: Irish-American Identity in Worcester, Massachusetts, 1880 to 1920
   Timothy J. Meagher   75

5. Intrepid Men: Three Philadelphia Irish Leaders, 1880 to 1920
   Dennis J. Clark   93

6. The Development of Catholic Identity among Irish Americans in Chicago, 1880 to 1920
   Ellen Skerrett   117

7. Kerry Patch Revisited: Irish Americans in St. Louis in
    the Turn of the Century Era
    Martin G. Towey   139

8. Exiles of Confidence: The Irish-American Community of
    San Francisco, 1880 to 1920
    Timothy Sarbaugh   161

9. Conclusion
    Timothy J. Meagher   181

    Bibliographical Essay   189

    Index   195

    About the Contributors   201

tables

2.1. Estimate of Relative Sizes of Agricultural Classes, 1841–
1881   31

7.1. St. Louis Occupational Statistics: 1900 Census   148

acknowledgments

A collection of essays is truly a collective effort and I would thus like to first thank all the authors who contributed to this collection. I thank them not only for their excellent work, but for their patience with my panicky entreaties and their prompt responses to my requests. I am grateful to Greenwood Press for many reasons, but perhaps the most important is the opportunity they gave me to become friends with so many excellent scholars who are also very generous people.

I appreciate, too, the efforts of those who have helped to prepare this manuscript. Teresa Cushing and Beth McNeill typed the manuscript and labored faithfully, cheerfully, speedily, and efficiently under the pressure of deadlines. I am thankful for their great contribution.

I would also like to thank a number of historians who offered their advice at various stages of this project: my advisors at Brown University, Howard Chudacoff and James T. Patterson; my colleagues at Worcester Polytechnic Institute, especially James P. Hanlan and Peter Onuf; my good friend Roy Rosenzweig; and a number of distinguished professors of Irish American history, James P. Walsh, Lawrence Mc-Caffrey, Jay Dolan, Kerby Miller, and David N. Doyle. I am also very grateful to James M. O'Toole of the Archives of the Archdiocese of Boston for his expert editing of portions of the manuscript.

Not all of my advice has come from professionals. I am also indebted to three close friends who are immigrants or the children of immigrants and who have helped me to understand the joys and sorrows of new-comers and their American born children. Eric Law, Lester Wong, and Vichit Souvanpong have offered me more than information and insights—they have also been great and good friends whose confidence and affection I cherish.

The same might be said of friends like Warren Leon, Cindy Robinson, Theresa McBride, and John Flessas whose support and comfort have been invaluable to me in some of the dark days that afflict every scholar. Finally, of course, my family, my father and mother, Hon. John H. Meagher and Elizabeth C. Meagher, and my brothers and sisters, Sean, Dermot, Andrew, Padric, and Mary, have been a continuing source of love and strength.

SERIES FOREWORD

"Contributions in Ethnic Studies" focuses upon the problems that arise when peoples with different cultures and goals come together and interact productively or tragically. The modes of adjustment or conflict are various, but usually one group dominates or attempts to dominate the other. Eventually some accommodation is reached, but the process is likely to be long and for the weaker group painful. No one scholarly discipline monopolizes the research necessary to comprehend these intergroup relations. The emerging analysis, consequently, inevitably is of interest to historians, social scientists, psychologists, and psychiatrists.

The experiences of every ethnic group that has migrated to the United States have been somewhat similar and dissimilar in many respects. The Irish whose background in Ireland and whose successes and frustrations in six American communities are described in these pages originally left their own country, as every school child knows, after suffering the "Great Potato Famines" of the 1840s. They have come from a rich tradition, with its own mythology and folklore, which has included such modern literary figures as Yeats and Joyce as well as courageous rebels such as Parnell and Pearse. In the United States they have faced the hostility of Yankees, WASPs, and other so-called Americans. They have been exploited and humiliated. They have remained loyal to their religion, in this instance an active and strong Catholicism. They have formed their own hyphenated organizations. As the title of the book cryptically suggests, they have been socially and economically mobile. They have made significant contributions to American culture.

Aside from sharing the fate of other immigrants, the "American Celts" have also been somewhat unique. When they arrived, they did not have to learn another language: they spoke a pleasant version of English. Most of them continued to have a passionate, action-oriented interest in Ireland, especially as their countrymen back home struggled to secure independence from England and, more recently, as the tragic, intractable conflict in Northern Ireland dragged on. They have not forgotten and will never forget what they or their ancestors endured in the old country. They have been outstanding in local, state, and national politics. They have had no prejudice against vaudeville, boxing, or alcoholic beverages.

The editor of this volume himself first surveys conditions in Ireland at the turn of the century. Then he has wisely sought to avoid generalizations about "the Irish" in the United States by enlisting, instead, competent scholars to relate the history of these people in the critically important cities of Lowell, Worcester, Philadelphia, Chicago, and—a happier place for them—San Francisco. Their reception and reaction in these communities have been multifarious—for better or worse—as a result not only of preexisting and changing economic and political conditions there, but also of other ethnic groups simultaneously accommodating themselves to American society: Italians, Greeks, Germans, French Canadians, Poles, and Asians. As ever, both the social context and the attributes of an ethnic group have affected their inner thoughts, their deep emotions, and their overt behavior.

Leonard W. Doob

1   timothy j. meagher

introduction

It was June 26, 1916; the summer was new and the weather balmy and pleasant in Chicago. In a modest but respectable home on the South Side, Patrick J. Lonigan "his feet planted on the back porch railing sat tilted back in his chair enjoying his stogy." Lonigan's son, "Studs," and his daughter, Frances, were to graduate from St. Patrick's grammar school that night. Studs was sneaking smokes in the bathroom and Frances and Lonigan's wife, Mary, were hurrying to complete last minute preparations for the ceremony. It was a good time, then, for "Old Man" Lonigan to escape to the back porch, enjoy the comfortable night air, take a few drags on his cigar, and reflect.

Perhaps because his children were taking one of their first long steps to adulthood, or because he caught sight of some children playing in a nearby schoolyard, Lonigan began to recall the days when he, himself, had been a "young shaver" thirty or forty years before. He thought of his father, an "impoverished greenhorn," and the house his family had lived in, a house so drafty and cold that he and his siblings often had to sleep with their clothes on. Yet "even with all the privations, those were the days," thought Lonigan, as he reminisced about the parish picnics, the old songs, and the "boys that hung out at Kiely's saloon."

Lonigan took a meditative drag on his stogy and "informed himself that time was a funny thing." "Old Man Time just walked along and he didn't even blow how do you do through his whiskers. He just walked on past you. Things just change." Lonigan, a painting contractor, had fought his way up to "a station where there weren't no real serious problems like poverty." He had moved to a comfortable home on a decent street, leaving his old neighborhood and all the old Irish districts to the new groups, Poles, Italians, or Blacks who were pouring into the city. He was wealthy enough to dream of taking a trip back to the old country, but neither he nor anyone else doubted his allegiances. He was proud to proclaim himself: "a good Catholic and a good American." In short, he was "comfortable and content." Yet there was something missing, Lonigan admitted, "something gone from a fellow's life." Perhaps it was simply the excitement of youth. But maybe it was something more, another kind of life, and a different kind of people that he had left behind in Chicago's inner city neighborhoods thirty or forty years before, "Things change . . . just change," he mused sadly.[1]

There were thousands, perhaps millions, of men and women like Patrick Lonigan scattered throughout America in 1916. Like him they had grown up with America's burgeoning cities, reached maturity at the dawn of a new century, and and begun to settle into middle age on the eve of the First World War. Like Lonigan too, many members of this new generation had moved up the occupational ladder, beyond the impoverished status of their immigrant parents, to "where there weren't any real serious problems like poverty" anymore. They could take pride in that, and pride in the prominence of their fellow Irish Americans in politics, religion, business, organized labor, the theater, and athletics. What Daniel Patrick Moynihan and Nathan Glazer said of the Irish in New York could easily have been said about the Irish throughout the United States: "There were sixty or seventy years" straddling the turn of the century "when the Irish were everywhere."[2]

Yet when Patrick Lonigan mused on how things had "changed . . . just changed" he seemed as much befuddled, perhaps a little sad, as proud. He and millions of Irish Americans like him were trying to take the measure of those changes which had transformed their lives. They were trying to understand how and why such changes had occurred and what those changes meant for their own and their children's futures. They were also struggling to sort out what was new, what was enduring, and what of their old life had been lost forever.

In the words of William Shannon, the American Irish in the five decades spanning the nineteenth and twentieth centuries were caught in an "ambiguous, indeterminate state." Their links to the old country seemed to become attenuated as the floodtide of Irish immigration passed its crest and began to recede. Nevertheless, they were still conscious of their distinctiveness. If they were not foreigners, however, nor yet "true" Americans, who then were they? Inevitably such questions of identity became entangled in the dilemma of their changing social and political roles. No longer the newest of the new immigrants or the poorest of the poor, they were also not accepted by America's native stock elite in many parts of the country. Suspended somewhere between the newer races and the Mayflower descendants, they were in Shannon's phrase "the closest to being in while still being out."[3]

Irish-American efforts to resolve their dilemmas of identity and role at the turn of the century did not occur in a vacuum. Indeed, this Irish-American quest took place just when their ancestral home and their new home reached critical crossroads in their histories. In the seventy years from the Famine to the Easter Rebellion, Ireland moved inexorably if erratically from colonial subservience to independent nationhood. At the same time a quieter, but no less fundamental, revolution was remaking rural Irish society. The hapless cottier class of the pre-Famine era virtually disappeared. Stringent marital customs previously limited to the largest farmers hardened into universal norms. In sum, the feckless anarchic life of pre-Famine Ireland seemed to give way to a new Puritanism and cold calculation. At the same time changes were occurring in America which were even more profound if only because they marked a critical watershed in the history of the world's greatest power. Between 1870 and 1920 the United States was transformed from a rural agricultural society, peopled largely by Western Europeans or their descendants, to an urban industrial colossus, home to millions of newcomers from all parts of Europe and many parts of Asia. The nation had also moved from a parttime, often ineffective, player in hemispheric squabbles to a fulltime, if sometimes reluctant, power in world politics. The Irish-American quest to define their identity and role thus took place in an environment of fundamental and turbulent change, change that could not help but influence their search.[4]

Surprisingly, though William Shannon first pointed out the significance of the turn of the century era as a transitional period more than two decades ago, the history of American Celts in those critical years remains only sketchily depicted and vaguely understood. Existing scholarship on the Irish Americans in the late nineteenth and early twentieth century tends to be fragmented and disconnected. There are excellent studies of social mobility, the Irish role in the church, Irish-American support for Irish nationalism, and Irish politics in American cities, but almost no studies that link together these and other facets of Irish life on the national, regional, or even community level.[5]

The absence of community studies is perhaps the most serious deficiency. Such studies provide the very kind of analysis, the examination of a wide variety of interrelated aspects of Irish-American life with a sensitivity to changing environmental contexts, which is now missing in the historical study of Irish Americans at the turn of the century. They also establish the building blocks for larger regional or national interpretations. Nevertheless, though Oscar Handlin's path-breaking study of the Irish in mid-nineteenth century Boston has been replicated elsewhere, few historians of Irish-American communities have seen fit to extend their studies beyond the Civil War, or, at the very least, beyond 1880.[6]

In the past the prevailing "assimilationist ideology" in American history or social science may have been responsible for such neglect. If, in Robert Park's words, "in America it has become proverbial that a Pole, Lithuanian or Norwegian cannot be distinguished in the second generation from an American born of native parents," why would an historian or social scientist even attempt to continue to trace the history of ethnic groups or communities which no longer existed, not to mention the problem of how to conduct such an investigation.[7]

Recently historians and other social scientists have begun to question that assimilationist ideology. They have begun to appreciate the persistence of ethnic loyalties and culture in the face of modernizing processes which once seemed to doom such "irrational" allegiances and behavior. Still this new appreciation of ethnicity's enduring importance in American life has fostered few investigations of Irish-American communities in the post-Famine era. The reasons for this continued neglect are not easy to detect. Perhaps immigrants are simply more interesting than their children. Daniel Patrick Moynihan and Nathan Glazer have speculated that "popular writing, scholarly writing, novels and plays all seem to find the beginning of the process of assimilation most interesting. It is when the immigrants first arrive that everyone is aware of them. By the time the problems are less severe or have become largely personal, local color has been dissipated in the flush of Americanization and writers find less to write about."[8]

A more important reason has been the continuing failure of students of Irish-American life, or, indeed, of American ethnicity in general, to perceive American ethnic groups as dynamic, historical phenomenons. Ethnic values, customs, and allegiances were not implanted in the souls of American ethnic group members long ago in some far away country to be either simply washed away or stubbornly retained in the new environment. As William Yancey, Eugene Ericksen, and Richard Juliani have argued, "rather than a constant ascribed trait that is inherited from the past, ethnicity is the result of a process which continues to unfold." Yancey and his associates suggest that ethnic groups continually make and remake themselves in their ongoing efforts to adjust and adapt to new conditions. Political scientist Donald Horowitz echoes such sentiments in his more specific discussions of ethnic identification. Horowitz contends that ethnic identities are not fixed in a set pattern from the beginning of the migration process but are in fact remarkably fluid. While conceding that such identities are not "infinitely malleable," he nonetheless observes the "alacrity" which groups display in adjusting their identities over time, broadening their identifications to include members of new groups or narrowing them to exclude others as circumstances dictate. From this perspective, which emphasizes the dynamic historical nature of ethnic groups, it is clear that it is not enough to analyze only the immigrants, the beginning of an ethnic group's history, and contemporary ethnics, the present day conclusion of a group's story. It is necessary to study the "middle years" of a group's evolution in order to fully understand the nature of its development. Yet for the Irish, and for most other ethnic groups in America, for that matter, the "beginnings" and "ends" of their stories are far better documented than the "middles".[9]

There is another serious consequence of this failure to investigate Irish-American communities in the turn of the century era. Two decades ago William Shannon noted significant differences between the Irish-American experience on the East Coast, specifically Boston, and the fortunes of Irishmen in the west, most notably San Francisco. Recently historians such as Lawrence McCaffrey, David Doyle, and James Walsh have aggressively reasserted the significance of those variations. They have severely criticized studies which suggest that the history of the New England, principally Boston, Irish was typical of Irish-American experience throughout the country. These historians have pointed out the severe handicaps which confronted Irishmen on the East Coast, particularly in New England: maturing economies offering few opportunities; recurrent and powerful nativist movements; established, entrenched native stock elites which monopolized social status and economic power. Overwhelmed by these difficulties, McCaffrey contends, Irishmen in New England remained mired in poverty and sank into a sullen despair, viewing outsiders with a suspicion bordering on paranoia. By contrast,

Doyle and Walsh argue, Irishmen on the West Coast enjoyed the benefits of new dynamic economies and the fluid social structure of "instant cities." They quickly achieved considerable economic, political, and social success, which in turn bred an openness and confidence among western Irishmen unknown among their fellow Celts in the East. So far this hypothesis has been supported largely by evidence drawn from studies of Irish communities in the Famine migration era or slightly later. With the absence of community studies for later periods it has been impossible to test the continuing relevance of this distinction in the important transitional years of Irish-American history.[10]

The purpose of this collection of essays is to address both of these critical questions in Irish-American historiography: the importance of the turn of the century era as a watershed in the history of Irish-American communities; and the significance of geographical variations in the Irish-American experience. The collection begins with a broad analysis of the social, cultural, and political revolutions which transformed Ireland in this period. All of the succeeding essays focus on the histories of individual Irish-American communities during all or part of that era. They should then provide a good test of Shannon's hypothesis that that period was a critical juncture in Irish-American history. Perhaps as important, the essays were chosen to include analyses of communities in all the major regions of Irish-American settlement: New England, the Middle Atlantic states, the Midwest, and the Far West. Even the two essays on the New England Irish are studies of Irish-American communities in ethnically plural and medium sized cities, not the Irish dominated Boston metropolis which has stood so long as representative of Irish history for all of New England and, indeed, all of America. With this kind of geographical spread it will be possible to sift out both the common themes and regional variations in Irish-American experiences throughout the country.

If this collection addresses specific problems in Irish-American history, it, perhaps, also has a wider significance. By probing the "middle years" of Irish-American history, it begins to fill a gap not only in the historiography of Irish Americans but in the study of American ethnicity in general. It is important not only to the understanding of American ethnics, however, but also to the investigation of a critical transitional period in the life of the nation. Historians of that era discovered long ago that the Irish were, indeed, "everwhere" as Moynihan and Glazer have claimed. It is almost impossible to analyze the major trends or movements of the late nineteenth or early twentieth centuries without at some point stumbling across America's Celts. To historians of American politics in the late nineteenth century the Irish were the quintessential Democrats and the foremost practitioners of machine politics. The recent study of nineteenth century American social mobility literally began with the Irish, and analyses of family life at the turn of the century frequently focus on them as the principal examples of immigrant adjustment to an urban industrial world. Labor historians cannot escape examining them in detail, and students of American Catholicism can hardly write the history of the church without discussing them.[11]

Because of this scholarship, and the few recent studies that focus directly on Celtic Americans in the late nineteenth or early twentieth centuries, a great deal more is known about Irish Americans in this period than when William Shannon first wrote. Nevertheless, despite the evidence and insights derived from this literature, these works ultimately raise more questions than they answer about such important aspects of Irish-American life as the emergence of a new American born Irish generation, rising Irish occupational status, Irish American efforts to sort out their loyalties, and Celtic relations with groups both above and below them on the social scale. Rather than offering firm conclusions about these transitional years in Irish-American history, the literature of the last twenty years provides only a useful starting point for the further discussion of Irish-American communities in that period.

Allusions to the emergence of the second generation Irish figure prominently in most historical investigations of the Irish in the turn of the century period. Census statistics provide evidence of their growing numbers. By 1880, the American born Irish already outnumbered Irish immigrants in the United States, and in the next two decades the gap continued to widen. Between 1880 and 1900 the number of American born Irish men and women rose by almost 30 percent. At the latter date, there were nearly twice as many second generation Irish in America as foreign born Celts.[12]

Nevertheless, such statistics may underestimate the continuing substantial presence of Irish immigrants in Irish-American communities, while overestimating the pace of the second generation's emergence. Forty years after the Famine immigration of the 1840s and 1850s, the Irish born population was still growing. Until 1890, the institutionalization of emigration in Ireland sent more than enough Irish newcomers to the United States to replace the dying members of the Famine era migration. As important, almost all of these new Irish immigrants were adults, while a large proportion of the second generation counted in census statistics were children or adolescents. Thus while the total number of American born Irish was more than double the number of immigrants in 1900, second generation Irishmen in the work force outnumbered Irish born workers by only about 30 percent in that year. The influence of second generation Irish men and women in their ethnic communities cannot be measured, of course, by numbers alone. As early as the 1880s, they had captured powerful posts in the church, politics, and the labor movement. Nevertheless, the emergence of the American born generation and conversely the declining strength of the immigrants appeared to have occurred more slowly than previously thought.[13]

Paralleling the maturing of the new generation—indeed in large measure a result of that trend—was the noticeable improvement in the economic status of the Irish. Few changes in Irish-American life during this period seemed so noticeable to contemporaries. Finley Peter Dunne's gentle satire, Harrigan and Hart's broad farce, and Thomas Beer's savage sarcasm all took aim at the pretensions of the new Irish middle class. A new term, "lace curtain," even crept into the American vocabulary in the 1890s to describe these upwardly mobile Irish. Statistics suggest the real occupational progress made by Irishmen which was reflected in the new popular images. E. P. Hutchinson's review of occupational statistics from the United States Census of 1900 reveals that the American born Irish were overrepresented in modestly respectable low white collar positions such as clerks, salesmen, teachers, and bookkeepers. By contrast American born Celts in the same year were underrepresented in poorer jobs which had once been the marks of their people's degraded status.[14]

Nevertheless, Irish Americans were hardly shining examples of the American myth of rags to riches success. While some Irishmen made impressive progress up the American occupational ladder, a substantial number made little or none. As David Doyle has pointed out, no foreign stock group in 1900 (foreign stock includes both the foreign born and the children of foreign born parents) was more widely dispersed throughout the ranks of the American occupational hierarchy than the Irish. That year a full 25 percent of the immigrant men were unskilled laborers. Perhaps as important the social mobility studies of the last two decades have indicated that even the apparent gains of the American born Irish were limited and tenuous. Second generation Irish occupational mobility seemed small when compared to the rapid rise of such other ethnics as the Germans, Scandinavians, and even recently arrived Jews. These studies reveal that second generation Irishmen were also less successful than members of other ethnic groups in holding on to the gains they had made. The evidence of these analyses indicates that the Irish "slipped" more frequently from white collar posts back into manual labor.[15]

This depiction of Irish failure, like the previous portrayal of Irish-American success, may be overdrawn. A number of historians, including David Doyle and James Walsh, have argued that the recent gloomy picture of Irish-American economic difficulties is drawn almost exclusively from analyses of Celtic occupational mobility in eastern cities. Doyle and Walsh contend, and R. A. Burchell has substantially proved, that Irish Americans were far more successful farther west than on the East Coast. Doyle and Walsh suggest that the so-called Irish-American economic failure was less the result of their own defects than the lack of opportunities in the eastern cities where so many of them lived.[16]

Whatever the precise dimensions of Irish-American economic progress, it is nonetheless hard to deny that, among some Irish Americans at the turn of the century, attitudes about a respectable standard of living, proper conduct, and their public image were clearly changing. Lace curtain may have been less an occupational status than a state of mind. As William Shannon stated, the term lace curtain "connoted above all a self conscious anxious attempt to create and maintain a certain level of gentility . . . to live down the opprobrium deriving from the brawling hard drinking and raffish manners of the shanty Irish of an earlier generation." Even Irish immigrant workers of lowly economic status were straining, and according to John Modell's study of Irish-American family budgets, succeeding in raising their standard of living to an American level by 1900. Yet it was not so much what Irish Americans did consume, as what they did not, which best reflected the spread of lace curtain mores in the Celtic American population. Specifically, nearly 100,000 Irish Americans had taken the pledge to swear off alcoholic beverages by the later 1890s. When delegates representing these total abstainers gathered in New York City in 1895, a *New York Times* reporter noted with some surprise that though the participants were all Irish, they "did not look Irish." Indeed, he remarked, they "all looked like substantial American citizens."[17]

Old traditions were hard to shake, however. Most Irish Americans continued to drink, for example. Indeed, more Irish Americans suffered from alcoholic diseases or were incarcerated for drunkenness than members of almost every other American ethnic group until well into the twentieth century. Even Irish Americans who tried not to look Irish felt the influences of their ancestral island's culture. Reflecting attitudes embedded deep in Ireland's Catholicism, the most convinced Irish Catholic exponents of temperance cast a jaundiced eye on the race for riches that seemed pervasive in late nineteenth century American society. They worried that the zeal for self improvement among their total abstainers and other Catholics might easily turn to a spiritually corrosive lust for wealth and status. Some Irish Catholics also feared that in America, just as in Ireland, where the economy and society were so thoroughly dominated by Protestants, Catholics might easily be tempted to downplay or deny their faith in order to curry the favor of their Protestant neighbors. As Paul Messbarger has pointed out Catholics thus had their own Horatio Alger myth. In the Catholic version young men had to overcome the temptation to abandon their faith as well as all the other usual obstacles of heroic proportions, before they gained the rewards of true virtue.[18]

By 1900, then, Irish Americans were clearly enmeshed in a process of transition. Yet that transition is difficult to chart. The new generation was rapidly growing to maturity, but when did they begin to dominate Irish-American communities? Irish men and women were climbing America's occupational ladder, but how fast? Many of them sought a new respectability, but what cultural baggage did they leave behind forever, what did they fight to retain, and what did they simply find impossible to abandon? The paradoxes could be extended. Irish Americans, particularly the second generation Irish, participated eagerly in the new American urban mass culture. It was a Casey after all who was at the bat, a Sullivan or a Corbett in the ring, and Harrigans, Harts, Rooneys, and Cohans romping on vaudeville stages. The same American born Irish generation still adhered to norms inherited from Ireland, however, in making the most intimate decisions of their lives. They married late, later than native stock Americans and almost as late as their distant cousins in Ireland. Once married they also had far more children than Yankee couples and nearly as many as foreign born Irish parents. If there was much that was new in the new Irish Americans at the turn of the century, there was also much that was old.[19]

Little wonder therefore that those same Irish Americans should find it so difficult to define a suitable identity for themselves in the late nineteenth and early twentieth centuries. Were they Irish, American, Catholic, members of the working class, or some or all of these elements combined into a single self conception? The process of sorting out their allegiances had proven difficult enough for their immigrant predecessors of the Famine era, but at least all of the Famine immigrants remembered the old country with a concrete vividness and shared a uniformly low status. The later Irish, half immigrant and half American born and fragmented into a number of social classes, were a more diverse and divided people. For them the effort to define their loyalties and a comfortable identity would be far more complicated.

Irish-American involvement in Irish nationalist movements in the late nineteenth and early twentieth centuries suggests some of these complications. Historians agree that American Celts displayed enthusiastic interest in Ireland's quest for independence throughout much of this period. They also agree that the motives for this Irish-American interest in the homeland grew as much from the Hibernians' perceptions of their own American social, political, and economic circumstances as Ireland's plight. They do not agree, however, on what those motives were nor the American circumstances that nourished them.

The most provocative studies of Irish nationalism in America have focused on the Land League and Home Rule movements of the 1880s. Thomas N. Brown was one of the first historians to probe this decade of intense and widespread Irish involvement in the Irish nationalist cause. He has suggested that wealthy Irish Americans, many of them American born, took the lead in the nationalist movement in order to improve their standing in the eyes of native stock Americans. As Michael Davitt shrewdly observed at the time, and Brown later echoed, ambitious Irish Americans felt they could not achieve true acceptance and respect in the new world until the shame of Ireland's slavery had been wiped away in the old. Equally important to these respectable Irish Americans was how Ireland won its freedom. Violence would only reinforce hostile stereotypes of brawling Irishmen, but a constitutional and respectable agitation giving birth to a modern Ireland modeled on American principles would earn new respect for Irish Americans.[20]

Brown's analysis of Irish-American nationalism in the 1880s has long been the principal interpretation of the American nationalist crusade in that decade, but he has had his critics. Eric Foner has pointed to a very different group of supporters who backed the nationalist agitation for very different motives. Foner noted the strong support for Irish nationalism among Irish America's working classes. Rather than seeking respectability, these workers followed the lead of Patrick Ford who seized upon the Irish nationalist agitation as a rallying point for economic reform throughout the English speaking world. Ford envisioned an Ireland not only free of British interference, but revolutionized according to the radical theories of Henry George and thus an opening wedge for the application of George's theories to the English, and more importantly the American, economies.[21]

Irish-American nationalism did not end with Parnell's fall, but few historians have attempted to analyze the motives and goals of Irish Americans involved in nationalist causes after that date. There has been, for example, very little scholarly interest in the fortunes of Irish-American nationalism during the 1890s and early 1900s. One can only guess that nationalist leaders in America were unable to rouse the interest of most Irish Americans in Ireland's cause during this period. Historians have paid considerably more attention to the tide of nationalist fervor which swept America after Ireland's Easter Rebellion in 1916 and peaked after the end of the First World War in 1918. This literature, however, focuses largely on elite opinion within the Irish American population or the Irish Question as a diplomatic issue in the relations between Great Britain and the United States. It is still unclear why the Irish-American masses, many of them, by that date, American born and economically comfortable, should react so passionately and unanimously to Ireland's fight for freedom. Perhaps it was because Ireland had its first real chance for some form of independence in four centuries, or because Woodrow Wilson's rhetoric had provided Irish Americans with a unique opportunity to harmonize Ireland's cause with America's wartime ideals of self-determination for all nations. In their own eyes (if not in Woodrow Wilson's) Irish Americans could support Ireland's cause not as undigested hyphenates fighting for a foreign cause, but as patriotic Americans pursuing a logical extension of America's basic beliefs.[22]

The last point is significant, for if Irish Americans remained loyal to Ireland, America—not Ireland—was, nonetheless, now their home. In struggling to define their identity, it was even more important for them to clarify their allegiances to the United States than to sort out their loyalties to the old country. Because they were conscious that their foreign origins or alien religion made their American loyalties seem suspect to native stock Americans, Irish-American expressions of patriotism in this era often bordered on jingoism. Monsignor Denis O'Connell, for example, trumpeted the world mission of the American people with all the fervor of the most convinced Anglo-Saxon imperialist in the 1890s. Two decades later George M. Cohan, the second generation Irish "Yankee Doodle Boy," wrapped himself in the "Grand Old Flag" and made himself the symbol of patriotism for an entire American generation. Such superpatriotism was not confined to church leaders or vaudevillians but appeared to be widely based among Irish Americans, especially in the twentieth century. The best evidence of the spread of this fierce American patriotism was the growth of the Knights of Columbus. Mixing militant Catholicism with American superpatriotism, the Knights grew from their founding in 1882 to over half a million members by 1920. Though not exclusively Irish, the Knights' strongest support came largely from American born and upwardly mobile Irish Americans, suggesting the deeply rooted commitment of the new generation of prosperous Celts to the land of their birth.[23]

Some Irish Americans, particularly recent immigrants, were less enthusiastic about their new home. Kerby Miller has discovered an intense sense of alienation among thousands of Irish immigrants in late nineteenth and twentieth century America. For many of them, the United States would never be their home; they would always be "exiles." A smaller number, perhaps, saw America not simply as a haven but as a base to promote the liberation of their real homeland, Ireland. These fierce nationalists were interested in American politics only as a forum for embarrassing England and helping Ireland. Congressman Finerty of Chicago reflected their views aptly when he dismissed one House session with the quip: "Only American business today." For a larger group, including even men and women who felt some commitment to the United States, Ireland's tragic history of colonial subjugation was a more powerful influence than contemporary Irish interests. These Irish Americans could not in good conscience tolerate America's own slide toward imperialism in the late 1890s and early 1900s and thus severely criticized the colonial adventures of the United States.[24]

Irish-American superpatriots and fervid Irish nationalists in exile often had one loyalty in common, allegiance to Catholicism. Catholicism, of course, was rooted in Irish tradition. Indeed the identifications were so intertwined in Ireland, that to be Irish was to be Catholic and vice versa. For Irishmen in America, however, fidelity to Catholicism did not necessarily mean a commitment to preserving Irish culture or advancing Irish nationalist interests. Irish-American bishops like John Ireland or Cardinal James Gibbons even discouraged such Celtic attachments lest their religion seem too "foreign" to native stock Americans. The best way to Catholicize America, Ireland proclaimed, was to Americanize Catholicism. Conservative bishops like Michael A. Corrigan of New York and Bernard McQuaid of Rochester were more fearful that heretical American notions might infect their church, but they too looked forward to the emergence of an American, if strictly orthodox, Catholic church in the United States. They were also severely skeptical of militant Irish nationalist societies. Such a vision was not limited to members of the American Catholic hierarchy. Despite their fierce devotion to the Catholic church, the largely American born and upwardly mobile laymen who swelled the ranks of the Catholic Total Abstinence Union and the Knights of Columbus also seemed indifferent, or even hostile, to the preservation of Irish culture. Unlike many other American ethnic groups, then, Irish Americans did not feel the need to preserve their traditional Irish culture in order to preserve their faith.[25]

Nevertheless, no matter how Americanized they may have become, the fidelity of Irish Americans to their religion prevented them from entering the American mainstream. By the early twentieth century, if not long before, the walls of a Catholic ghetto had begun to rise, enclosing within a distinctly Catholic, if American, subculture and a separate Catholic subsociety. Despite a recent flurry of popular interest in this ghetto, its origins remain obscure. Specifically, it is not clear whether the Vatican, the American hierarchy, the laity, or anti-Catholic nativists played the decisive role in its formation. It is also not clear if the defensiveness and suspicion characteristic of the Catholic ghetto mentality varied in intensity from region to region or even city to city. The ghetto once created, however, had a long life in many parts of the United States. Gary Wills remembering his Catholic boyhood in the 1950s recalls that "we grew up different . . . there were places we went and others did not . . . and also places we never went and others could." We were members of a church, Wills contends, that was "stranded in America, out of place."[26]

Less enduring than their Catholic allegiances, but critically important in the turn of the century era, were Irish-American loyalties to the working class. Irish Americans supplied many of the members and much of the leadership for the Knights of Labor in the 1880s. They also provided significant support for labor political campaigns such as Henry George's race for mayor of New York City in 1886. Two decades later Irish Americans ruled fifty of the 160 national unions affiliated with the A. F. of L., and Irish-American legislators led the fight for social and economic reforms in state houses across the Northeast and Midwest.[27]

Irish American workers may have participated eagerly in the labor movement and reform politics in the turn of the century era but the strength of their loyalties to their class—their class consciousness—is hard to measure. Indeed, few questions have provoked more bitter historical debate recently than the attempt to determine the class consciousness of all American workers in the nineteenth century. Part of the problem lies in the fuzziness of the early labor movement's ideology, which seems a confusing mix of republican principles, class rhetoric, moral reform, and utopian nostrums. Recently labor historians like Leon Fink have argued that the Knights of Labor's philosophy had a greater coherence and sharper edge than previously thought. The extent of the Knights' radicalism, however, remains a controversial issue. It is also difficult to separate class interests from ethnic interests in early labor struggles, especially among a people like the Irish who were overwhelmingly blue collar workers in the 1870s and 1880s. Scattered evidence suggests, however, that even if many Irish Americans had, in fact, been class conscious and sympathetic to radicalism in the 1870s and 1880s, those sympathies had begun to dissipate by the early twentieth century. Fewer Irish Americans were blue collar workers by that time; fewer still were stuck at the bottom of the American economic hierarchy. There were other reasons for the decline of Irish-American radicalism as well, most notably: the Catholic church's virulent anti-socialist crusade in the 1910s, and the success Irish Americans enjoyed in pursuit of their own, exclusively ethnic, political interests. For these reasons and perhaps others a powerful Irish radical tradition failed to take root in America. Nevertheless, it would be a mistake to ignore the importance of class interests and allegiances in Irish-American calculations of their identity.[28]

Irish American attempts to sort out their allegiances to Ireland, America, Catholicism, and the working class were often profoundly influenced by their relations with their American neighbors. Their interest in Ireland's plight, their blustering expressions of American patriotism, their construction of a Catholic ghetto, and their efforts to forge a united

working class were all to some degree or another affected by the attitudes of the diverse groups which surrounded them. Their relations
with those groups were changing, however, just as Irish Americans
themselves were changing. Indeed, the generational transition and upward social mobility of the Irish (no matter how slowly those processes
may have occurred) not only enhanced the confusion of their cultural
behavior but vaulted them into an indeterminate position suspended
somewhere between the new immigrants and the native stock Americans. The dilemmas Irish Americans confronted, therefore, included
more than choices between American and Irish norms, customs, values,
or even allegiances. They included decisions about how they should
relate to their neighbors. Should they seek to accommodate the native
stock elite (join the ins) or mobilize the new immigrants (lead the outs)?
Answers to this dilemma, as William Shannon implied, could best be
found in the roles Irish Americans played in urban politics and the
American Catholic church. In both settings American Celts struggled
almost constantly to define patterns of relations with other groups which
would best serve their interests.

The traditional depiction of Irish political relations with native stock
Protestants is a simple one of unremitting antagonism: Irish Democrat
versus native stock Republican; Celtic Boss versus WASP reformer; or
Hibernian rebel versus Yankee Brahmin. Such a portrayal, however, is
vastly oversimplified. It seems particularly inaccurate in describing the
political interaction between Protestants and Irish Catholics in western
states. In California, as James Walsh has stated, Irish Catholics
achieved political prominence quickly and easily, due in large part to
the relative absence of anti-immigrant (or at least anti-*European* immigrant) and anti-Catholic feeling there. Paul Kleppner has contended that
intense ethno-religious sentiments seemed to play little role in partisan
divisions throughout the entire west, not just in California. Characterizing Irish political relations with native stock Protestants in simple terms
of mutual antagonism seems to distort the history of many eastern Irish
communities as well as western ones. It ignores, for example, cities
where the Irish never achieved sufficient strength to challenge the local
WASP Republican political hegemony, such as in Philadelphia, and
thus were forced into practical compromises with the "enemy." Even
in New York where the Irish led Tammany machine seemed to dominate, the sources of the Hall's power appear fragile upon close inspec-
tion. Its success derived as much from negotiation and trading with a

number of factions, including various elite groups, as the mobilization of brute voting power. Finally, in Boston, where the characterization of unrelenting antagonism between Irish and Yankee has seemed most appropriate, recent research suggests a surprising degree of cooperation between the two groups in the late nineteenth century.[29]

While Irish political relations with native stock Protestants in the turn of the century era may have been a good deal better than previously imagined, their relations with the newer immigrants may have been a good deal worse. It is true that by the late 1920s, a number of diverse ethnic elements had been fused together in powerful Democratic coalitions throughout the United States. Nevertheless, Irish Americans were not always the principal builders of such coalitions. In Chicago, for example, Anton Cermak, a second generation Czech, assumed that role since none of the city's Irish Democratic leaders seemed capable of performing it. Even when Irish Americans were the principal architects of new multiethnic Democratic majorities, the construction of those alliances was often painful and difficult. In New York, despite the efforts of skillful Irish practitioners of "United Nations politics" like "Big Tim" Sullivan, Tammany actually lost votes among the new immigrants throughout the 1910s. In New England, Irish Democrats also experienced severe difficulties in luring French Canadians or Italians into their party until the 1920s.[30]

The problems Irish Americans encountered in dealing with the new immigrants should not be surprising. The diversity of languages and cultural traditions among the new ethnics posed truly monumental obstacles to effective coalition building. As important, however, Irish Americans had to try to satisfy the ambitions of the new groups without jeopardizing their own interests. Wealthy native stock Protestants who were not dependent on politics for income or status, could, perhaps, more easily yield political recognition to new groups than Irish Americans for whom politics was often their lifeblood. From that perspective, the successes of Irish-American politicians in helping to forge multiethnic coalitions, though more limited than once thought, are still impressive.[31]

Irish-American churchmen were more restricted in dealing with other American groups than Irish politicians, for they were responsible not merely to their own faithful but to their Vatican superiors as well. Nevertheless, the Irish led church's relations with American Protestants, for example, can no more be categorized in simplistic terms of unrelieved suspicion and hostility than could Celtic political relations with their WASP neighbors. Indeed, in the late 1880s and early 1890s a liberal movement appeared in American Catholicism seeking to bridge the social and cultural chasms which separated American Catholics and Protestants. The general outlines of this movement and the actions and attitudes of its leaders and principal opponents have been well documented. It seems clear for example that Irish-American bishops were divided over many of the questions raised by the liberal movement. Archbishop John Ireland and James Cardinal Gibbons emerged as Liberal Catholicism's principal spokesmen while Archbishop Corrigan of New York and Bishop Bernard McQuaid of Rochester were its most effective opponents. Much about this Liberal Catholic movement remains obscure, however. Most important, there has been little exploration of the connections between the movement's leaders and ordinary Catholic priests or laymen. Whether Liberal Catholicism was simply a factional quarrel fought out in the upper reaches of the American and Vatican hierarchy or a mass movement of broad dimensions is not yet known. Thomas McAvoy, one of the early historians of Liberal Catholicism, suggested two decades ago that the movement was strongest in the Midwest or Far West where lay Catholics enjoyed more prosperity and more amicable relations with their Protestant neighbors than their cousins in the East. There has been no serious attempt to test McAvoy's hypothesis, however, nor any new interpretations of the possible connections between the social and political circumstances of Catholic laymen and the policies of Liberal Catholic leaders.[32]

One of the principal issues in the debate over Liberal Catholicism centered on the place of foreign language Catholics in the American Church. Irish Catholic conservatives often looked to German and other Catholic ethnics for support in their battle against the Liberal Irish Americanizers. Yet even Irish Catholic conservatives objected to German Catholic proposals which threatened the balkanization of American Catholicism. The defeat of those proposals in 1891 may have prevented the American Church from cracking into separate ethnic fragments, but it did not resolve the problem of ethnic diversity confronting the Irish dominated church. Indeed, as the sources of American immigration shifted from Northern and Western to Southern and Eastern Europe the problem became even more difficult.[33]

The performance of Irish-American priests and bishops in handling this problem is difficult to judge. There is no doubt that some of them dealt with non-Irish Catholics roughly. The list of squabbles between German, French Canadian, Polish, Lithuanian, and Italian Catholics on the one hand and their Irish bishops on the other is a long litany. Some of these squabbles even erupted into open revolts leading to excommunications or the founding of schismatic churches. Nevertheless, just as Irish-American politicians may have been given too much credit in the past for their skillful dealings with the new immigrants, so Irish Catholic prelates may have been judged too severely for their handling of the newcomers. Recent research on the relations between Irish Catholic bishops and the new immigrants in Connecticut and Chicago suggests that Irish-American clerics displayed considerable respect and sensitivity for the ethnic traditions of the non-Irish members of their flock. The problems that did appear in those dioceses were often rooted in internal conflicts within the new immigrant groups themselves, rather than frictions between the hierarchy and the non-Irish ethnics.[34]

"The Irish, in short," William Shannon wrote in 1963, "stood at the opening of the twentieth century with a foot in each world. The desire to join the 'ins' conflicted with the desire to lead the 'outs.' The wish to climb socially ran counter to the impulse to champion the rebellious, restless poor." The dilemmas, he notes, could be extended virtually endlessly: "conventional success or frustrated insurgency; . . . assimilation or the chauvinism of the Irish community; . . . the American style idealism of Gibbons and Ireland or the clerical reaction of Corrigan and McQuaid," and on and on. As Shannon notes, the Irish "had come a long way in seventy years. They knew they still had a long way to go."[35]

NOTES

1. James T. Farrell, *Studs Lonigan: A Trilogy* (New York: Vanguard Press, 1935), pp. 12–20.

2. Nathan Glazer and Daniel P. Moynihan, *Beyond the Melting Pot: The Negroes, Puerto Ricans, Jews, Italians and Irish of New York City* (Cambridge, Mass.: M.I.T. Press, 1970), p. 217.

3. William Shannon, *The American Irish: A Political and Social Portrait* (New York: Collier Books, 1974), pp. 131–143.

4. Joseph Lee, *The Modernization of Irish Society* (Dublin: Gill and McMillan Co., 1973); George Dangerfield, *The Damnable Question: A Study of Anglo Irish Relations* (Boston: Little Brown and Co., 1976); Robert Wiebe, *The*

Search For Order: 1877–1920 (New York: Hill and Wang, 1967); Samuel P. Hays, *The Response to Industrialism 1885–1914* (Chicago: University of Chicago Press, 1957).

5. For studies of social mobility see Stefan Thernstrom, *The Other Bostonians: Poverty and Progress in the American Metropolis* (Cambridge: Harvard University Press, 1973) and Clyde and Salley Griffen, *Natives and Newcomers: The Structure of Opportunity in Mid Nineteenth Century Poughkeepsie, New York* (Cambridge: Harvard University Press, 1977). On the Irish role in the Catholic Church see, for example, Thomas T. McAvoy, *The Great Crisis in American Catholic History* (Chicago: Henry Regnery Co., 1957) and more recently Charles Shannabruch, *Chicago's Catholics: The Evolution of an American Identity* (Notre Dame, Ind.: University of Notre Dame Press, 1981) and Robert E. Curran, *Michael Augustine Corrigan and the Shaping of Conservative Catholicism in America 1878–1902* (New York: Arno Press, 1978). On Irish-American nationalism, see Thomas N. Brown, *Irish American Nationalism: 1870–1890* (Philadelphia: J. B. Lippincott, 1966) and Eric Foner, "Class Ethnicity and Radicalism in the Gilded Age: The Land League and Irish America," *Marxist Perspectives* Vol. I, no. 2 (Summer 1978), pp. 20–44. On Irish politics in American cities, see Ronald Formisano and Constance McLaughlin Burns, eds., *Boston, 1700–1980: The Evolution of Urban Politics* (Westport, Conn.: Greenwood Press, 1984), John Allswang, *A House for All Peoples* (Lexington, Ky.: University of Kentucky Press, 1971) and Nancy J. Weiss, *Charles Francis Murphy 1858–1927: Respectability and Responsibility in Tammany Politics* (Northampton, Mass.: Smith College, 1969).

6. Oscar Handlin, *Boston's Immigrants: A Study in Acculturation* (Cambridge, Mass.: Harvard University Press, 1959). Examples of other studies of mid-nineteenth century Irish immigrant communities include: Douglas V. Shaw, *The Making of an Immigrant City: Ethnic and Cultural Conflict in Jersey City, New Jersey 1850–1877* (New York: Arno Press, 1976); R. A. Burchell, *The San Francisco Irish: 1848–1880* (Berkeley, Calif.: University of California Press, 1980) and Jo Ellen Vinyard, *The Irish on the Urban Frontier: Detroit 1850–1880* (New York: Arno Press, 1976). The few recent studies of Irish communities in the turn of the century era remain unpublished dissertations. One such excellent dissertation by an author not included in this book is Margaret Connors, "Their Own Kind: Family and Community Life in Albany New York 1850–1915" (Ph.D. dissertation, Harvard University, 1975).

7. Rudolf Vecoli, "Ethnicity: A Neglected Dimension of American History" in Herbert Bass, ed., *The State of American History* (Chicago: Quadrangle Books, 1970), pp. 70–88. For Park's quote see Vecoli, "Ethnicity," pp. 77–78.

8. Moynihan and Glazer, *Beyond the Melting Pot,* p. 22.

9. William Yancey with Eugene Ericksen and Richard Juliani, "Emergent

Ethnicity: A review and Reformation,'' *American Sociological Review* (Vol. 41, No. 3 June 1976), p. 399; Donald Horowitz, "Ethnic Identity" in Nathan Glazer and Daniel P. Moynihan, eds., *Ethnicity: Theory and Experience* (Cambridge, Mass.: Harvard University Press, 1973), pp. 112–140 and Horowitz, "Cultural Movements and Ethnic Change," *Annals of the American Academy of Political and Social Science* Vol. 433 (September 1977), pp. 7–12. For sociological studies of contemporary ethnics see Andrew Greeley, *The Irish Americans: The Rise to Money and Power* (New York: Harper and Row, 1981); Richard Gambino, *Blood of My Blood: The Dilemmas of Italian Americans* (Garden City, N.Y.: Anchor Press, 1975); Michael Novak, *Rise of The Unmeltable Ethnics: Politics and Culture in the Seventies* (New York: McMillan, 1972); and Richard Krickus, *Pursuing the American Dream: White Ethnics and the New Populism* (Bloomington, Ind.: Indiana University Press, 1976). The few investigations of the "middle years" of other ethnic groups include largely contemporary sociological studies such as Irwin Child's *Italian or American: The Second Generation in Conflict* (New Haven: Yale University Press, 1943). One unique and concrete reason for the lack of studies of the middle years of Irish Americans, specifically, may have been the unavailability, until very recently, of manuscript schedules of United States Censuses beyond 1880. Vinyard, *Irish on the Urban Frontier* and R. A. Burchell, *The San Francisco Irish* are examples of studies tied closely to the manuscript schedules of United States Censuses from 1850 to 1880.

10. Shannon, *American Irish*, pp. 86–94, pp. 183–200; John Higham "Another Look at Nativism," *Catholic Historical Review* Vol. XLIV, No. 2 (July 1958) pp. 155–158; James P. Walsh, "The Irish in the New America: "Way Out West," in David Noel Doyle and Owen Dudley Edwards, eds., *America and Ireland, 1776–1976: The American Identity and the Irish Connection* (Westport, Conn.: Greenwood Press, 1976), pp. 165–177; David N. Doyle, "The Regional Bibliography of Irish America, 1880–1930: A Review and Addendum," *Irish Historical Studies* Vol. XXIII, No. 1 (May 1983) pp. 254–255; Lawrence J. McCaffrey, *The Irish Diaspora in America* (Bloomington, Ind.: Indiana University Press, 1976), pp. 77–79. See also Burchell, *The San Francisco Irish* and Vinyard, *The Irish on the Urban Frontier.*

11. On Irish Americans as Democrats in politics see Paul Kleppner, *Cross of Culture: A Social Analysis of Midwestern Politics, 1850–1900* (New York: 1970) and John Allswang *A House for All Peoples* and as machine politicians, see Weiss, *Charles Francis Murphy* and William Bullough, *A Blind Boss and His City: Christopher Augustine Buckley and Nineteenth Century San Francisco* (Berkeley: University of California Press, 1979). On social mobility see Stefan Thernstrom, *Poverty and Progress: Social Mobility in a Nineteenth Century City* (Cambridge, Mass.: Harvard University Press, 1964). For a more recent example see Dean R. Esslinger, *Immigrants and the City: Ethnicity and Mobili-*

ty in a Nineteenth Century Midwestern Community (Port Washington, N.Y.: Kennikat Press, 1975). For studies including analysis of Irish-American families see, for example, Tamara K. Hareven and Maris A. Vinoskis, "Marital Fertility, Ethnicity, and Occupation in Urban Families: An Analysis of South Boston and the South End in 1880," *Journal of Social History* Vol. VIII (1975) pp. 65–93 and Michael Katz, *The People of Hamilton Canada West: Family and Class in Mid Nineteenth Century City* (Cambridge: Harvard University Press, 1975). Labor historians studying Irish Americans include: Roy Rosenzweig, *Eight Hours for What We Will: Workers and Leisure in an Industrial City 1870–1920* (New York: Cambridge University Press, 1983); Daniel J. Walkowitz, *Worker City, Company Town: Iron and Cotton Worker Protest in Troy and Cohoes, New York, 1855–1884* (Urbana, Ill.: University of Illinois Press, 1981); and Leon Fink, *Workingmen's Democracy: The Knights of Labor and American Politics* (Urbana, Ill.: University of Illinois Press, 1983). For Irish Americans in the Church see, for example, Curran, *Michael Augustine Corrigan* and Shannabruch, *Chicago's Catholics.*

12. E. P. Hutchinson, *Immigrants and Their Children: 1850–1950* (New York: John Wiley and Sons Inc., 1950), p. 5.

13. *Reports of the Immigration Commission, U.S. Senate Documents, 61st Congress: 3rd Session* Vol. I, "Abstract of Reports," p. 136, p. 825; Vol. III, "Distribution of Immigrants," p. 552.

14. Hutchinson, *Immigrants and Their Children,* p. 174.

15. David Doyle, "Unestablished Irishmen," in Dirk Hoerder, ed., *American Labor and Immigration History: Recent European Research* (Urbana, Ill.: University of Illinois Press), pp. 199–205; Thernstrom, *The Other Bostonians,* pp. 111–175.

16. David Doyle, *Irish Americans: Native Rights and National Empires* (New York: Arno Press, 1976), pp. 86–95, pp. 182–200; Walsh, "The Irish in the New America," pp. 166–169; Vinyard, *The Irish on the Urban Frontier.*

17. Shannon, *The American Irish,* p. 142; John Modell, "Patterns of Consumption, Acculturation and Family Income Strategy in Late Nineteenth Century America," in Tamara Hareven and Maris K. Vinoskis, eds., *Family and Population in Nineteenth Century America* (Princeton, N.J.: Princeton University Press, 1978); Sister Joan Bland, S.N.D., *Hibernian Crusade: The Story of the Catholic Total Abstinence Union of America* (Washington, D.C.: Catholic University of America Press, 1951), p. 201.

18. Robert F. Bales, *The Fixation Factor in Alcohol Addiction: On an Hypothesis Derived from a Comparative Study of Irish and Jewish Social Norms* (New York: Arno Press, 1980), pp. 13–37; Jay Dolan, *Catholic Revivalism: The American Experience* (Notre Dame, Ind.: University of Notre Dame Press, 1978), pp. 157–164; Paul Messbarger, *Fiction with a Parochial Purpose: So-*

cial Uses of American Catholic Literature, 1884–1900 (Boston: Boston University Press, 1971), pp. 80–95.

19. Shannon, *The American Irish*, pp. 95–106, pp. 259–260; Carl Wittke, *The Irish in America* (Baton Rouge, La.: Louisiana State University Press, 1956), pp. 246–251; Michael Katz, *The People of Hamilton West*, pp. 279–290; Albert Gibbs Mitchell, "Irish Family Patterns in Nineteenth Century Ireland and Lowell, Massachusetts," (Ph.D. dissertation, Boston University, 1976); David M. Heer, "Marital Status of Second Generation Americans," *American Sociological Review* Vol. 26, No. 2 (1961) p. 237; *Reports of The Immigration Commission: 62d Congress* Vol. 28, No. 1, "Fecundity of Immigrant Women," pp. 820–821.

20. Brown, *Irish American Nationalism*, pp. 22–34, p. 64, pp. 154–156.

21. Foner, "Class, Ethnicity and Radicalism," pp. 20–44. See also Michael Funchion, *Chicago's Irish Nationalists* (New York: Arno Press, 1976).

22. On Irish-American nationalist activity in the 1890s and early 1900s see Charles Callan Tansill, *America and the Fight for Irish Freedom 1866–1922* (New York: Devon Adair, 1957), pp. 114–134; Alan J. Ward, *Ireland and Anglo American Relations* (Toronto: University of Toronto Press, 1969), pp. 10–29; Leon O'Broin, *Revolutionary Underground: The Story of the Irish Republican Brotherhood, 1858–1924* (Tottowan, N.J.: Rowman and Littlefield), pp. 65–93. On Irish-American nationalism during World War I and after, see Ward, *Ireland and Anglo American Relations;* F. M. Carrol, *American Opinion and the Irish Question, 1910–1923* (New York: St. Martin's Press, 1978); J. E. Cuddy, *Irish Americans and National Isolationism: 1914–1920* (New York: Arno Press, 1976); Patrick J. Buckley, *The New York Irish: Their View of American Foreign Policy, 1914–1921* (New York: Arno Press, 1976); Margaret Sullivan, "Fighting for Irish Freedom: St. Louis Irish Americans, 1918–1922" in James Walsh, ed., *The Irish: America's Political Class* (New York: Arno Press, 1976); William M. Leary, "Woodrow Wilson, Irish America and the Election of 1916," *Journal of American History* Vol. 54, No. 1 (June 1967) pp. 57–62.

23. McAvoy, *The Great Crisis in American Catholic History*, p. 207; Doyle, *Native Rights and National Empires*, pp. 271–281; Dorothy Dohen, *Nationalism and American Catholicism* (New York: Sheed and Ward, 1967), pp. 109–110; Shannon, *The American Irish*, pp. 259–260; Maurice F. Egan and John Kennedy, *The Knights of Columbus in Peace and War* (New Haven, Conn.: Knights of Columbus Publishers, 1923), p. 83; Christopher J. Kauffman, *Faith and Fraternalism: The History of the Knights of Columbus, 1882–1982* (New York: Harper and Row, 1982), pp. 73–94, p. 227; William Halsey, *The Survival of American Innocence: Catholicism in an Era of Disillusionment, 1920–1940* (Notre Dame, Ind.: University of Notre Dame Press, 1980) pp. 3–4.

24. Kerby Miller with Bruce Boling and David N. Doyle, "Emigrants and Exiles: Irish Culture and Irish Emigration to North America, 1790–1922," *Irish Historical Studies* Vol. XXII, No. 86, (September 1980) pp. 97–125; Doyle, *Native Rights and National Empires*, pp. 227–234.

25. Dohen, *Nationalism and American Catholicism*, p. 71; Curran, *Michael Augustine Corrigan;* Aaron Abell, *American Catholicism and Social Action 1865–1956* (New York: Garden City, 1960), p. 43; Kauffman, *Faith and Fraternalism*, pp. 121–124. For discussion of religious and ethnic loyalties among Catholics see Philip Gleason and David Salvaterra, "Ethnicity, Immigration and Catholic History," *Social Thought* Vol. III, No. 3 (Summer 1978); and for such loyalties among all American ethnic groups see Timothy L. Smith, "Religion and Ethnicity in America," *American Historical Review* Vol. 83, No. 5 (December 1978) pp. 1155–1185.

26. Martin Marty, "The Catholic Ghetto and All Other Ghettoes," *Catholic Historical Review* Vol. LXVIII, No. 2 (April 1982) pp. 185–205; Curran, *Michael Augustine Corrigan;* Robert Cross, *The Emergence of Liberal Catholicism in America* (Cambridge, Mass.: Harvard University Press, 1967), pp. 189–195; Halsey, *Survival of American Innocence*, p. 37; Samuel J. Thomas, "The American Periodical Press and the Apostolic Letter, Testem Benevolentiae," *Catholic Historical Review* Vol. XLII, No. 3, pp. 413–414; David J. O'Brien, "Some Reflections on the Catholic Experience in the United States," in Irene Woodward SNJM, ed., *The Catholic Church: The U.S. Experience* (New York: Paulist Press, 1979), pp. 13–14; Garry Wills, *Bare Ruined Choirs: Doubt, Prophecy and Radical Religion* (New York: Dell, 1972), p. 15, p. 18.

27. Walkowitz, *Worker City, Company Town;* Fink, *Workingmen's Democracy;* David Montgomery, "The Irish and the American Labor Movement," in Doyle and Edwards, eds., *America and Ireland*, pp. 205–218; Martin Shefter, "The Electoral Foundations of the Political Machine: New York City, 1884–1897," in Joel Sibley, Alan G. Bogue, and William Flanigan, eds., *The History of American Political Behavior* (Princeton, N.J.: Princeton University Press, 1978), pp. 263–298.

28. For the most recent example of the bitter debate over the American workers' class consciousness see John Patrick Diggins, "Comrades and Citizens," *American Historical Review* Vol. 90 No. 5 (June 1985) pp. 614–639. An older interpretation of the Knights of Labor ideology emphasizing its fuzziness and backwardness is Gerald Grob, "Knights of Labor versus the American Federation of Labor," in David Brody, ed., *The American Labor Movement* (New York: Harper and Row, 1941), pp. 30–43. Another interpretation suggesting its radicalism is Leon Fink, *Workingmen's Democracy*, pp. 3–37, pp. 219–233. For Irish contributions to this ideology see Foner, "Class, Ethnicity and Radicalism," pp. 20–44; Montgomery, "The Irish and the American Labor Movement," p. 216; and Sean Wilentz, "Industrializing America and the

Irish: Towards the New Departure,'' *Labor History* Vol. 20, No. 4 (Fall 1979) pp. 579–595. On the decline of Irish-American radicalism because of social mobility and ethnic politics see Walkowitz, *Worker City, Company Town*, pp. 254–257. On the effects of the anti-socialist crusade see John O'Dea, *History of the Ancient Order of Hibernians and the Ladies Auxiliary* (Philadelphia, Pa.: National Board of the A.O.H., 1923), Vol. III, pp. 1450–1451; Thomas McLean Henderson, *Tammany Hall and New Immigrants: The Progressive Years* (New York: Arno Press, 1976), pp. 87–88; and Mark Karson, *American Labor Unions and Politics* (Carbondale, Ill.: Southern Illinois University, 1958), pp. 212–284.

29. Walsh, "The Irish in the New America," pp. 169–170; Paul Kleppner, "Voters and Parties in the Western States," *Western Historical Quarterly* Vol. XIV (January 1983) pp. 59–65; Dennis Clark *The Irish in Philadelphia: Ten Generations of Urban Experience* (Philadelphia: Temple University Press, 1974), pp. 126–144; David C. Hammack, *Power and Society: Greater New York at the Turn of the Century* (New York: Russell Sage Foundation, 1982), pp. 110–147; Geoffrey Blodgett, "Yankee Leadership in a Divided City," in Formisano and Burns, *Boston 1700–1980*, pp. 87–100.

30. John Allswang, *A House for All Peoples*, pp. 105–106; Henderson, *Tammany Hall and the New Immigrants*, pp. 127–156; Ronald Arthur Petrin, "Ethnicity and Political Pragmatism: The French Canadians in Massachusetts 1885–1915," (Clark University: Ph.D. dissertation, 1983); J. Joseph Huthmacher, *Massachusetts People and Politics, 1919–1933* (Cambridge, Mass.: Belknap Press, 1959), pp. 116–123.

31. Edgar Litt, *Beyond Pluralism: Ethnic Politics in America* (Glencoe, Ill.: Scott Foresman, 1970), pp. 26–28.

32. Cross, *The Emergence of Liberal Catholicism*, pp. 27–105; Curran, *Michael Augustine Corrigan*, p. 316; McAvoy, *Great Crisis*, pp. 17–18, pp. 79–83.

33. Corrigan and McQuaid opposed the first German American protest to the Vatican in 1886, and Corrigan later wrote a letter condemning Peter Paul Cahensly's proposals in 1891: Rev. Colman Barry OSB, *The Catholic Church and German Americans* (Milwaukee: Bruce Publishing Co., 1953), p. 67, pp. 150–151, p. 160.

34. Charles Shannabruch, *Chicago's Catholics;* Dolores Liptak, "The National Parish: Concept and Consequences for the Diocese of Hartford, 1890–1930," *Catholic Historical Review* Vol. LXXXI, No. 1 (January 1985) pp. 52–64; Philip T. Sylvia Jr., "The Flint Affair: The French Canadian Struggle for Survivance," *Catholic Historical Review* Vol. LXV, No. 3 pp. 414–435; Rudolf Vecoli, "Prelates and Peasants: Italian Immigrants and the Catholic Church," *Journal of Social History* Vol. 2 (Spring 1979) pp. 217–268.

35. Shannon, *The American Irish*, p. 145.

"man overboard": change and stability in post famine ireland

> Monday morning fog continued until night sailing was very short in consequence we had weighty rain in the evening the sea is as calm as a lake we have lots of (salt?) beef coffee and spuds gruel bread and tea but for the first day while sick we could not look at them one person overboard a vessel should have her own butter there is lots of butter in the vessel but you could not smell it.
>
> emigrant from the Clancy family of Clare, ca. 1885[1]

From our modern perspective this is a strange journal entry. Was the loss of human life of as little consequence as it appears? Or, more likely, are we so distant from this world that we cannot understand its language? Perhaps weather and food were so significant to the whole group that they superseded the importance of any individual's fate; or was the form of written language available to this young person unable to deal with the emotional distress and ominous prophecy which this "one person overboard" represented? Perhaps such trauma was dealt with by public ritual rather than by individual and private emotional expression. In any or all cases, the distance between this voyager and the modern reader is clear.[2]

Yet he sailed from the same island that was the home of Charles Stuart Parnell, the quintessential parliamentary sophisticate; the young W. B. Yeats, master of the English language; and the infant James Joyce, the linguistic genius of our century. Together these three serve well as symbols of much of the best of twentieth century Irish, and indeed Western, language and politics. Was the young man from Clare simply separated from his more illustrious countrymen by education and class, or was there a more profound and universal difference between urban and rural *mentalite* in nineteenth century Ireland?

The clear delineation of such a difference would be of great assistance in understanding Irish culture and society since 1850. It would also add greatly to our understanding of an Irish-American society which drew its membership from this rural world but provided a predominately urban experience. Connections are striking during our period. On both sides of the Atlantic the issues were similar. The quest to form a workable Catholic identity within a larger society ordered by Anglo-Protestant values, a parallel problem of reconciling the new found prosperity of a significant minority with the continued poverty of the majority, the pioneering task of building effective democratic political machinery from the bottom up, and the often painful restructuring of family and moral values in rapidly changing social and economic circumstances. It would be a mistake to presume that these parallels represent the simple "importation" of Irish culture into an American world, but it would be an equally serious error to assume that later nineteenth century American Irish society can be studied in isolation from its European counterpart. Irish Victorian experience provided Irish America with a constant supply of individuals schooled in the problems of survival in an increasingly capitalized and Anglicized world. In a sense Ireland supplied these migrants with the tools, psychological, cultural, and social, with which to do their American work. Irish people did not carry blueprints for family or political organization, but they did carry with them a set of widely shared personal and community goals which strongly influenced how they individually and communally reacted to American realities.

Because of the consequent importance of understanding rural and urban society in Ireland this essay will concentrate on the more visible aspects of post-Famine society and the ways in which it interacted with the urban world. Of course, even so limited a task is difficult, for this was a revolutionary era during which the Irish people won control over their own land; aggressively asserted themselves politically through both constitutional and revolutionary politics; regained their ability to maintain an independent cultural identity and language; and took the penultimate steps toward the defeat of British military and political control of their island. Simply to list the names of the significant organizations and movements which originated in these years illustrates the energy of the era: the Tenants Rights Party, the IRB, the Home Rule Party, the Land League, the Ladies Land League, the National League, the Plan of Campaign, the GAA, the Gaelic League, Sinn Fein, the co-operative movement, the Literary Renaissance, the Ulster Unionist Party, the IGTWU, the UVF, the Irish Volunteer Force, the Irish Citizen Army, the Pioneers, and the Cumman Na Bann.

There is no doubt that a revolution was underway. Like all revolutions, there were often innocent casualties, untouchable villains and unexpected results. And like most revolutions, it was also incomplete. Yet, from the perspective of most of the survivors it was successful: when compared to the endmarks of this era, the Great Famine and the Great War, this was a remarkable bloodless revolution. In many ways the transformation which the Irish experienced, however painful and costly, was one which many developing nations today can envy.

The revolution itself is usually dated from the 1916 Rising but, as Emmet Larkin has pointed out, the emergence of an independent Irish nation predates the struggle for military superiority on the island.[3] The social, political, and religious institutions and traditions of modern Ireland were well established before the end of the century. And as Joseph Lee has argued, Ireland by 1916 had already undergone one of the most rapid and thorough periods of modernization of any nation in Europe.[4] Of course much remained unchanged and unaccomplished and the process did not run strictly according to theory.

We often think of modernization and the development of capitalism as requiring a process of social fragmentation and specialization with consequently complex social relationships. Yet in post-Famine Ireland the process of economic development required a simplification of social and economic structure. The Famine itself began the process by exercising selectivity in choosing its victims. Rural Pre-Famine society had one basic social and economic division based on access to land. The more prosperous members of the community held land as tenants from the aristocratic landlords. Those who held enough, say 15 acres of decent land, often held their land by leasehold, had some legal rights of occupation, and in good years approached prosperity. Even the smallest tenancy offered some opportunity for economic initiative and was desperately sought after by those on the other side of this great divide: the landless. Those without land were in a much more vulnerable position. They were dependent upon tenant farmers for both employment and for their "gardens" where they raised potatoes, their only food supply. These were the Irish people who were annihilated by the Famine.

In the post-Famine period emigration continued to draw disproportionately from landless families. (See Table 2.1.) As a result while the absolute numbers of farming families remained relatively constant they came to dominate the local community. Their goals were increasingly identified as community goals, their definitions of social responsibility and respectability became increasingly indistinguishable from community mores and their political voice dominated the more public side of the national debate.

By the 1870s rural society had nearly completed a quiet social and moral revolution: nearly all of the customs and practices surrounding marriage, procreation, and family reproduction had been vastly simplified into what some twentieth-century commentators have misleadingly labeled the "traditional pattern" of Irish marriage and family life. In reality it was a great departure from pre-Famine family experience which managed to reconcile the coexistence of extremely high marital fertility with two wildly different patterns of infant mortality and marriage age. This pre-Famine demographic diversity represented the coexistence within a single community of different patterns of marriage, family, and sexual experience.

Those holding land attempted to maintain their precarious hold on what passed for material prosperity by delaying marriage for males, arranging appropriate matches (those which preserved wealth within the family while forming an alliance with another family of roughly equal economic status) and restricting inheritance to one male who would receive the farm and one female who would receive a dowry. (Ownership of the farm, of course, remained in the hands of a landlord, only the right—legally not recognized—of possession was transferred.) Other siblings were encouraged to emigrate, find a secure place within the church, or to enter into trade in a nearby village or town. For all of these children of farming families the desirability of delaying sexual initiation as long as possible was obvious. In this pre-contraceptive and patriarchal society sexual activity threatened impending marriage and its inherent restrictions on savings, mobility, and independence. This was especially true for the heir for whom this prolonged celibacy was essential.[5]

The existence of this specific pressure upon general social practice was partially masked (and confused) by the presence within the commu-

Table 2.1
Estimate of Relative Sizes of Agricultural Classes, 1841–1881

AGRICULTURAL CLASS	ESTIMATED PERCENTAGE OF ADULT MALE AGRICULTURAL LABOR FORCE	
	1841	1881
Farmers and Sons	42	60
Laborers	56	38
Other	2	2
Total adult male agricultural labor force	1,604,034	970,835

Source: Samuel Clark, "The importance of agrarian classes: agrarian class structure and collective action in nineteenth-century Ireland" in Ireland: Land, Politics and People ed. P.J. Drudy, Cambridge University Press, London, 1982.

nity of a large number of individuals, perhaps the majority (see Table 1) who had a very different sort of relationship with the economic life of the land. Landless laborers, artisans, and textile workers generally held no property worth consideration in the marriage market. Their survival depended either upon wage income or subsistence farming carried out upon land provided by a willing farmer. In either circumstance there was little security and very little incentive to delay marriage. Earning capacity peaked very young (by about age 16 males could claim the adult wage) and was lost relatively soon. As a result early marriage and large numbers of children actually provided the best available assurance for a family's survival. In such circumstances there was little social or economic rationale for extreme sexual repression of the young. This does not imply free sexuality: where sexual intimacy went too far (or perhaps 'far enough' would be more accurate) a marriage normally followed. Still the fact that courtship, sexual exploration, and eventual early marriage were considered acceptable for the children of laboring families implies a very different adolescence than that of their farming neighbors.

The existence within small and highly integrated communities of such contradictory patterns of marriage and sexual experience led to some conflict in pre-Famine Ireland.[6] The churches, of course, favored the more 'victorian' views of the prosperous section of the community, but they had been doing so since the Reformation with very little success. One very clear example of the failure of the clergy to exercise much influence in this area can be found in their inability throughout the nineteenth century to curtail or even substantially tone down the traditional Irish wake. (In this case the 'traditional' does apply.) The Irish ritual for dealing with loss included adolescent sexual games and mock marriages, both remnants of pre-Christian ritual emphasizing the continuity of death, life, and sexuality.

This survival of pre-modern ideas about the basic elements of human life was shared by the whole community. Its existence should remind us that while differing attitudes and practices on family issues represent real division within the community, there was still a considerable area of agreement. Indeed it would be accurate to characterize these divergent marriage patterns as two different strategies for achieving the common communal goal: the security and reproduction of the family. For while it may be true that generations of Irish children were "sacrificed" to preserve the rules of economics,[7] it is equally true that for both those who remained to inherit and those who were driven to North America, Great Britain, or Australia, family identity and survival remained a central and at times ferocious element of individual as well as collective consciousness. And as the decades of the nineteenth century played themselves out, this family identity, especially in its collective sense, was increasingly defined in terms of the realities of farming life.

When seen from the perspective of the entire century the "traditional" Irish marriage pattern of late marriage, frequent celibacy, and consequent sexual repression therefore appears as the surviving element of a more complicated and flexible eighteenth century social system. Even at the risk of redundancy, it is worth re-emphasizing the irony here: the pre-Famine rural world was *more* complex and flexible than that which followed. There was little that was 'stable' or conservative about it except in the most literal sense. The pre-Famine world could accommodate different patterns of marriage and sexuality because its social structure required different means to achieve the basic goal of the entire community and nearly all of the individuals within it: the creation and maintenance of family households, which in turn required the individual prerequisites of adulthood, marriage, and a means of providing sustenance for the household.

The process by which the possible strategies for achieving this adult status was narrowed to the "traditional" late marriage-celibacy pattern was not one of choice between past and future any more than it was a choice between Christian and pagan. The process was really one of coerced realignment. Those elements of pre-Famine society which continued to provide the family continuity valued by the community were maintained, those that did not were modified if possible, or if not, they were relegated to the collective consciousness of popular thought and practice to be recalled when circumstances changed—as they would for many migrants from these communities. In this way change was not a process of choice, or of decay, but of conservation of the community ethos. Indeed it is a remarkable example of the adaptability which is the true peasant "conservatism."

In the post-Famine period the Catholic church played a major role in facilitating the consolidation of the farmer's moral hegemony; but again we should note that the church had always favored prudent marriages, chastity, and modesty. And the clergy had always served as an example of the highest form of Christian sexuality, celibacy. What changed in the post-Famine period was the relevance of the church's teaching to the majority of its members. As chastity and celibacy became increasingly necessary to the successful functioning of the social and economic system, the role of the church and its clergy gradually shifted from that of a familiar nagging and largely ineffective conscience to that of an efficient moral police. This was possible only because the majority of the adult community wished it to be so.

Unfortunately for relationships between the generations, the hopes and expectations of the youth of Ireland did not harmonize with the wishes of this majority. Disputes between generations and among siblings arising over the designation of heirs (Ireland did not practice primogeniture) and the timing of succession were always a potential source of tension and violence. But the actual incidence of intra-family violence was certainly reduced by the availability of North America as a safety valve drawing off the angry and discontented. Inter-family conflict was certainly more responsible for the high level of violence in rural Irish society.[8] Most commentators have rightfully identified the land system as the ultimate cause of most of this violence. Generally they identify the rent system as the mechanism which ensured that a static land supply operated to produce a cannibalistic type of competition between farming families. This view is too simplistic. Most Irish tenant farmers were quite happy to work within a truly open competitive system: what distressed them, and often drove them to violence, was the generally corrupt, often arbitrary and occasionally prejudiced way in which the land system operated.

The presence of conflict within the tenantry does not negate the concept of the tenantry as a single class, nor does it call into question the existence of an emerging homogeneous community dominated by this class.[9] Nearly all of the inter-family violence was caused by the inability of the community to peacefully protect its communal values against the rising threat of individual opportunism. As long as the occupation of their farms remained subject to landlord caprice and British property law the existence of a community sense of justice and discipline could only be maintained by communal persuasion, either of the moral or violent kind. Obviously this was a situation ripe for abuse and error: but it would be wrong to assume that the crisis entailed in communal violence marked the breakdown of the community. The very persistence of such violence may be evidence of the endurance of communal economic mores radically different than those protected by the British state. Indeed what is most remarkable about post-Famine Ireland is the continued reassertion of community values in the face of social and economic factors which conspired for their annihilation.

The concept of "community" is always problematic; it is used by many urban folk, including some academics, to refer to a harmonious state of existence bordering on Utopia. Traditional peasant communities were, of course, far different. Their very existence was predicated upon the shortage of the basic necessities of life and their unequal distribution within a local population. Communal values in Ireland did recognize the right of every individual to survival, but the majority of folk practices and customs had as much to do with validating the unequal distribution of the community's surplus production as with enforcing a type of corporate responsibility upon the more fortunate. For example, the right of hospitality which the less fortunate could claim from the privileged provided a legitimizing logic (and ritual explication) for the more prosperous farmers of the community. The great difference between the older communal value system and the individualism which threatened to replace it was the relationship (or lack of same) between these two groups. In the traditional community these groups were defined by their reciprocity; in the 'modern' world they existed as independent, or more likely, hostile entities. In the post-Famine era the increasing numerical dominance of the more prosperous farming group removed much of the danger of resistance from the less fortunate. By a process of "unnatural selection" emigration continued to carry away those who despite the steadily falling population of the country were unable to find a space for themselves in an increasingly specialized Irish economy.

Without the control of a farm or the prospect of steady employment and the position as a head of a household, the majority of Irish young people could not hope to achieve adult status within the traditional Irish community. These things receded with subsistence and tillage farming. Dairy production, which the British market necessitated, created very different labor patterns which made the existence of independent laborers increasingly marginal. Together with the inherent stability and impartible inheritance practice of the land system this greatly narrowed the horizon of opportunity for most Irish young people. Indeed by the 1870s it would not be hyperbolic to speak of an "opportunity famine" in Ireland.

Emigration, of course, served as the 'solution' for many of these young people, and during the post-Famine period the channels of the Irish emigration flood were worn so broad and so deep that the turbulence subsided as the flow increased. But it is important to recognize that those who physically escaped from the opportunity famine in Ireland did not abandon the Irish community or its values. From the servants quarters and slum tenements of North America they sent millions of pounds home to subsidize the family farm and to assist their siblings, cousins, nephews, nieces, and friends to escape the nets of poverty, oppression, and sexual repression. A priest from Roundstone in Connemara reported a typical though unusually graphic example of the practical results of the ties which bound young emigrant women to their families in Ireland: "There are two horses engaged in the little holding in performing work done heretofore on the backs of the young girls . . . namely carrying seaweed, often for miles, to manure the land. The price of the horses was remitted by the girls of the family who emigrated."[10]

Perhaps the clearest sign of the strength of the Irish rural community and its ethos is to be found in the attempts of these migrants to re-establish their families and communities in a new and utterly different environment. It is probable that most emigrants already had some family or community contact in North America and that many chose their destinations within North America for its connection with home. James Waldron, parish priest of Ballyhaunis, reported in the 1880s that "out of every 20 girls who left the parish for America 19 went to join their uncles or aunts and other near and dear relatives in the 'Land of the West'."[11] And these same migrants sought out other Irish migrants as marriage partners. These young men and women did not flee Ireland to escape its patriarchal and repressive ethos, they left because they could not find room in it for themselves.

This was particularly true for young Irish women, who by 1880 outnumbered Irish men as migrants.[12] Young men had the possibility, however slim, of employment in service industries as dockers, teamsters, and general laborers. For women there was virtually no opportunity for employment outside of agriculture. The one exception, domestic service, precluded marriage and hence adult status in the community. The family farm was the only realistic opportunity for most women. Those who could find such an opportunity took it. Those who did not (the majority) had to choose between emigration and spinsterhood (which meant permanent economic dependence on male relations). Those who chose emigration were often, in an ironic way, choosing tradition, i.e., they sought the opportunity to marry freely and create a family of their own. This required initiative, perseverance and hard work—just as it did at home—but it did not require a rejection of traditional attitudes to marriage and family.[13]

By the 1870s the combined effect of constant emigration, declining population, church efforts, and British market pressure had insured the dominance of the farming class. Indeed by this time only those institutions beyond the reach of the Irish people as a whole remained outside of the farmer's control: the land system and the state itself. Both of these were controlled by the Anglo-Irish aristocracy and their British elite sponsors. By a combination of ingenious mass political organization and revolutionary activity the Irish people would capture these in the next half-century. The land war of 1879–1882 began the final stage in the struggle for the land of Ireland. It also served as a catalyst for the rapid crystallization of institutional and cultural connections between rural and urban society which would lead to the struggle for an independent Ireland.

The Land League, the mass rural political organization that would lead this effort had complex origins. It was partly the logical maturation of traditional forms of local agrarian resistance; partly a psychological response to the humiliation of the famine holocaust; partly an expression of class conflict and partly the practical development of republican politics. The Land League was, in short, the institutional expression of the social and economic change which had taken place within Irish rural society since the famine. This was not the rural community of Gaelic romanticists, nor was it a blind peasant jacquerie, nor a narodinic black rebellion. It was instead a war fought by an Irish rural community which despite internal tensions, continuous hemorrhage of population, and most formidable opposition was able to mobilize for a massive disciplined struggle with the entrenched colonial elite and its imperial ally.

Their victory here and in the subsequent struggle for independence depended upon their ability to build alliances with other Irish and Irish-American groups, most notably the increasingly visible urban and provincial middle class, and their new political vehicle, the Irish Parliamentary Party founded by Issac Butt in 1870.

This critical development had actually begun a decade earlier when two middle class veterans of Young Ireland launched a new republican revolutionary organization, the Irish Republican Brotherhood. Although based on traditional Irish republican principles the new organization was much more successful than any previous group at recruiting members from the lower economic strata of society. As a result the movement became the first secular populist movement not dominated by an urban elite. Rigorously non-sectarian, to the point of anti-clericalism, the IRB advocated a radical egalitarian and democratic Irish Nation.

An abortive revolution in 1867 revealed the weakness of the IRB's exclusively military policy in confronting a major military power. But the strong popular support which the IRB prisoners and 'martyrs' received signaled both the end of deferential politics and the great emotional potential of militant separatism. The Irish people were not the only ones to offer a positive response to the attempted revolution. IRB courage and idealism prompted the great Victorian himself, W. E. Gladstone, to undertake a solution of the 'Irish Question.' His first attempt, the Disestablishment Act of 1869, brought him into conflict with Ireland's Protestant leadership, and in one of the great ironies of a very ironic history, led (or pushed) the conservative Protestant leader, Issac Butt, into the forefront of Irish nationalism. Butt by 1869 was already a distinguished veteran of Irish sectarian politics, having earned his spurs as a forceful opponent of Daniel O'Connell and his pre-Famine Catholic nationalism. Like Gladstone, Butt was shocked into new action by the revolutionary fervor of the IRB. He performed an invaluable ecumenical service by leading the amnesty movement for IRB prisoners who were held under appalling punitive conditions in British (not Irish) prisons.

Butt also began rethinking his position on the proper constitutional arrangement between the two British Isles. A traditional conservative, he was no friend of democracy, but the determination of the IRB radicals convinced him that some sort of local government would be necessary to defuse Irish nationalism. His thoughts turned to action in the dismay and rage with which he and other Irish Protestants (not Presbyterians) reacted to Gladstone's disestablishment of the Church of Ireland. Unable to see either the logic or justice of removing the most obvious (though probably not the most insidious) aspect of religious discrimination in Ireland, Butt and other members of the Protestant ascendancy launched their Home Government Association to seek Home Rule, a limited form of local government. With a Home Rule parliament in Dublin they believed that they could protect their privileged position in Ireland from the dangerous meddling of an increasingly middle class Liberalism.

Butt's initiative was a political blunder of truly imperial proportions. The franchise reform acts of 1850 and 1868, the emergence of the IRB, the demand for the secret ballot, and the rise in the power of the Catholic Church should have been enough to alert a talented politician that the old forms of control and intimidation would no longer be adequate in an increasingly democratic system. But Butt was blinded by his belief in the inherent superiority of Protestant and aristocratic leadership. He believed that the only way to avoid the anarchy of democracy was through a paternalistic local government which would use the talent of the ascendency and the ''natural'' deference of the peasantry to block the emergence of an egalitarian democracy. Unfortunately for Butt and his class the stores of ascendency political talent and peasant deference were running very low. Soon after its founding, both Protestant and Catholic voters recognized the real meaning of Home Rule, and the party began to receive the majority of its electoral support from some very undeferential Catholic voters.

It was in this atmosphere that a generation of young veterans of the IRB joined with local rural leaders on the west coast of the country, in the county of Mayo, to launch the first phase of the Irish liberation struggle; the war for the land of Ireland. Michael Davitt, one of the early leaders of the struggle, was well aware of the potential of the new political party as a vehicle of advanced nationalism. In 1878 he joined with John Devoy and Patrick Ford in New York in an unsuccessful attempt to forge an alliance with Charles Stuart Parnell, a young, outspoken backbench member of Butt's Parliamentary party.[14] Davitt was also rebuffed in Paris by the Supreme Council of the IRB when he sought their approval for a departure from the exclusive military policy. Undeterred, he returned to his home county of Mayo for the first time since his family had been evicted during the Famine. There, probably to his great surprise, he found the people far in advance of their 'leaders.' They were already organizing on their own to resist the payments of high rents after a disastrous agricultural year. Together with other IRB men and James Daly, editor of the *Connaught Telegraph,* the local newspaper, they founded the Land League of Mayo in 1879. The League sought radical land reform with peasant proprietorship as the major goal.

From an outsider's perspective (and there were few outside of Mayo who knew anything about what was going on) the prospects did not appear very favorable. The organizers had already encountered strong clerical condemnation caused by a combination of the Leagues' 'socialistic' goals and the prominence of so many IRB men on its platforms. The Home Rule Party with Butt as its leader was obviously uninterested and even its most 'radical' and ambitious member, Charles Stuart Parnell, refused Davitt's initial invitations to join the League's leadership. Beyond all this, the remote areas of Mayo, with their tiny farms, extreme poverty, and disastrous potato harvest, seemed better positioned for famine than for fight. But this was precisely what Michael Davitt, a child of the Great Famine, and the local leadership understood so much better than the national leadership of the Church, the Party, or the IRB. Davitt may have shocked some of his audience when he suggested that those who starved during the Famine deserved to die because they had not fought to save themselves, but he did not confuse them. The residual anger and terror left by the Famine was to be the decisive weapon both in maintaining solidarity among tenants risking eviction and in encouraging the American Irish to contribute the money necessary to underwrite this campaign and to assist those actually injured by landlord and government retaliation.

Eventually, when Parnell realized just how explosive and powerful an organization the people of the West were creating, he accepted Davitt's invitation to participate in the creation of a National Land League and he became its president, with Davitt as its vice president. Parnell moved quickly to identify himself with the rural struggle. He did this in a particularly courageous and visible way when he personally led the resistance to evictions at Balla in November of 1879. The presence of the aristocratic landlord M.P. on the right side of agrarian combat was a powerful image of the possibilities of the future, and of the success of Davitt and company in organizing the rural population.

The emergence of Parnell as a national leader marked a crucial turning point in Irish history, one which under less imperialistic conditions in England might have led to a peaceful solution to Ireland's demand for independence. By positioning himself at the point of convergence between the radical populist organization and the very moderate constitutional party Parnell had gained leverage over both. With the heightened visibility this conferred, he would draw both groups closer to his own political position and eventually he would consolidate control over both and merge their identity to form the great constitutional movement of Irish nationalism. By 1882, after the Land League agitation had won both legal recognition for the concept of dual ownership of the land of Ireland and greatly reduced rents, Parnell was the undisputed leader of Irish nationalism.[15]

He consolidated his newfound position of control (he had also been elected as chairman of the Irish Parliamentary Party) by shifting the emphasis of the rejuvenated popular feeling toward his own goal of Home Rule. Davitt and others saw this as a betrayal of their rural agenda, and indeed it was. But Parnell, who shared their goal of peasant ownership (though for very different reasons) was opposed to extra-parliamentary activity wherever and whenever there was an alternative.[16]

By 1886 Parnell had completely reorganized the party into the most disciplined, efficient, and effective group in Parliament; Parnell's skill as a power broker between Liberal and Conservative seemed momentarily to solve the Irish problem when in 1886 Gladstone announced his famous 'conversion' to Home Rule. Parnell was able to achieve these amazing results through the exploitation of several electoral reforms and through several creative initiatives of his own. The Secret Ballot Act (1872) and the Franchise Act of 1884 provided nearly automatic Home Rule victories in all but the most Protestant areas of Ulster, and South Dublin, and the Trinity College seats. The party itself instituted a written pledge which bound candidates for office to obey the party whip once elected, and the party introduced the first stipends for Members of Parliament. Both British parties cried foul at what they saw as limitations on individual ''freedom,'' but both were absolutely essential to prevent the traditional erosion of Irish party membership through British corruption. Far more importantly, the payment of M.P.s opened up the Parliamentary Party to the majority of Irish men (later the Irish would elect the first woman to Parliament) and began the democratic revolution within the House of Commons itself. The entrance of men such as John Finncane, farmer from East Limerick, and John Stack, farmer and draper from Listowel who had received only a 'private' education, raised many eyebrows at Westminster and provided material for much savage ridicule. It also marked the end of elitist monopoly in the House of Commons.

The presence of largely uneducated farmers and rural merchants in Parliament marked the 'nationalization' of rural Ireland as well as the democratization of Irish politics. Nearly all of the new members of the Parliamentary party 1880–1890 had Land League connections and most were elected to represent their home constituency. (A rarity in British or Irish politics of the time, Parnell, a Wicklow native and resident, sat for Cork.) This local, popular representation gave the party an identity unique in British politics. Balanced with Parnell's sophisticated style of leadership, it provided a nearly perfect 'ecumenical' image for the Irish party.

There was, of course, an inherent contradiction between the apparent local expression of democracy and the strong centralization and discipline required by Parnell's Parliamentary Strategy. There were also other forces now seeking to influence the party, most notably the Catholic Church and the middle class. But successful politics in a democratic world are organized around such contradictions and pressures. As long as Parnell was in control of the party these forces coexisted easily enough, partly because of their satisfaction at exercising *any* real power, and partly because all recognized that for the party to achieve its goal all would have to submerge their separate interests.

In these circumstances the Catholic clergy were well placed to play a major role in constituency affairs. Because they had both a local presence and a national voice, they could serve as the connective tissue that bound rural and urban as well as local and national interests together. Parnell also found them to be an effective counter weight to the more radical agrarian elements within the party. Also, though surprising to some, Parnell's moral and social goals also coincided to a remarkable extent with those of the Catholic Church.

As a result of all these factors the actual balance within the Party shifted slowly but steadily away from the agrarian radicals who had given new life to Irish politics. The very success of the rural radicals had created a new institution which they were poorly equipped to control. Their place was gradually taken by an urban middle class who were better placed and prepared to exercise influence on a now established political party.

This Irish middle class of the last quarter of the century was a curious social grouping. Coexisting within the same political and economic framework as their British counterparts, they might be presumed to resemble them. Externally they did. The houses they built in suburban Dublin or Cork, the furniture they imported, or copied, the clothing they wore, or longed to wear, all were of British design. But beneath the surface it is clear these people were not members of the British middle class. On the most basic economic and social level they occupied a different space. Whereas the British middle class were predominately involved in industrial activity, their Irish counterparts were almost exclusively concerned with agricultural trade, service or processing, or the professions; activities in which the value of caution exceeded that of innovation. In this they were structurally closer to the French rather than the British middle class. They were also by virtue of their religion generally alienated from the established leaders of the business and professional community. Banks, insurance companies, and professional organizations were all still under ascendency control. And most of the middle class of 1880 also had parents or grandparents who had been legally barred from political, military, and civil positions in the years before Catholic Emancipation. In all this they resembled the European Jewish middle class rather than the British middle class.

All of these factors helped to mark the Irish middle class as different from the British; but on the cultural and psychological level there was an even more profound division between these groups. The British middle class confidently celebrated its sense of identity with its nation and its monarch. They believed that they as a class were primarily responsible for the sense of peace, order, and prosperity which they saw as the hallmarks of their age. England had had its Peterloo, but the middle class had responded by supporting authority and later by ensuring the defeat of the Chartists. They could claim with naive pride that they *were* the nation. Their respectability, their confidence, and, above all, their wealth did give this era the external appearance of equipoise by which it has become so well known. [17]

The Irish grain merchant or doctor lived in a very different kingdom. Perhaps old enough to remember the Famine, certainly old enough to share its psychic and cultural legacy, these people controlled wealth compromised by guilt; wealth which threatened their identity. The popular British and Irish definitions of 'Irishness' might vary on certain peripheral areas such as intelligence or honesty, but they were surprisingly close to agreement on the essentials. To be native Irish was to be poor, Catholic, rural, and rebellious. By definition the middle class were never poor, seldom rural, and rarely rebellious. For many only their Catholicism confirmed their Irishness. Small wonder that many who felt some guilt at their plenty amidst the general poverty had difficulty in asserting any independence from their church.

There was another, less appealing, reason for many middle class people to cling tightly to their church. Those who were proud of their acquisitions and equally insecure in their enjoyment were often ashamed of their connection with the impoverished rural world from which they had only recently escaped. From these people the social and moral aspects of class distinction assumed an almost maniacal importance. The British cult of respectability served to confirm the superiority and permanence of their world and it coincided in an amazing way with the sexual puritanism and hierarchical deference ascendent in the Catholic Church of the period.

For some, respectability and religion were enough to provide a sense of identity, but this was a small and extremely narrow space, and most felt some tension between their privileged economic position and their identity as Irish people. These people who invested heavily in the cult of respectability should resemble the self assured middle class described by W. L. Burn or Harold Perkin; instead, like Joyce's character, they were misfits. Partaking of the externals of Victorian life, the material possessions and fashions, the sentimental vision, and the drawing room social life, they also maintained a deep and seemingly unalterable sense of alienation that was never far from an emotional despair and violence unacceptable in the age of equipoise.

In the 1890s these people would express this anxiety through the cultural revival movements, but here in Parnell's prime there was a far more immediate way to express their Irishness without endangering their middle class status and respectability. Participation in Home Rule activities allowed the majority of Irish middle class people to stress their separateness from Great Britain and to enjoy the thrill of Parnell's verbal confrontation with Britain's elite; all this without risking their property, careers, or lives. Furthermore the Party allowed them to exercise power and influence within Ireland under the guise of patriotism. In a strange way the party came for a short time to replace the function of many communal practices of rural Ireland noted earlier: i.e., it provided the privileged an opportunity to expend some of their wealth, power, and energy in the pursuit of a communal goal; to use their private privilege for the public good. This helps to explain their investment in the Party. It also helps to explain the strange circumstances surrounding its tragic crisis in 1890–1891.

In October 1890 one Captain William O'Shea filed suit for divorce from his wife Katherine on the grounds of adultery. The co-respondent was named as Charles Stuart Parnell. The events which followed are among the most familiar in Irish history because they have become mythologized in Irish popular history and because both Yeats and Joyce made this public myth part of their private art. For these same reasons these events are also among the least understood.

The most compelling and familiar form of the myth is found in the Christmas dinner scene of Joyce's *Portrait of the Artist as a Young Man*. In this scene all of the elements of the myth are present: an indelible image of Parnell materializes within the dining room of the Daedelus household; a noble, heroic figure; a king, hounded to death by a small minded people dragooned by a fanatic ignorant clergy. The issues of the room and of the myth are priestly power, moral cowardice, and hypocrisy, the props of the cult of respectability.

Yet the reality of what happened was somewhat more complicated, and rather different in its implications for the understanding of Parnellite Ireland. Most historians would now agree that Parnell was not destroyed at the initiative of the Catholic Church but by the leaders of his own creation, the Irish Parliamentary Party, and most especially by the more progressive and independent members of the party.[18] Furthermore, these men, the "hounds" of the myth, educated by Parnell to place party goals above all questions of personal advancement, emotions, or loyalties, were reacting to a pragmatic reading of British, not Irish, sexual puritanism. As F.S.L. Lyons demonstrated, it was British Low Church fanaticism which forced the British Parliamentarian, Gladstone, to confront his Irish allies with a painful choice: loyalty to Parnell or Home Rule. Gladstone was responding to his party's middle class and sectarian identity. The Irish Parliamentary Party, overwhelmingly Catholic, were quite ready to re-elect as their leader Charles Stuart Parnell, the adulterer. They did so on November 25, 1890. Party members believed then that they could still carry the Irish people and the Catholic Church whichever way they turned because all knew that the achievement of Home Rule required nationalist solidarity. But when Parnell was publicly denounced by Gladstone he could no longer offer the effective leadership which the Irish as a minority community required. Allegiance was therefore withdrawn. This was rational in terms of the Party's development and pointed to the community's future. This was the democratic response. The Irish party and later the Irish voters rejected the divine right of some to rule and others to follow. While members of the decaying ascendancy such as W. B.

Yeats might resent this outrageous assumption of equality, it was a crucial step in the emergence of the popular democratic tradition in Ireland.

The Fall of Parnell then did not reveal the "priest ridden" nature of the Irish but instead the puritanical cult of respectability which ordered the politics of the Big British Isle. From the Irish perspective it revealed much more: indeed save for the Great Famine, it was the most disturbing moment in nineteenth century collective experience. Although it only claimed one life, the crisis of 1890–1891 revealed the most humiliating aspect of Irish National suppression: the utter dependency of the Irish upon the whims of British public opinion and political expediency. The Irish could achieve nothing within the Parliamentary system without the approval of the British political elite. And clearly Irish self-determination was not on their agenda. In essence, the Irish were once again forced to recognize that despite the masquerade of the Act of Union they were little different than the other 'native' populations which the Victorian British empire encountered.

None of this was terribly surprising or disturbing to the radical Irish nationalists. They had been trying with varying success to convince the Irish people of these realities. The IRB had considerable success in rural areas and among the urban working class; but the middle class Catholic and Presbyterian refused to recognize the simple fact of their servile status. Of course they could not take such a leap of understanding without relinquishing the false sense of status which their class membership gave them. Instead they bought bowler hats and umbrellas, sang "God Save the Queen," voted for Parnell's Party, and hoped they could pass as genuine Victorian people. The destruction of their leader, and the bitter fragmentation of their party, shattered this illusion that they could have their privilege and their liberation. It is in the shock and disillusionment which followed that the more perceptive middle class members focused their attention on the conflict between respectability and liberation. It is here that the myth had its genesis.

The myth of Parnell's martyrdom at the hands of middle class and Catholic fanatics deflected an amorphous anti-British hostility away from British politics where it had little useful function and refocused it, intensified it, and aimed it at the major obstacles to radical and revolutionary political activity within Ireland: the Catholic church, the Irish Parliamentary Party itself, and the most dangerous weapon of British imperialism, the cult of respectability. The myth allowed some members of the Irish middle class to transfer the hostility engendered in their alienation away from its ultimate target, Great Britain, and towards the immediate and more vulnerable evil, the Victorianization of Irish society. Once again we are observing a great irony: the most anglicized group in Catholic Irish society opted to move outside of their own main line politics and to encourage the most anglophobic elements in Irish nationalism to attack the Irish institutions which both checked revolution and upheld middle class values, the Church and the Party. The vicious self-criticism which the myth encouraged would eventually lead a small but critical group of middle class activists to take their place beside the agrarian radicals and the just emerging socialist working class in the revolutionary coalition which would prove strong enough to overthrow British rule in Catholic Ireland.

Two new movements, the Gaelic League and Sinn Fein, facilitated the radicalization of the middle class. Both sought to redefine Irishness in terms appropriate to a disillusioned and confused middle class. Both provided a form of separatism and both were peculiarly middle class forms of radicalism that would lead a generation of young middle class Irish men and women into increasingly turbulent waters.

The Gaelic League founded in 1893 by Douglas Hyde, Eugene O'Growney, and Eoin McNeill, sought to save the Irish language from imminent extinction.[19] All three men were concerned for the survival of the language as a symbol of identity and as a repository of traditional Irish culture. They also saw the language as a buffer which could protect the Irish people from the vulgarity of British industrial civilization. They viewed the League as a nonpolitical educational movement and worked carefully to insulate it from political influences. But its goals of reviving the Irish language and protecting Irish life from British contamination were highly charged with political meaning, and while the League would remain scrupulously detached from political parties, many of its members would not.

Arthur Griffith's Sinn Fein offered a similar separatist alternative. Griffith, a peculiarly conservative revolutionary, offered a gaelicized version of Samuel Smiles' self help philosophy. He argued that Ireland's future could only be assured if the Irish people choose to lift themselves up via the familiar boot straps and create an independent and self-sufficient society and economy. Despite the obvious desirability of offering some sort of accommodation to the poor, the movement remained vigorously middle class and not only rejected any connection with the emerging labor movement, but openly attacked it.

Both of these movements epitomized the ambivalent nature of the

Irish middle class's position. Their division of the world into a simple anglo-gaelic polarity was an attempt to redefine Irishness in safe terms which would remove all doubt of their identity. But despite its initial conservatism the Gaelic Ireland movement did provide a powerful answer to those middle class Irish people who were most insecure in an Anglo-Irish world. And by attempting to isolate a 'perfect' Ireland they were sailing into uncharted waters. Obviously those ensnared in the grim realities of rural life or trying to negotiate the slums of Dublin found little use for the Gaelic mists which the League emitted. Yet, even within the League, the more active and intelligent began to find their way through the Celtic maze toward a more modern revolutionary definition of Ireland and its future.

It was Joyce's generation that produced the successful multiple answers to the questions of Irish identity. Ultimately Joyce himself provided much of the intellectual impetus for this achievement, but in the critical years 1900–1916 Patrick Pearse was by far the most important voice of Ireland's future. He led the disenchanted young middle class into an alliance with the rural community and the emerging urban working class. Pearse accomplished this by presenting the Irish middle class with an intelligent synthesis of traditional republicanism, new gaelic revivalism, and Catholic mysticism. A student of the Gaelic League, he accepted the idealism of the movement, indeed he infused it with an eschatological spirit that often brought him to dizzy rhetorical heights, as in his description of the future of the Irish people: "The Gael is not like other men, the spade, and the loom, and the sword are not for him. But a destiny more glorious than that of Rome, more glorious than that of Britain awaits him; to become the saviour of idealism in modern intellectual and social life."[20] It is easy to ridicule the heady chauvinism here. Just as it is easy to dismiss his infamous glorification of violence. But to reach any conclusion about Pearse or his role in Irish politics based on these instinctive academic reactions would be both unfair to Pearse and a grave distortion of Irish and European history.

It is necessary, though not sufficient, to point out that most of Europe and much of the world could agree with Pearse's arguments connecting "manhood" and the spilling of blood. But Pearse was not part of the Anglo/Teutonic club defending the right of the strong to dominate the weak. Pearse was not a proto fascist; his arguments justifying violence were always connected with discussions of "slavery" or "martyrdom," not "mastery" or "victory." Pearse's fixation with violence stems from the dilemma which faces a peaceful individual who confronts the realities of violence endemic in a divided colonial society. Even so, *his* dedication to violence was not a simple reflex response to the violence directed against the Irish people. It represented carefully worked out conclusions regarding the seductive power of imperial culture and the need to provide a catalytic shock to precipitate the psychological liberation he sought.

Serious students of Pearse's work are also keenly aware that the quotations on violence that are often repeated in essays such as this represent only one thread in a complex and dynamic theory of society and liberation. His extraordinary effort on behalf of the revolution of Irish education serves not only as a reminder of his 'constructive' side but also as evidence of his role as one of the great apostles of modernization in Ireland.[21] This forward-looking orientation was critical to Pearse's personal success in forming alliances within the IRB and with James Connolly's socialist Irish Citizen Army. Pearse and his philosophy may have contained elements of mysticism confusing to materialists, but it was clear that he was a man with more than a sense of the spiritual. He also had a clear vision of the future, a future which included a secular, egalitarian society and which would provide for all of its children equally: urban and rural, Protestant and Catholic, male and female. This vision launched the Irish Revolution of 1916; it was the first successful liberation theory of the twentieth century. It was a vision worth pursuing.

Pearse's success at leading a significant minority of the Irish middle class into a revolutionary alliance with the urban working class and the agrarian community permitted the liberation of all but the six most Unionist counties. It also did much more. Like the Parnell myth which played a role in its genesis, the existence of a middle class Catholic revolutionary "vanguard" permitted those who walked what Pearse described as the "pleasant path" of material acquisition to maintain a sense of vicarious subversiveness. This, in turn, allowed the majority of the middle class to negotiate the revolutionary period with great self assurance and little of the counter revolutionary hysteria which a more consistently conservative and Catholic group might have displayed.

Unfortunately, despite the passage of time, it is still too soon to assess the legacy of Pearse and the revolution of 1916. We are left instead with the task of providing some final observations on the issues explored in this essay. Unless we recall the starting point of this essay it might be difficult to find a connection between the family experience of rural Ireland at mid-century and Pearse's blood sacrifice of 1916. Like the young man from Clare, most of rural Ireland spoke with a different language until the events discussed here transpired. Ireland at the conclusion of the Famine was a divided, exhausted, and impoverished country whose very survival was questionable. The rural people who emerged from this nightmare shaped the successful future of their nation. Their social and economic reorganization permitted the modest economic growth which confirmed both the permanence of the high emigration/late marriage social regime and the now simplified rural class structure. Simultaneously these same Famine survivors launched those organizations which dominated the political history of Ireland until its independence: the IRB, the Land League, and the revivified Parliamentary Party. These organizations drew rural and urban Ireland closer together and led to their union during the successful liberation movement.

NOTES

1. Emigrant Diary of a member of the Clancy Family of Islandbawn. 1888. In the National Library of Ireland: Ms21, 666.

2. See Kerby A. Miller, "Emigrants and Exiles: Irish Cultures and Irish Emigration to North America 1790–1922," *Irish Historical Studies* XXII, 86 (1980) 97–125.

3. See Emmet Larkin, *The Roman Catholic Church and the Creation of the Modern Irish State 1878–86* (Philadelphia, 1975) and Larkin, "Church, State and Nation in Modern Ireland," in *American Historical Review* 80, No. 5, pp. 1244–77.

4. See Joseph Lee, *The Modernisation of Irish Society 1848–1918* (Dublin, 1973).

5. In the parish of Killashandra, Cavan, in 1841 the mean age of first marriage for males was:

Farmers (all)	26.0
Farmers (with more than 25 acres)	28.4
Laborers	24

For further details see Kevin O'Neill, *Family and Farm in Pre-Famine Ireland: The Parish of Killashandra* (Madison, Wisconsin, 1984).

6. See O'Neill, *Family and Farm* and O'Neill, "A Demographer Looks at Cuirt and Mhean Oiche," *Eire-Ireland* (Summer, 1984) pp. 135–142.

7. Lee, *The Modernisation of Ireland*, p. 5.

8. See David Fitzpatrick, "Class, Family and Rural Unrest," in *Ireland: Land, Politics and People,* ed. P. J. Drudy (Cambridge, 1982).

9. Samuel Clark, "The Importance of Agrarian Classes: Agrarian Class Structure and Collective Action in Nineteenth-century Ireland," in *Ireland: Land, Politics and People,* ed. P. J. Drudy (Cambridge, 1982).

10. *Report of Mr. Vere Foster's Irish Female Emigration Fund October 1884* in National Library of Ireland, Ms13, 552.

11. *Report of Emigration Fund October 1884*, Ms13, 552.

12. See David Fitzpatrick, *Irish Emigration 1801–1921* (W. Tempest, 1984), pp. 3–13.

13. For a different interpretation see Hasia Diner, *Erin's Daughters in America: Irish Women in the Nineteenth Century* (Baltimore, 1983).

14. See Thomas Brown, *Irish American Nationalism 1870–1890* (Philadelphia and New York, 1966) and T. W. Moody, *Davitt and Irish Revolution 1846–82* (Oxford, 1982), pp. 221–71.

15. See F. S. L. Lyons, *Charles Stuart Parnell* (London, 1977) and Conor Cruise O'Brien, *Parnell and His Party 1880–90* (Oxford, 1957).

16. Paul Bew, *C. S. Parnell* (Dublin, 1980) pp. 26–30.

17. See W. L. Burn, *The Age of Equipoise: A Study of the Mid-Victorian Generation* (New York, 1964) and Harold Perkin, *The Origins of Modern English Society 1780–1880* (Toronto, 1969) for a very useful discussion of this ethos.

18. See Bew, *Parnell*, pp. 115–24.

19. See Garret Fitzgerald, "Estimates for Baronies of Minimum Level of Irish-Speaking Amongst Successive Decenial Cohorts: 1771–1781 to 1861–1871," in *Proceedings of the Royal Irish Academy* Vol. 84, C. No. 3, pp. 117–155.

20. F. S. L. Lyons, *Ireland Since the Famine* (London, 1971), p. 332.

21. Lee, *Modernisation of Ireland*, pp. 141–148.

"they Do not DIffeR GReatly": the pattern of community Development among the IRIsh In late nineteenth century lowell, massachusetts

With the success of Samuel Slater's "Rhode Island" system, American textile production, and thus American industry, generally entered a new era. Entrepreneurs throughout New England quickly grasped that more mechanization meant more profits. In Massachusetts, a group of investors, the Boston Associates, opened an experimental mill at Waltham, Massachusetts, which took the production process one step further than Slater's mills by constructing a workable loom. This development permitted them to produce cotton cloth cheaply, efficiently, and in large quantity. Using water to power their machines, the Boston Associates searched for a site with greater waterpower potential than Waltham.[1] They settled upon East Chelmsford, Massachusetts, where the Merrimack River dropped thirty-two feet, renaming the site of their factory village "Lowell."[2]

Lowell grew rapidly. By 1836, the Boston Associates developed a large factory complex which included numerous mills, boardinghouses, an agent's home, bleacheries, dyeworks, and outbuildings. They employed recruiting agents who combed the northern New England countryside working to attract Yankee farm women into Lowell's labor force. These agents promised opportunity, excitement of city life, and cash wages. To safeguard the virtue of these women and to enhance Lowell's reputation as an industrial showcase, they enforced a strict moral code among mill employees.[3] By 1836, Lowell's population was eighteen thousand and it had become the third largest city in Massachusetts. Lowell's fame increased and the "Lowell Plan" was copied widely throughout New England.[4]

Lowell's rapid growth presented opportunities not only for Yankee farm women but also for unskilled laborers. Lowell's agents employed hundreds of laborers when building a new industrial village with its canals, streets, and mills. As early as April, 1822, a group of thirty Irish men left their homes on Boston's docks and journeyed to Lowell to participate in the construction boom.[5] The harsh New England winters discouraged winter employment. Still, work was available from April until November and a permanent Irish settlement soon appeared on the scattered Irish workers' encampments; a new neighborhood, the Acre, arose by 1830.[6] A year later, Boston's Bishop Fenwick dedicated St. Patrick's Church there.[7]

The Acre remained separate from the Yankee factory village. Compromises were reached between the two groups, notably on education, but any early efforts toward an amicable assimilation of Irish immigrants, even an assimilation on Yankee terms, disappeared as the Famine Irish flooded into Lowell in the later 1840s.[8] Despite the failure of assimilation, the Irish played a crucial role in the transformation of Lowell's economy. In an effort to maintain the level of profit, the Boston Associates and their descendants abandoned the paternalism for which their management had been noted. They cut wages, increased the number of looms for which workers were responsible, and speeded production. Their actions encouraged labor unrest among Yankee factory women who formed the Lowell Female Labor Reform Association under the banner of the Ten Hour Day. Such labor unrest caused the Boston Associates to turn to Irish immigrants[9] and the Irish poured into the mills. By 1850 one-third of Lowell was Irish.[10]

While the Irish obtained mill employment, they generally worked at the lowest-paying jobs. At the Hamilton Corporation, for example, Thomas Dublin has found that the highest percentages of Irish employees were in the carding and spinning departments, while Yankee women retained their control over more specialized and better-paying positions in weaving and dressing. Such advances as Irish women made into better-paying positions resulted from the inability of the corporation to attract Yankee women in sufficient quantity.[11] Even within the mill, Yankee and Irish women worked separately within the same department.[12] Among Irish men, a few obtained employment in the Lowell Machine Shop; most, however, worked as unskilled laborers in the Yard, bleachery, or dyeworks.[13] From the broader perspective shared by many of Lowell's citizens, the startling increase of Irish in

Lowell's mills was a cause for real alarm and precipitated a number of nativist outbursts culminating in the rise of the Know-Nothings in the 1850s.[14]

Despite the large numbers of Irish in the mills, effective political leadership never developed in the Acre. Irish women benefited the most by the change in the pattern of employment and, yet, while their income was important to a family wage economy, their employment did not significantly enhance the political position of the Irish in Lowell. The rapid turnover of Irish mill employees, the failure of Irish men to move beyond unskilled labor, the transient nature of Lowell's Irish population, the Know-Nothing agitation, and the business recession of 1857 also discouraged political development. Finally, that small group which constituted an "Irish middle class"—shopkeepers, foremen and artisans—generally supported Whig politics in Lowell. A few Irish Whigs even held minor political offices.[15] Among the Irish community in general, the Whigs and Democrats split the Irish vote evenly until the mid-1850s; and, even more important, most of Lowell's Irish remained unnaturalized emigrants until those years.[16]

When the Civil War broke out, Lowell's agents closed the mills and many Irish enlisted in the Union forces.[17] After the war, Lowell underwent a crucial transformation which affected the way that natives and even the Irish thought about the notion of being Irish in Lowell. Whereas the Irish had accounted for almost half of Lowell's population and the vast majority of its foreign born in 1860, the percentage of Irish in Lowell's general population decreased steadily throughout the nineteenth century. By 1900, when the population of Lowell was 94,969, the percentage of first and second generation Irish among Lowell's residents had decreased to 30 percent where it remained throughout much of the twentieth century.[18] The absolute numbers of the Irish, of course, had not fallen. They were in fact increasing. The Irish, however, were no longer the only immigrant people in Lowell, and as thousands of newcomers from a host of new lands flooded Lowell, the relative strength of the Irish in the city's population shrank.

The largest number of these newcomers came from French Canada. Attracted by mill employment and discouraged by persistent economic and social problems at home, they poured into the textile cities of New England. By 1880, there were almost ten thousand French Canadians in Lowell.[19] By that date they had already carved out a segment of Lowell's working class districts for themselves and rapidly transformed that area into a "Little Canada."[20] As early as 1868 they had organized a French parish, the first national parish in the history of the Boston Archdiocese.[21] In the last two decades of the nineteenth century their numbers more than doubled, and they soon surpassed even the Irish as the city's largest ethnic group. New "Little Canadas" sprouted near the railroad station and across the Merrimack River in those years. Hosts of French clubs and societies, a French credit union, and even a French language newspaper also appeared.[22]

The nature of the development of Lowell's French-Canadian community precluded any possibility of real accommodation with the Irish at the turn of the century. There were a number of reasons for this failure. First, the notion of community in New England's "Little Canadas" rested firmly in the concept of "survivance," or ethnic survival. As Ronald Petrin has suggested, French Canadians preferred to "remain always *Canadiens* at heart, and thus relatively unpredictable in politics."[23] As Frances Early has argued, the two dominant institutions, the family and church, encouraged such clannishness contributing to the easy ability of outsiders to depict the French in the worst possible light as degraded, immoral transients. The Massachusetts Bureau of Labor Statistics even dubbed them the "Chinese of the East" in 1881.[24] The Irish who had once been described in similar fashion now took great pains to distance themselves from Lowell's new pariahs.

There were other reasons for the emerging hostility between Irish Catholics and French Canadians as well. Early found that, despite some tentative steps toward accommodation, the two groups had exhibited a "history of ill-will from the beginning." In both groups, the church was a dominant institution but they differed on the direction of church growth. The Irish preferred a hierarchical, American, English-speaking church, while the French Canadians wished for a decentralized grouping of national parishes. At work, the Irish held better-paying jobs in the mills, which French Canadians naturally resented. Both groups passed on their discontent to their children with little evidence of intermarriage or even a blurring of neighborhood ethnic territorial lines. Finally, as elsewhere, survivance among French Canadians presumed "*a priori* loyalty to the ideal of ethnic exclusiveness" and prevented French Canadians from joining the Irish in developing a religious or broadly Catholic consciousness.[25]

The arrival of French Canadians heralded the entry of successive waves of immigrants into Lowell. In the 1890s, the first Greeks, Poles, and Jews settled there. Like French Canadians, they formed distinct neighborhoods which hosted a range of institutions to meet specific immigrant needs. After 1900, thousands of Portuguese settled in Lowell where they joined nearly forty ethnic groups there. In the early twentieth century, Lowell joined Fall River, Lawrence, Massachusetts, and Manchester, New Hampshire, as the four cities with the largest percentage of foreign born among their residents. Lowell also was among the leaders in the percentage of Americans with foreign born parents. Only Lawrence, Chicago, and Fall River boasted more than Lowell. The figure for Lowell was an amazing 77.92 percent of the population.[26] The impact of successive waves of immigrants upon Lowell was immediate, and it created a strikingly cosmopolitan city. In 1900, for example, only about one-half of Lowell spoke English.[27]

Among the Irish, the foreign born represented about 40 percent, or 11,000, of the over 27,000 Irish men and women living in Lowell in 1905.[28] The percentage of foreign born among Lowell's Irish was about the same as the average for the city's general population and significantly lower than among newer immigrants, including the French Canadians. In the general population, 41.7 percent of the residents were foreign born, while about 75.1 percent were of foreign parentage. Among newer immigrants, about 60 percent of French Canadians were foreign born with the figure rising to 96 percent among Lowell's Greeks.[29] In this sense the percentage of Irish born indicated that the Irish were an intermediate group, not as foreign as those who came later than them but still containing a high percentage of foreign born. Put another way, they had become "old stock" immigrants.

As the number of Irish increased in Lowell, they spread throughout the city. The Acre remained a strong Irish neighborhood with particularly heavy concentrations of Irish in Ward One and the eastern end of Ward Five.[30] The crude huts of early "paddy camps" in the Acre gave way to more substantial tenement blocks and gable-roofed workers' cottages.[31] In the midst of the Acre stood a new St. Patrick's Church, a grand edifice dedicated at the height of Know-Nothing harassment in 1854.[32] The Irish settlement at the opposite end of the mill district on Chapel Hill also flourished. In 1841, local Irish built St. Peter's Church there. By 1900, the Irish neighborhood which spread out beyond Chapel Hill had become the largest in the city.

With the extension of horsecar and, later, electrified trolley lines, the Irish spread into other areas, particularly to the northeast and north of the mills. In 1869, Irish parishioners built the Church of the Immaculate Conception for those living on the hills across the Concord River in Lower Belvedere.[33] Another cluster of Irish crossed the Merrimack to settle in Centralville. Lowell's officials had annexed Centralville in 1851 but the first large-scale movement of Irish began with the extension of horsecar lines in the 1860s. While they faced scattered pockets of discrimination, inexpensive land and convenient access proved attractive inducements to settlement. Such development had a "middle class" stamp, and, so long as the Irish clustered on flat land or the lowest reaches of hills which ringed the city, they faced no organized opposition. In 1883, Centralville's Irish joined with all Catholics living on the north bank of the Merrimack River, including those in the adjacent town of Dracut, to construct St. Michael's Church.[34]

The pattern of Irish settlement in Lowell indicates that the Irish no longer perceived the need to live in close proximity to one another. Lowell was a small, self-contained city of thirteen and one-half square miles, and settlement in new Irish neighborhoods on Lowell's periphery still placed these Irish well within the range of existing neighborhood, church, and family institutions. Using an "Index of Dissimilarity," for example, A. Gibbs Mitchell measured the degree of concentration among Lowell's Irish in the late nineteenth century. He found that the index for the Irish was 19.1 as early as 1855 and decreased to 17.7 by 1880, well below the figure of 25.0 which indicated heavy ethnic concentration in a given ward. By comparison, Lowell's French Canadians attained a level of 30.6 in 1880. While the Index is based upon ward populations and is insensitive to ethnic territorial boundaries, it is clear that the Irish lived throughout Lowell.[35] Obviously, the wealthier Irish tended to settle in the new neighborhoods on the periphery in which they constructed small single-family homes or solid wooden tenement blocks.

The nearly even mix of foreign born and second generation among the Lowell Irish at the turn of the century, and their dispersal throughout the city's neighborhoods, reflected their status as the intermediate group in Lowell. This status was of course not unique to the Irish of Lowell alone, but in William Shannon's opinion characterized the position of Irishmen throughout America. Like the Irish elsewhere, the intermediate position of the Lowell Celts forced them to confront a puzzling dilemma. Would the Irish unite with other recent immigrants to become the leaders of the "outs?" Or on the other hand, would they assimilate into America as their economic, social, and political circumstances improved?[36] The solution worked out by Lowell's Irish suggests one possibility which reflects the national dilemma but was also shaped by local conditions.

Shannon suggested that there were some basic trends common to the American Irish in the late nineteenth century. First, there was a level of ethnic loyalty among them encouraged, at least in part, by interest in the great political debates occurring in Ireland over Home Rule and independence. Such debates nurtured a nationalist outlook among the American Irish and served to maintain their ties to Ireland.[37] In addition, a set of common institutions also encouraged the persistence of ethnic identity among them. In most Irish communities, the workplace, the labor union, the political machine, and the Catholic Church governed the actions of Irish men "urbanized abroad."[38] While the Irish in America favored assimilation and exhibited a kind of "super patriotism" toward the United States, they never rejected their Irish identity. Irish patterns of ethnic loyalty proved a barrier toward assimilation on "American" terms and precluded inter-ethnic cooperation, even in areas such as employment where ethnic groups frequently interacted with one another.

The pattern of employment among ethnic groups in Lowell demonstrates the limits of ethnic cooperation. In 1855, Lowell had fifty-two mills with 11,773 looms producing 2.25 million yards of cloth per week. By 1878, Lowell had one hundred mills with 18,261 looms producing 3.44 million yards of cloth per week. During that time, the number of mill employees increased from 4,367 to 7,625 workers, or over 70 percent.[39] It was in the effort to provide this additional labor that mill agents extended the range of their recruiters in an effort to attract French Canadians into the textile mills. By 1900, almost eleven thousand French Canadians worked in Lowell, or over four times the number living there in 1870.[40] By then, French Canadians had been joined by a host of other ethnic groups, with particularly heavy concentrations of Greeks, Poles, Portuguese, and Jews.[41]

In the midst of this vast influx of new workers from a host of nations an interesting pattern of ethnic segmentation appeared among Lowell's mill workers with important ramifications for the city's Irish. In 1910, the seven largest cotton mills employed 16,905 workers. Among them, the foreign born numbered 72.41 percent and, of these, nearly three-fourths were from non-English-speaking ethnic groups.[42] By contrast, these same mills had employed Irish and Yankee labor almost ex-clusively as late as 1870.[43] Within the mills, therefore, there was a shift toward the employment of new ethnic groups. In that these seven large cotton mills provided much of the mill employment available in Lowell, their actions raise a number of interesting questions. First, what was the position of the Irish within these mills? Second, does the pattern in the seven large mills hold for mill employment generally in Lowell? Third, and perhaps most interesting, does the shift in the pattern of em-ployment indicate that the Irish moved up or were forced out?

By 1900 over fifteen thousand Irish worked in Lowell. Among all Irish, including native born, about two-thirds of those employed worked in the mills. The Irish generally held more skilled jobs within them but they failed to retain their hold on entry-level unskilled labor. Overall, the percentage of Irish in the mills remained about the same throughout the late nineteenth century. Beyond the mill, the Irish comprised about 75 percent of the workers employed in domestic and personal service.[44] For the Irish working class, two trends are apparent. First, the Irish continued to hold skilled mill employment but the largest cotton mills had shifted away from employing them toward hiring newer ethnic groups in the lowest-paying mill jobs. Second, traditional opportunities for the Irish in domestic service remained important sources of em-ployment. In this sense, the Irish both held and lost ground among the seven largest mills and in Lowell's employment picture generally.

By comparison, 8,523 employees worked in textile companies other than the seven largest cotton mills. Most of these employees were men. Among them, there was a significantly higher proportion of natives and Irish with far fewer employees coming from new immigrant groups. The Irish represented about 12 percent of the total but, when their number is added to that of native employees, the total was about 50 percent of all workers employed. While the large cotton mills opened to new immigrants, the shift in the pattern of employment did not extend as rapidly to other textile firms nor to those concerns which employed men.[45] To this end, the Irish still enjoyed an opportunity for mill employment in Lowell's mills, but that employment was conditioned by the particular mill, position held, and sex of the employee. It is less that the Irish moved ''out'' than that they moved ''up'' or ''over,'' i.e., out of entry-level unskilled labor at the seven largest cotton mills.

At the same time, the Irish made significant advances beyond the mill; indeed, over 50 percent of them worked elsewhere by 1900. While many were laborers, about 40 percent of those who worked outside the mill held white-collar jobs or were artisans. From within this group emerged an Irish middle class. Lowell had boasted an Irish middle class of shopkeepers, foremen, and artisans as early as 1860 when Hugh Cummiskey, the *pater familias* of the early Acre Irish, reported his occupation to the census as "gentleman."[46] By 1900, about 2 percent of Lowell's Irish were government officials, doctors, and lawyers, while much larger numbers were merchants, bookkeepers, salesmen, and selling agents. A few Irish had also moved into newly created job occupations such as electricians, and as many as 5 percent of Lowell's Irish men had found positions as policemen, firemen, watchmen, steam railroad employees or as workers on the street railway system. Finally, about eight hundred Irish held skilled positions in the mills or machine shops as engineers and machinists.[47]

Together, this group represented perhaps 25 percent of Lowell's Irish men.[48] For them, movement had been "up" to skilled positions within the mills or "out" of the mills altogether. There was a small but highly visible core of Irish professionals best illustrated by the election of Irish-American banker John J. Donovan as Mayor in 1881.[49] Even more significant, two brothers, John and Edward Harrington, founded a hard-hitting, labor-oriented Democratic weekly newspaper, the Lowell *Sun,* which published daily shortly thereafter and grew steadily in influence.[50] In addition, the Irish middle class generally remained part of a family wage economy and the employment of large numbers of Irish women in the mills contributed to the family's economic vitality. In 1900, 4,864, or 39 percent of Lowell's mill women, were Irish. They also accounted for almost 50 percent of the women employed in domestic and personal service.[51]

The Irish middle class had become an important social, economic, and political force in Lowell by 1900. Historically, the Irish middle class had supported the position of Lowell's corporate and political leaders, and this pattern continued into the twentieth century. Many of the Irish had benefited directly from securing skilled and better-paying positions within the mills, and family wages still were crucial to their continued prosperity. In addition, the rapid increase of "foreign" immigrants made the Irish seem less foreign and reinforced the position of the Irish as the intermediate group. Significantly, when George Kengott compiled his bigoted, racist account of Lowell's ethnic groups in 1910, *The Record of the City,* he clearly identified the "special case" situation of the Irish. Kengott noted that, unlike more recent ethnic groups, the Irish, like other English-speaking immigrants, "generally speaking . . . do not bring habits or institutions differing greatly from those of the Americans themselves."[52] The absence of a Yankee-American upper class neighborhood in Lowell also enhanced the perception of the Irish as an intermediate group. While the Irish seldom, if ever, reached the crest of the hills which ringed the city, they began moving in that direction.

The position of the Irish would seem to offer real opportunity for the development of a political machine in Lowell by the end of the nineteenth century. Two factors worked against Irish political power in Lowell. First, the Democratic Party, which claimed the allegiance of most Irish by 1900, was badly splintered after the Civil War. Its titular local leader, Civil War General Benjamin F. Butler, carried a Republican standard in his Congressional victory. By the early 1880s, the situation improved and Butler was elected Governor of Massachusetts as a Democrat in 1882 thanks to a coalition of Irish and reform-minded Yankees.[53] On a local level, John J. Donovan used the Butler coalition to win as Mayor. Donovan slowly rebuilt the Democratic Party locally but even he failed to develop an effective political leadership which went beyond narrow coalition politics.[54]

The reason for Donovan's inability to form a Democratic political machine lay with Lowell's French Canadians. While the Irish were the city's best organized immigrant group, the French Canadians were also politically active and became increasingly aware of their potential political power. Lowell's French-language newspaper, *L'Etoile,* regularly editorialized on important political issues but with an outlook which reflected a staunchly "Little Canada" perspective. Due to heavy Irish influence in the Democratic Party, the French-Canadian perspective tended to be Republican, further exacerbating the historic ill-will between the two groups.[55] While a virulent local chapter of the American Protective Association with ties to the Republican Party dampened French-Canadian enthusiasm for local Republican politics in the 1890s, French Canadians never joined the Irish as Democrats. Instead, they wisely preferred to exercise their position as the pivotal immigrant group which held the balance of power in Lowell's politics.[56]

The inability of the Irish to convince other immigrants to accept Irish leadership also contributed to the failure of the Irish to assume leadership in union organization. At the heart of the problem was the failure to organize workers into one industry-wide union. In the early twentieth century, the United Textile Workers, affiliated with the American Federation of Labor, organized groups of Lowell mill workers into unions of skilled craftsmen. At the first sign of a strike, Lowell's mill agents moved aggressively against the strikers, closing the mills to all workers. In addition, they played each immigrant group off against another, moving newer immigrants such as Poles and Portuguese into better-paying skilled positions formerly occupied by Irish or French-Canadian strikers. The actions of the mill agents discouraged any sense of working class consciousness from developing among Lowell's immigrants. The sharp business downturn of the 1890s further discouraged unionization.[57]

An even deeper problem lay in the climate of mutual suspicion shared by immigrant groups toward one another. Craft union organization was beneficial only to those immigrant workers in skilled positions, i.e., the Irish and, to a lesser extent, the French Canadians. Among the French Canadians, there was only moderate sympathy toward unionization, in part, because many of them viewed employment as an opportunity and questioned any effort which might disrupt those advances they had made. As one indication, the French-Canadian clergy were always neutral regarding unionization. Among newer immigrant groups, there was even more suspicion of unions. As the IWW inspired ''Bread and Roses'' strike in nearby Lawrence spread to Lowell in 1912, for example, Lowell's Greeks reluctantly agreed to strike but only on their own terms. Those terms included refusal of relief assistance from any unions, even the moderate United Textile Workers. In the end, the Greeks negotiated a separate settlement with Lowell's millowners.[58]

By 1900, it was obvious that ''survivance,'' exercised in a climate of mutual distrust, would prevent Lowell's ethnic groups from organizing effective political leadership in common, either in the mills or in local politics. The Irish shared in these parochial ethnic loyalties, negotiating to their own advantage and never providing leadership which transcended their immediate concerns. To a large extent, the same pattern of ethnic provincialism permeated local church affairs. Within Lowell, there were territorial Irish parishes literally within sight of the French-language churches. While church relations were generally cordial, local, diocesan, and national patterns of development affecting American Catholicism prevented the Church from becoming a common meeting ground. Each ethnic group took polite note of the others' festivals, feast days, and fund raisers, but separate institutional growth characterized parish development among Lowell's Catholic ethnic groups.

As such, it was impossible for the Irish to exercise leadership over the "outs." At the same time, however, an undercurrent of native hostility as well as Irish ethnic loyalties prevented the Irish from assimilating into the "ins." They were, and would remain, the intermediate ethnic group in Lowell. The pattern of development within the Irish community was unique to them, meeting their own needs in a stagnating industrial city slowly moving toward economic collapse. To this end, labor unions protected Irish workers in skilled crafts, and local politics offered the Irish some hope of influencing conditions beyond the mill. Of all the "Irish" institutions which played a role in the pattern of community development locally, however, the one which had the greatest impact upon that development was the Catholic Church.

The institutional growth of the Catholic Church had been slow during the first years of its development in Lowell. By 1848, however, strong church leadership emerged with the arrival of Fathers John and Timothy O'Brien, the first of the "O'Brien Dynasty" who would run St. Patrick's from 1848 to 1922. Under their direction, old wounds caused by factional fights within the parish healed quickly.[59] The O'Briens combined charisma, a tradition of service, and a sense of discipline and authority to create at St. Patrick's what the historians of Massachusetts Catholicism have called the most highly organized parish in the Boston Archdiocese in 1900.[60] A speaker at the St. Patrick's "Silver Jubilee" recalled that Fr. John O'Brien was "a man of big frame and bigger heart, the tender father of his people, and the dear friend of all his brother priests. . . . His courtesy, his hospitality, united to every manly, sacerdotal virtue, made him truly loved, and his company sought after."[61] The speaker characterized O'Brien as a "faithful priest and a true gentleman, he had a hearty welcome for all, but he knew how to combine politeness and duty."[62]

The success of the O'Brien Dynasty was due to four important factors. First, the O'Briens assumed control of St. Patrick's at precisely the moment of heaviest Famine immigration to Lowell and at the same time as the transformation of the pattern of employment to Irish labor. The O'Briens offered service, building a parish network of educational, health, and relief organizations which met the needs of Irish men, as Dennis Clark put it, "from cradle to career."[63] In the process, they earned the respect of Lowell's Irish. Second, they expanded the role of the Catholic Church by creating missions in new Irish neighborhoods and in suburban towns which later became Irish parishes in the "O'Brien" stamp. Third, the O'Briens cooperated with French Oblates in the creation of French-language parishes to meet the needs of Lowell Catholics. At the funeral of Fr. John O'Brien, the French-language parish sent a delegation to honor his memory.[64] Finally, the O'Briens formed a close alliance with Lowell's Irish middle class, using that support to establish a financial, social, and political foundation for subsequent growth.

The O'Briens' actions gave them enormous political influence over local Irish affairs. Before the Civil War, the Irish middle class had been small and badly divided. Their support for corporate policies had damaged their political effectiveness at the moment it was needed most, in the 1850s when the Know Nothing crisis erupted into a series of mob attacks on St. Patrick's parish and general harassment of innocent Catholics.[65] The O'Briens arrived in Lowell as the crisis erupted and stepped immediately into the political vacuum caused by the absence of Irish middle class leadership. In response to the visit of the infamous Hiss "Smelling Committee's" investigation to the parish school, Fr. Timothy O'Brien, an elderly, cultured gentleman who had personally pledged the funds to construct the school, was reported to have said: "They shall not harm a hair of your (the Sisters') heads, the black-hearted villains." The O'Briens' actions marked the end of any early efforts to assimilate on native terms, placing instead an "Irish" and "Catholic" stamp upon the pattern of Irish development in Lowell. Despite Lowell's acclaimed public schools, the O'Briens constructed sectarian schools because of their fears of "godless" education.[66] In short, the O'Briens provided an attractive alternative to joining the "ins"; they would create a distinct, if respectable, Irish Catholic identity in Lowell.

To do so, they needed the support of the Irish middle class. The development of an Irish Catholic community in Centralville offers an appropriate example. Originally part of neighboring Dracut, Lowell's officials annexed Centralville following a petition to annex from area residents to the Massachusetts legislature. After tolls were abolished on the bridge which connected Centralville with Lowell's mills, a steady expansion ensued. Rapid growth came with the extension of horse car lines along Bridge Street, a thoroughfare which led from the Central Bridge through Centralville and into New Hampshire. By 1900, a number of small commercial businesses and industries located there.

Bridge Street ran along a steep incline called "Christian Hill," and most of the early settlement spread out along streets lined with workers' cottages at the base of the hill or paralleling the river along Lakeview Avenue and Front Street. A number of imposing homes for Lowell's Yankee middle class graced the tree-lined slopes of Christian Hill.[67]

By 1900, the pace of Centralville's development had sharpened. With the extension of horse car lines and the construction of an additional bridge at Aiken Street in the western end of the neighborhood, new residents poured into Centralville. Attracted by the accessibility to the mills and the availability of cheap land, residents constructed gable-roofed workers' cottages. As the neighborhood became more congested, rows of wooden tenements lined the streets near the Merrimack River. What had been a pleasant, comfortable, middle class neighborhood had become home to Irish, French Canadians, and Poles. By 1900, one-half of Centralville's residents were immigrants and their descendants.[68]

About 30 percent of these residents were Irish.[69] Despite the growth of Centralville's Irish population, most Irish maintained their allegiance to St. Patrick's, which had jurisdiction over them, or to the two other Irish parishes in Lowell. In addition, Centralville's Irish were active in such city-wide organizations as the Mathew Institute and the Hibernian Society. Despite the strong "Irish Catholic" stamp upon them, there was the possibility that the inconvenience of attending St. Patrick's across the river, together with the "rural" and "Yankee" atmosphere of Centralville, could weaken old associations in time. Complaints arose that Centralville's Irish "attended any church" or, worse yet, that they might not attend any at all.[70] To solve this dilemma, a new parish arose.

The process began with Archdiocesan decree. In November 1883, Archbishop Williams announced that Lowell would be divided into parishes with set territorial boundaries and that two parishes, one in South Lowell and a second in Centralville, would be established. The latter would serve all Catholics living in Lowell on the north bank of the Merrimack River as well as in the adjacent town of Dracut.[71] Williams appointed Fr. Michael O'Brien, the pastor of St. Patrick's, to organize the new parish. O'Brien promptly turned over daily development to his cousin and assistant, Fr. William O'Brien, who held Mass in December 1883 in a city firehouse on Fourth Street in Centralville.[72] Although never expressly detailed, it was understood that the new parish was to be Irish and that Centralville's growing French-Canadian community would continue to worship at churches in Little Canada until their numbers were sufficient to establish one of their own in Centralville.

Fr. William O'Brien faced a difficult task. He quickly recognized that his most cumbersome problem would be to break down existing loyalties among Centralville's Irish and to forge new but similar ones in their place. To accomplish his goals, O'Brien adopted two strategies. First, he visited his new parishioners individually, urging them to develop new loyalties and to contribute to his building campaign. Personal charisma had always been a hallmark of the O'Briens' approach in Lowell, and his appeal for support worked nicely.[73] Second, he enlisted the assistance of the Irish middle class living in Centralville. They had been drawn to the neighborhood ever since an Irish tailor, Hugh McEvoy, moved to Christian Hill thirty years earlier.[74] Fr. Michael O'Brien's brother, Timothy, was one of them and donated land for a church site.[75] O'Brien utilized the business acumen of Centralville's Irish middle class to good effect. By combining a personal appeal to the general Irish population in the development of the parish, Fr. William O'Brien successfully launched his development drive.

Perhaps nothing better indicates the importance of the alliance between local church leaders and the Irish middle class than the location of the new Centralville church. The first site proposed was on Jewett Street to the west of the Bridge Street bridge and in the heart of its working class Irish neighborhood. After a problem arose in securing land title, O'Brien abandoned this site and selected one proposed by his allies within the Irish middle class.[76] Despite vocal opposition from Yankees in Centralville, the new church arose to the east of Bridge Street on the lower slopes of Christian Hill.[77] In June 1884, church officials dedicated the new parish, called St. Michael's to honor the patron saint of Fr. Michael O'Brien. As expected, his cousin, William, became pastor.[78]

The location of the church signified that St. Michael's had become a parish of the Irish middle class. They had made a case for its location by suggesting that proximity to trolley lines and to the commercial district along Bridge Street would ensure that the church would become the center of the new parish. They were right, although the process took fifty years.[79] In fact, the location spoke more to the spirit of cooperation shared by O'Brien and the Irish middle class. St. Michael's would be situated among the "lace curtain" Irish and on the periphery of the working class Irish district in Centralville. Its site symbolized the hopes and dreams of the Irish middle class as they made their way up Christian Hill. On another level, the Irish working class had already accepted the philosophy which governed the selection of the church's site by virtue of their move from largely immigrant districts into an "American Irish" neighborhood. All Irish groups in Centralville loyally supported the on-going development drive. By 1900, a brick edifice with a seating capacity of twelve hundred had arisen.[80]

In the case of Lowell, the answer to the question of whether Irish would join the "ins" or become the dominant ethnic group among the "outs" rests somewhere in between. On a national level, the Church, political machine, and labor union would provide a framework upon which all Irish would assume an American-Irish identity. The mix among Irish institutions varied, however, with the specific community. In Lowell, a "one-industry" economy and the absence of an upper class allowed the Irish an opportunity to place their mark upon a community in which everyone belonged, in one fashion or another, to the working class. In the absence of successful labor organization, and with an Irish political machine still in its infancy, the Church became the dominant Irish institution in Lowell. Backed by the loyalty of the Irish middle class, it flourished as it shaped Irish community development.

Ultimately, the Irish joined the "ins," particularly after World War II, but the process occurred only gradually and reflected conditions in postwar America.[81] Until then, compromises reached as early as the mid-nineteenth century dominated Irish attitudes. By becoming a church of the Irish middle class while also providing service and a sense of direction to its working class, the Church created a framework for institutional growth which matched the conditions faced by the Irish. As the Irish moved beyond the old immigrant parishes, Catholic leaders modified their system to meet the improving circumstances of many Irish while grounding that system firmly in a notion of service. There was no effective labor organization in Lowell in the late nineteenth century; economic conditions, especially those affecting the make-up of the labor force, precluded it. Catholic leaders had nothing to fear from officers in the Hibernian Society or Catholic politicians; they were respected parishioners upon whom the success of the parish rested. It was not that the Irish begged off the issue of deciding whether or not to join the "ins" or lead the "outs," it was more that the Irish found a route somewhere in the middle which was far more practical and effective.

NOTES

1. See, for example, Fredericka Bremer, *The Homes of the New World: Impressions of America* 2 vols. (New York: Harper and Bros., 1868; reprint ed., New York: Negro University Press, 1968); Anthony Trollope, *North America* 2 vols., (New York: Harper and Bros., 1862; reprint ed., New York: Kelley, 1970); Michel Chevalier, *Society, Manners and Politics in the United States: Letters on North America* (Boston: Weeks, Jordan and Co., 1839; reprint ed., New York: Kelley, 1966); Charles Dickens, *American Notes for General Circulation* (New York: Harper and Bros., 1842; reprint ed., Penguin, 1972). Nathan Appleton, *Introduction to the Power Loom and Origin of Lowell* (Lowell, 1858), p. 19.

2. Harry C. Dinmore, "Proprietors of Locks and Canals: The Founding of Lowell," in Arthur L. Eno, Jr., ed., *Cotton Was King* (Lowell: Lowell Historical Society, 1976), pp. 69–73.

3. In the "Regulations for the Boarding Houses of the Middlesex Company," issued by Agent Samuel Lawrence in 1846, for example, Lawrence ordered that the doors be closed at 10:00 P.M. and "no one admitted after that time without some reasonable excuse: and that "the keepers of the Boarding Houses . . . give an account of the number, names, and employment of their boarders, when required, and report the names of such as are guilty of any improper conduct, or are not in the regular habit of attending public worship."

4. By 1850, the Boston Associates had developed mills in Chicopee, Taunton, and Lawrence, Massachusetts; Manchester, Dover, Somersworth, and Nashua, New Hampshire; Saco and Biddeford, Maine, and, shortly after, in Holyoke, Massachusetts.

5. George O'Dwyer, *Irish Catholic Genesis of Lowell* (Lowell, Mass.: Sullivan Brothers Printers, 1920), p. 7; John F. McEvoy, "Letter to the City of Lowell at the Semi-Centennial Celebration of the Incorporation of the Town of Lowell," 22 February 1876, *Proceedings at the Fiftieth Anniversary of the Incorporation of the Town of Lowell* (Lowell, 1876), p. 132.

6. Paul Hill, "Reminiscenses of Lowell, Fifty Years Ago," *Old Residents Historical Association* 5 (1894): 280; McEvoy, p. 132; A. B. Wright, "Lowell in 1826," *ORHA* 3 (1887): 405; and Charles Cowley, "The Foreign Colonies of Lowell," *ORHA* 2 (1881): 2 among others accounts.

7. *United States Catholic Miscellany*, 23 July 1831 as quoted in O'Dwyer, p. 19.

8. See Brian C. Mitchell, *The Paddy Camps: The Meaning of Community among the Irish of Lowell, Massachusetts, 1821–1861*. (Urbana: University of Illinois Press, 1986) for the initial effort and eventual failure to assimilate Irish immigrants in Lowell on Yankee terms and as to the effect of this failure upon the development of community.

9. "Irish Girls in Lowell," Boston *Pilot*, 16 August 1851, p. 7.

10. In the 1855 State Census, for example, the foreign born Irish living in Lowell exceeded the total number of Irish, whether foreign, naturalized, or American born, who had lived in Lowell in 1843. By 1855 over ten thousand native born Irish lived in Lowell. State Manuscript Census (1855), Commonwealth of Massachusetts, Lowell, v. 16.

11. Thomas Dublin, *Women at Work: The Transformation of Work and Community in Lowell, Massachusetts, 1826–1860* (New York: Columbia University Press, 1979), pp. 147–49, 158.

12. Dublin, *Women at Work*, pp. 154–56.

13. As early as 1835, Richard Cobden, who was then a little-known English businessman visiting Lowell, noted that on a visit to the Lowell Machine Shop "*even the Irish* always wash their hands before leaving his [the overseer's] shop." Elizabeth Hoon Cawley, ed., *The American Diaries of Richard Cobden* (Princeton: Princeton University Press, 1952: reprint ed., Greenwood Press, 1969), p. 117.

14. Lowell voted overwhelmingly in 1854 for a Know Nothing mayor, Ambrose Lawrence, and boasted a Know Nothing paper for several years, the *American Citizen*.

15. In 1833–1834, for example, two Irish men, Hugh Cummiskey and Samuel Murray, served as town constables. O'Dwyer, p. 58.

16. "The Whig Party in Lowell," Lowell *Advertiser*, 16 November 1854, p. 2.

17. Catholic priests actively supported the Union position from the pulpit. "The Lowell Pulpit on the War," *Lowell Daily Courier*, 29 April 1861, p. 2.

18. Table 59, Census Reports, Vol. I, *Twelfth Census of the United States, Taken in the Year 1900*. There were 25,466 Irish with foreign born parentage among the 94,969 residents of Lowell in 1900.

19. George F. Kengott, *The Record of a City: A Social Survey of Lowell, Massachusetts* (New York: Macmillan, 1912), pp. 29–30.

20. Kengott, *Record of a City*, pp. 29–30; pp. 51–52.

21. The Two Oblates priests, Lucien Lagier and André Marie Carin, purchased a vacant Unitarian Church with a $3,000 down-payment from parishioners. Peter F. Blewett, "The New People: An Introduction to the Ethnic History of Lowell," in Eno, pp. 195–196.

22. Kengott, *Record of a City*, pp. 29–30; pp. 51–52.

23. Ronald A. Petrin, "Culture, Community and Politics: French Canadians

in Massachusetts, 1883–1915,'' in *Little Canadas of New England*, Claire Quintal, ed., p. 68.

24. Frances Early, ''The Settling-In Process: The Beginnings of Little Canada in Lowell, Massachusetts, In the Late Nineteenth Century,'' in Quintal, pp. 30–31.

25. Early, ''The Settling-In Process,'' pp. 32, 34.

26. Kengott, *Record of a City*, p. 37.

27. Kengott, *Record of a City*, p. 40.

28. Kengott, *Record of a City*, Table 7, pp. 38–40.

29. Kengott, *Record of a City*, pp. 38–40.

30. Albert Gibbs Mitchell, Jr., ''Irish Family Patterns in Nineteenth Century Ireland and Lowell, Massachusetts,'' (Boston University, Ph.D. dissertation, 1976), p. 205.

31. Lowell National Historical Park and Preservation District, *Cultural Resources Inventory:* Prepared for Division of Cultural Resources, North Atlantic Regional Office, National Park Service, by Shepley, Bullfinch, Richardson, and Abbott, including ''the Acre through Broadway Street,'' ''Centralville,'' and scattered references, Special Collections, University of Lowell.

32. ''St. Patrick's Church,'' *Daily Journal and Courier*, 12 October 1854, p. 2.

33. Early, ''The Settling-In Process,'' p. 33, on the division of parish responsibilities by ethnic consideration among Lowell's Oblates, 1870.

34. Brian C. Mitchell, *On the North Bank: A Centennial History of the Parish of St. Michael* (Lowell: Sullivan Brothers Printers, 1984).

35. A. Gibbs Mitchell, ''Irish Family Patterns,'' pp. 201–203.

36. William V. Shannon, *The American Irish: A Political and Social Portrait* (New York: Macmillan, 1974), pp. 131–32.

37. The editors of the regional Irish Catholic newspaper, the Boston *Pilot*, worked particularly hard to foster a nationalistic view of Ireland. See also Shannon, *The American Irish*, pp. 132–33, on this outlook.

38. See Lynn Lees and John Modell, ''The Irish Countryman Urbanized: A Comparative Perspective on the Famine Migration,'' *Journal of Urban History* 3 (1977): 391–408 for the impact of urbanization on Irish emigration experience.

39. Eno, *Cotton Was King*, Appendix B.

40. Table 43, *Special Reports on Occupations of the Twelfth Census under sup of William C. Hunt* (Washington: GPO, 1904, pp. 598–60).

41. Lowell's Jews generally worked outside the mills.

42. Kengott, *Record of a City*, p. 34.

43. As early as 1870, however, mill agents sent recruiters north into Quebec in an effort to attract French Canadians to Lowell. Early, p. 24.

44. Table 43, *Statistics of Occupations*.

45. Kengott, *Record of a City*, pp. 34, 36.

46. Federal Manuscript Census (1860), Microcopy 653, Roll 507.

47. Table 43, *Statistics of Occupations.*

48. Of the 8,983 Irish men employed, 2,378, or 26%, worked at a variety of occupations including salesmen, banking, bookkeeping, restauranteurs, shipping, tailoring, and as bakers. Among the group were a number who worked in skilled mill jobs such as engineers (168) and machinists (656) and, together, they constituted a rough middle class among Lowell's Irish.

49. Mary Blewett, "The Mills and Multitudes: A Political History," in Eno ed., *Cotton was King,* pp. 174–75.

50. Shortly before World War II, the descendants of the Harringtons bought out the other surviving newspaper, the *Courier Citizen/Evening Leader,* and became the only newspaper in Lowell.

51. Table 43, *Statistics of Occupations.*

52. Kengott, *Record of a City,* p. 40. He also noted that there was "no particular 'Little Ireland' in Lowell"—a fact more imagined than real (p. 51).

53. Mary Blewett, "The Mills and the Multitudes: A Political History," pp. 174–176.

54. Mary Blewett, "The Mills and the Multitudes," pp. 175–76.

55. *L'Etoile* remained a force in Lowell's politics until the 1930s.

56. Blewett, "The Mills and the Multitudes," pp. 175–76.

57. Fidelia Brown, "Decline and Fall: The End of the Dream," in Eno, *Cotton Was King,* pp. 148–49. Prior to then, union activity had centered in the Lowell Textile Council comprised of members of skilled workers' unions. They numbered about 10 percent of all mill employees.

58. Brown, "Decline and Fall," p. 149 on the clergy's reaction to the 1903 strike; pp. 150–52 on the 1912 strike and the Greek role in it.

59. These persistent feuds had led to the separation of the feuding groups with the foundation of St. Peter's in 1841.

60. Robert H. Lord, John E. Sexton, and Edward P. Harrington, *History of the Archdiocese of Boston* (New York: Sheed and Ward, 1944), 3 vols., 3:307.

61. *History of the Archdiocese of Boston,* 2: 306.

62. *History of the Archdiocese of Boston,* 2: 306. The speaker also reported that "their reign here was the epitome of religion and piety."

63. Dennis Clark, *The Irish in Philadelphia: Ten Generations of Urban Experience* (Philadelphia: Temple University Press, 1973), p. 99.

64. Early, "The Settling-In Process," p. 33.

65. Brian C. Mitchell, *The Paddy Camps.*

66. *History of the Sisters of Notre Dame de Namur by the Pioneer Sister,* St. Patrick's Convent, Lowell, Massachusetts; Archives, Sisters of Notre Dame de Namur, Ipswich, Massachusetts, pp. 7–8; 12–14. For a more general discussion, see Brian C. Mitchell, "Educating Irish Immigrants in Antebellum Lowell," *Historical Journal of Massachusetts* 11 (1983): 94–103.

67. "Centralville," *Cultural Resources Inventory.*

68. Federal Manuscript Census (1900), J 623, Rolls 659, 660, 661.

69. Federal Manuscript Census (1900). J623, Rolls 659, 660, 661. In the late 1890s, Fr. William O'Brien estimated that the parish had grown from 1,100 to 3,800 parishioners. *The Story of St. Michael's* (Lowell, Ca. 1896), p. 9.

70. "Episcopal Register," 16 April 1884, Archives, Archdiocese of Boston.

71. In effect, the territory extended from the Merrimack River to the border of New Hampshire.

72. "Episcopal Register," 16 April 1884; *Story of St. Michael's*, p. 4.

73. Many of the prospective parishioners knew Fr. William O'Brien well in that they had continued to affiliate with St. Patrick's despite residing in Centralville.

74. Lowell Tax Assessments (1835), (1863), Assessor's Office, Lowell City Hall, Lowell, Massachusetts.

75. *Story of St. Michael's*, p. 22.

76. Even at the founding of the parish, there were already "lace curtain" and "working class" districts within Centralville.

77. Lowell's Mayor, William F. Courtney (1895–96) and publisher John J. Harrington were also among St. Michael's parishioners.

78. *Story of St. Michael's*, p. 5.

79. Much of the movement to Christian Hill occurred in the years around World War II. The process continued even more rapidly after the war.

80. There are a variety of accounts which deal with the dedication of St. Michael's upper church See, for example: Frederick W. Coburn, *History of Lowell and Its People* (New York: Lewis Historical Publishing Co., 1920) vol. II, pp. 555–556; *Illustrated History of Lowell* (Lowell: Courier Citizen, 1897) p. 722; and *Parish Reunion Celebrating the 90th Anniversary of the Founding of St. Michael's Parish* (1974) "St. Michael's," on Patrick Keeley as architect.

81. A large percentage of the Irish which still identifies itself as "Irish" now lives in suburban Lowell.

ırısh, amerıcan, catholıc: ırısh-amerıcan ıdentıty ın worcester, massachusetts, 1880 to 1920

On July 4, 1826, two hundred Irish construction workers descended on Worcester, a small town in central Massachusetts. Even in the midst of the town's jubilant celebrations of the fiftieth anniversary of the new Republic, the arrival of the Irish did not go unnoticed. The rugged Irish laborers trudging into the town inspired dreams of imminent economic prosperity among Worcester's natives, for the Irish had come to complete a canal linking Worcester to Providence, Rhode Island, and the sea, promising lucrative new trade for the Massachusetts town and its residents. Yet the sight of the Celts also roused nightmarish visions of future social and cultural fragmentation. Worcester in 1826 was a homogeneous community. Virtually all of its residents were descendants of stalwart Anglo-Saxon Puritans. Over the years Worcester's citizens had jealously guarded their village from the encroachment of outsiders, even chasing an earlier group of Irishmen, Ulster Presbyterians, out of town a century before. The bounties to be reaped from the canal seemed undeniable, but few of Worcester's natives could view the advent of the Irish workers who were building it as anything but a mixed blessing.[1]

Worcester would have its prosperity. Indeed, its economy would expand beyond the wildest imaginings of the townfolk in 1826. Though the canal's benefits would prove transitory, the advantages reaped from the railroads which quickly followed the canal would not. A mixture of wide ranging railroad connections, Yankee mechanical ingenuity, and sharp investments by local capitalists would make Worcester the thirteenth largest manufacturing center in the nation by 1890. In 1895 over fourteen hundred Worcester companies, employing nearly 22,000 men and women, would produce $41 million worth of manufactured products. Further, as the city's boosters never tired of boasting, Worcester's economy differed radically from those of neighboring Massachusetts cities like Lawrence, Lowell, or Fall River. While the economic fortunes of those cities rose and fell with a single trade, textiles, Worcester's diverse industrial base fostered steadier, more stable but no less substantial economic development. Though world renowned for the manufacture of wire, machinery, and machine tools, Worcester's companies produced everything from corsets to breakfast cereal. Thus even when the growth of the city's economy began to peak and slow in the early twentieth century the subsequent decline was by no means as catastrophic as the rapid descent of the state's textile centers. In addition, the city's boosters, again distinguishing their home from most other Massachusetts cities, could also claim that most of Worcester's companies were home grown—established, financed, and managed by local entrepreneurs and capitalists.[2]

Yet if the rise of industry brought prosperity to Worcester, it also doomed forever the small, homogeneous town which the natives had guarded so jealously for so long. By 1880 Worcester was an industrial boom town of over fifty thousand people coping with rutted streets, an overloaded sewer system, and spreading tenements. By 1920 it was a small metropolis with nearly four times as many residents, some already dreaming of suburban homes in nearby towns. Perhaps the most dramatic change in Worcester's population, however, was not its rising numbers but its growing diversity. There were still Yankees in Worcester by 1900, over thirty thousand of them, and they still controlled the city, its economy, its premiere social clubs, and even its politics to a remarkable degree. Many of these Yankees, however, were themselves newcomers to Worcester, largely farm boys and girls from Vermont, Maine, New Hampshire, and rural Massachusetts. Worcester's Yankees were not only divided by different origins but by class and religion. In the 1880s a newly self conscious Yankee elite began to consolidate and draw away from the native stock middle and working classes. In the same decade, the city also exploded with new Protestant churches of a variety of sects. Still Worcester's Yankees were but a minority of the city's population by the end of the nineteenth century. Over 70 percent of the city's residents in 1900 had themselves been born, or their parents had been born, in foreign countries. Included in that proportion were ten thousand French Canadians and eleven thousand Swedes (a surprisingly large number for a Northeastern city). In the first twenty years of the new century these immigrants and their children would be joined by over twenty-five thousand Poles, Lithuanians, and Italians.[3]

The Irish, the first of the foreign ethnics, however, were still the largest ethnic group in Worcester in 1900, or even 1920. Many of the construction workers who came to build the canal in 1826 stayed on, and in the 1830s and 1840s more Irish arrived to build Worcester's railroads. Still, the number of Irishmen in Worcester was small, only about six hundred or 5 percent of the town's population until the Famine disaster struck Ireland in 1846. Then the trickle of Irish immigrants into Worcester became a flood, and by 1865 there were more than five thousand Irish born in the city. The background of Irish immigrants changed, too, in the Famine years, as the sources of Worcester's Irish immigration shifted from Ireland's eastern provinces and southern sea-coast to the island's more economically backward and thoroughly Gaelic western counties. After the Famine a river of Irish immigrants continued to flow into Worcester. The number of foreign born Irish in the city did not peak until 1900. Yet by that time there were already twice as many American born or second generation Irish men and women as immigrants. That number is somewhat misleading, for the bulk of the second generation Irish, even in 1900, were still children. Nevertheless, as the new century opened, the number of American born Irish adults (men and women age eighteen or over) nearly equalled that of Irish immigrant adults.[4]

By the turn of the century the Irish were as much an established fact of Worcester's life as the city's railroads, factories, and traffic-choked streets. Yet if they had set down roots in the city, they were not necessarily accepted. To many Yankees the Irish were still outsiders, suspect for their ancestry and their foreign faith. In 1920 Irish Catholics would be little more welcome in Yankee social circles than they had been nearly one hundred years before, when the Celtic canal workers first appeared in Worcester. Their progress up the city's occupational ladder or out of their old tenement neighborhoods was also disappointing, not only in retrospect when compared to the social and geographic mobility of other groups, but to themselves as well. The history of the Worcester Irish in the turn of the century era, then, clearly reflects the apt distinction made by historians of Irish America between the experiences of Irishmen in the east versus those of Hibernians living in western America. Even the Worcester Irish themselves sometimes bemoaned the fate that had set them down in cold, hostile, Yankee New England, while permitting their more fortunate cousins to enjoy the freedom and dynamism of rapidly growing western cities.[5]

Yet as apt as such a regional distinction is, it may tend to oversimplify the history of eastern Irish communities such as Worcester's. It suggests an inevitability to the history of the Worcester Irish, as if the paths of their evolution were unalterably set when the first Irish Catholic arrived in the city, or even long before when Cromwell's troopers slashed through Catholic Ireland while Puritans of equal zeal were nursing their bible commonwealth in Massachusetts. Such a depiction masks the complexity and dynamism of Irish-American history in Worcester and perhaps other eastern cities during the turn of the century era. If Irish progress up Worcester's occupational ladder was sluggish, for example, the Irish did, nonetheless, make substantial progress. Likewise if their movement out of their old neighborhoods proceeded at a slow pace, it still took place and with growing momentum.

Most important perhaps, if their permanent exclusion from Yankee society seemed destined looking backward from 1920, it did not appear so to the Irish themselves looking forward in 1880. It would take the Worcester Irish the better part of forty years and a series of wild fluctuations in their conceptions of themselves and their place in Worcester society before they would finally define who they were and where they fit in the social, political, and cultural life in Worcester. In part, the volatility of these conceptions was a product of the changes within their own population, the emergence of a new generation and a growing lace curtain class. To a large extent, however, it also reflected significant trends in the particulars of their environment. The past may have bequeathed them a maturing economy and more important a well entrenched and suspicious native population, but the structure of local politics remained fluid throughout the turn of the century era, the economy still fluctuated in cycles of boom and bust, and the city still grew with the arrival of new immigrants from a host of different nations. These alterations in the particulars of their environment would have a considerable influence on how the Worcester Irish defined their identity and their role in the city.

In short, the Irish in Worcester and important elements of their environment were both changing in the turn of the century era, and such changes caused a considerable amount of confusion in the city's Celtic community. Perhaps no Irish population in America at the turn of the century better fit William Shannon's characterization of a people caught in an ''ambiguous indeterminate state'' as well as the Irish in Worcester. Perhaps none wrestled so intensely with questions of who they were and what kind of Americans they were either, or puzzled more anxiously over the dilemma of whether to join the ''ins'' or lead the ''outs'' of their city.[6] For the Irish in Worcester, the turn of the century period was truly a time of difficult and painful transition.

In 1899 John F. O'Connor, a Worcester schoolteacher, lamented the slow occupational progress of his people: ''We (the Irish) are only halfway up the ladder.'' Worse, he suggested, there were new groups in Worcester, immigrants from Germany and Sweden who had settled in the city after the Irish and yet had achieved greater success. It would take the Irish two or three more generations, O'Connor asserted, before they could match the achievements of even those recent nordic arrivals to Worcester.[7]

Many Irishmen in Worcester shared O'Connor's pessimism. Frustrated complaints about the economic ''failure'' of the city's Irish filled the columns of the local Irish press at the turn of the century. One of the most frequent refrains in such laments was the utter failure of the Worcester Irish to compete with the city's Yankees for control of Worcester's major industries or banks. As late as 1919 only 8 of the 104 first or second generation Irish listed in the biographical sections of Charles Nutt's *History of Worcester* were manufacturers. By contrast thirty of the thirty-six Swedes listed in Nutt's *History* were manufacturers, and many of them were immigrants. The achievements of the Irish in finance were nearly as dismal. By 1920 they controlled only two marginal ''Irish'' banks and had made almost no inroads into the city's largest financial institutions.[8]

The performance of the Irish on a lower level also lent substance to contemporary complaints about Irish failure. The economic stagnation of Worcester's Irish immigrants, for example, was clearly evident. In 1900, nearly seventy-five years after the first Irish Catholics arrived in Worcester, only 9 percent of the city's Irish immigrants were white-collar workers and only another 20 percent toiled at skilled blue-collar jobs. Over two-fifths could find only the meanest kind of unskilled jobs at the bottom of Worcester's economic hierarchy. Of course, many of these were recent arrivals from Ireland. Nevertheless, only 23.8 percent of those who had been in the United States as long as fifteen to twenty years were white-collar or skilled blue-collar workers. The economic status of foreign born Irish women was much the same. In 1900 only 3.8 percent of the single Irish women in Worcester were white-collar workers. A majority were domestic servants, and almost all the rest labored in low skill industrial occupations.[9]

Restricted opportunities accounted, at least in part, for this Irish failure. Though Worcester's economy was relatively healthy in the turn of the century era, it would pass its peak period of growth during those years. The prosperity of its diverse industries also varied significantly throughout the late nineteenth and early twentieth centuries. The boot and shoe trade, for example, was Worcester's largest industry in 1880 but collapsed to near insignificance by 1890. Since 11 percent of the city's Irish immigrant workers labored in the boot and shoe shops in 1880, the death of the industry undoubtedly severely hindered their occupational progress. In other branches of manufacture, such as the metal working or machine tool industries, the city's Celts confronted discrimination and competition from other ethnic groups. The Yankee owners of the Washburn Men Wire Company and the Norton Grinding Wheel Company, two of Worcester's largest firms, seemed to prefer Swedish Protestant workers over Irish Catholics. Irish women also encountered discrimination even in their search for jobs as servants. Classified advertisements seeking "American girls only" appeared frequently in Worcester's newspapers during the late nineteenth century.[10]

Restricted opportunities, however, were only one hindrance to the Irish upward climb; their cultural inheritance from Ireland also proved to be a handicap. As O'Connor noted in 1899 the most important defect in their cultural inheritance was simply their lack of useful skills. While many of the Swedish immigrants came to Worcester with experience in the iron trade and even some of the French Canadians could boast carpentry or construction skills, the Irish could offer little of value to a burgeoning industrial city. They had not only come from an overwhelmingly agricultural country, but many of them, perhaps most, had come from western Ireland, the most economically backward region of an economically backward country. They may have also suffered from their homeland's ambivalent attitudes about the very worth of ambition and upward mobility. Their priests in Worcester, like clerics in Ireland, often railed against the evil of materialism. Priests and lay spokesmen also frequently worried aloud that the excessively ambitious might be tempted to deny their faith or ancestry in exchange for advancement in an economy and society still tightly controlled by native stock Protestants.[11]

For these reasons and more perhaps, the Irish occupational advance was slow in the turn of the century era, but the sluggishness of that advance should not obscure the real occupational progress which Irishmen made in Worcester. Despite all the obstacles they confronted or hindrances of their culture that slowed them, the number of white-collar Irish workers rose 91 percent between 1880 and 1900 and skilled blue-collar workers by 31 percent in the same two decades. Most of these gains were made by the new generation. Though the American born Irish hardly threatened the Yankee monopoly on the top spots in Worcester's economic hierarchy, a large proportion of them had nonetheless secured a modest prosperity and status. Nearly one quarter of the second generation Irish men and unmarried women were white-collar workers in 1900, and another third of the men worked in skilled blue-collar occupations. Conversely only 10 percent of the American born Irish men were unskilled laborers and only 10 percent of the second generation women were domestic servants. John F. O'Connor was only partially correct in 1899. A larger proportion of Swedes and French Canadians may have been skilled blue-collar workers in 1900, but far more Irish had climbed into white-collar jobs. If the Worcester Irish were only half way up the ladder, that still meant that a substantial proportion had escaped its bottom rungs.[12]

The sluggish economic progress made by the Worcester Irish in the late nineteenth century had a significant influence on their slow dispersal from their old neighborhoods. When the Irish canalworkers first came to Worcester in 1826, the town fathers had rigidly segregated them on Worcester's East Side, safely distant, or so Yankee leaders thought, from the village proper and its respectable native stock Protestant inhabitants. By the turn of the century when the vast majority of the city's Yankees lived on the West Side, nearly 84.7 percent of the city's Irish immigrants still lived on the East Side not far from the original canalworkers' camp. In part this pattern of segregation reflected the impact of Yankee hostility. In the 1890s, for example, the anti Catholic American Protective Association was very popular in middle or lower middle class Yankee residential areas, discouraging even those Irishmen with the means from buying or renting in those districts. Some Irishmen, especially newly arrived immigrants, also seemed to prefer the older Irish districts, where churches, clubs, saloons, groceries, and boardinghouses run by their own people were numerous. Yet to a great degree Irishmen remained in their older neighborhoods simply because they could not afford to leave. Cheap tenement housing was plentiful in their districts, and virtually all of the city's factories were in or near those neighborhoods, permitting Irishmen an easy walk to work. These constraints coupled with the slow development of the city's transportation system gave the Irish few alternatives but to remain where they were. In 1893, Irish school committeeman John Duggan aptly described a Worcester divided between "the East and West Sides . . . the Irish and the Americans, the Catholics and Protestants."[13]

In the twentieth century the geographical distinction between an Irish East Side and a Yankee West Side in Worcester no longer held. As more and more Irishmen, particularly of the new generation, climbed the occupational ladder, their economic resources improved. The streetcar system also began to spread to all corners of the city, and Irish real estate agents began to play a critical role in the development of new residential sections. As the *Catholic Messenger,* Worcester's Irish newspaper, proclaimed in 1911: "As Fortune favors us and better things which others have enjoyed come within our reach we seek to secure them. Among these are quiet homes far removed from the turmoil, the dirt, and the smoke of the busy center and such as these, the Catholic people are seeking." The paper predicted that year that the "spires" of Catholic churches would soon be as numerous on the West Side as they were on the East Side. Within the next decade, the *Catholic Messenger's* prediction had begun to be fulfilled, as four new Catholic churches appeared in the peripheral western and northeastern sections of the city. Not all Irish families left the old neighborhoods, at least in part because not all could afford to leave. In the 1910s, the vast majority of the Irish families which settled near the new churches in the west or southwest had at least one white-collar member. Nevertheless, the degree of the Irish dispersal throughout Worcester became so great that by 1950 a Clark University geographer found no group in the city, not even the Yankees, more widely scattered about Worcester's neighborhoods than the Irish.[14]

Though their progress up the occupational ladder or dispersal from the old ghettoes was slow, the Worcester Irish still found it easier to escape old jobs or neighborhoods than the influence of subtle norms and customs inherited from Ireland. To some Worcester Yankees their Irish neighbors seemed so thoroughly acculturated by the dawn of the twentieth century as to seem invisible, especially in comparison with the more colorful, recent immigrants from Southern and Eastern Europe. Even within the Irish community, immigrants bitterly lamented that the new American born Irish generation seemed thoroughly "Americanized." It is true that the new generation had eagerly adopted many of the customs of their native America. Old Irish folk songs had given way to tin pan alley tunes, jigs to the "turkey trot," and the hurley stick to the baseball bat. "I'm makin for Macon Georgia" even crept onto the concert bill of one St. Patrick's Day program in 1915. Yet beneath that veneer of Americanization, Irish values and norms continued to shape the most intimate decisions of even the American born. Second generation Irishmen and women in Worcester married late, for example. In 1900 American born Irishmen married on the average at age thirty-one and second generation Irish women on the average at age twenty-eight. These ages were not only later than any other groups in Worcester but even later than Irish immigrants in the city. Second generation Irish couples also continued to have large families. In 1900 second generation Irish wives gave birth to far more children than married Yankee women, and once married bore children at about the same rate as Irish immigrant wives.[15]

The turn of the century era then was a confusing period for the Worcester Irish. A new generation grew to maturity, while the immigrants remained numerous. Celts began to move up the economic ladder or out of their old neighborhoods, but only slowly. The American born Irish participated avidly in American popular culture but were still sensitive to Irish norms in their private lives. This confusion made the search for a definition of their identity and their place in Worcester society very difficult. Changes in their environment complicated that search even further. The Worcester Irish would fluctuate wildly in their responses to their dilemma of identity over the forty years straddling the turn of the century: from earnest attempts to prove their acculturation to American norms and to accommodate their Yankee neighbors in the 1880s, to a retreat into a belligerent social and cultural ethnocentrism in the late 1890s, to finally a more or less permanent definition of themselves as militant Catholics and yet patriotic Americans in the early twentieth century.

In the 1880s and early 1890s Worcester's Irishmen seemed eager to overcome the cultural and social differences which separated them from their longtime Yankee antagonists. A spirit of optimism and reconciliation seemed to pervade Worcester's Irish community in those years. The evidence of that spirit was widespread. Irish Catholic priests cooperated frequently with their Protestant counterparts in local charitable enterprises, and the editor of Worcester's local Irish weekly, the *Messenger*, took great pains to praise Protestant institutions and organizations. Parochial schools and the divisive issues they raised found little support from either Irish priests or laymen. Both instead lauded the "ennobling influences" of public education. Acutely conscious of Yankee stereotypes, young Irishmen, particularly second generation Irishmen, flocked to Catholic temperance societies to learn how to become "more American than the Americans themselves." Between 1883 and 1888 the number of Irish teetotallers in Worcester rose from a little over two hundred to over twelve hundred. Even the Irish nationalist movement reflected the yearning of the Worcester Irish to prove their American patriotism and reconcile their differences with their Yankee neighbors. Leaders of the movement consistently eschewed violence and militance. After a short lived rebellion by followers of Patrick Ford's brand of radical nationalism, they also studiously avoided any mention of revolutionizing Ireland's economy as well. Espousing conservative rhetoric laden with invocations of American ideals, Worcester's Irish nationalists worked diligently, and successfully, to solicit hefty contributions to the Home Rule Cause from members of the Yankee elite.[16]

The causes of this Irish effort to seek a rapprochement with their Yankee neighbors were complex. Memories of cooperation between Yankees and Irishmen in the Civil War still lingered in Worcester until the 1880s. In addition the local economy rebounded well in the early 1880s from the depression of 1873, inspiring confidence among workers as well as manufacturers. Parnell's direction of Irish nationalism along a moderate constitutional line and the spread of Catholic liberalism in America also encouraged Worcester's Irishmen in their search for respectability and a reconciliation with their Yankee neighbors. Ultimately, however, mutual accommodation between Irishmen and Yankees in Worcester was rooted in local political mutual self interest. In the 1880s the Irish were too weak to rule the city by themselves, and if the Yankee Republicans had been united, Irish Democrats would have been doomed to the plight of a powerless minority. Yankee Republicans were not united, however, and severe factionalism within the GOP offered the Irish unique opportunities for alliances across party lines. Tied together by mutual need, neither Irish Democrats nor Yankee Republicans wished to see the emergence of ethnic chauvinism on either side which might disrupt the city's fragile balance of power.[17]

These economic and political conditions which had fostered mutual tolerance and accommodation in the 1880s would not survive in the 1890s. Parnell fell in 1891 and Worcester's moderate Irish nationalist movement collapsed. The Vatican began a crackdown on the alleged excesses of American Catholic Liberalism and the term Catholic Liberal was reduced to an epithet in the vocabulary of the Worcester Irish. In 1893 Worcester's economy, like the nation's, plunged into depression. Besides undermining the faith in economic self improvement which had so long buoyed Worcester's Irish temperance men, the depression sparked a new nativist revolt among the city's Yankee middle and working classes. This revolt was aimed as much at the Yankee leaders who had coddled the Irish in the previous decade as the Irish themselves, and by the late 1890s few Republican politicians were still willing to risk any further flirtations with Irish Democratic allies. At the same time, the Irish themselves were growing tired of the old alliances. Bolstered by the increasing numbers of American born Irish maturing in the 1890s, Irish political expectations had risen. They would no longer be junior partners in a coalition led by Yankee factions but would seize the leadership for themselves. In 1900 they deliberately rejected consideration of a possible alliance with dissident Yankee Republicans and nominated and elected the first Irish Catholic mayor in Worcester's history.[18]

In the wreckage of the old dreams of reconciliation, the Worcester Irish struggled to define a new conception of their identity and role in Worcester society. Some Irish workingmen hoped to create a multiethnic class based alliance of laboring men out of the depression's suffering and disillusionment. Yet interethnic cultural conflicts were too deeply rooted to permit this as a practical alternative. Most Irishmen themselves, their tastes for political recognition whetted by recent successes, preferred to advance the interests of their own group rather than experiment with radical working class ideologies and organizations.[19]

The largest number of men and women in the Irish community found a belligerent ethnocentrism more suitable to their aspirations and circumstances than socialism or workingmen's parties. The new ethnocentrism mixed an aggressive assertion of Irish interests with a fierce pride in Irish culture. The Worcester Irish of the 1890s and early 1900s were no longer interested in accommodating their Yankee neighbors. Indeed, the new editors of the *Messenger* proclaimed in 1905 that they feared "the openly avowed enemy of our faith far less than he who masks his purposes under pretended liberality and friendship." The best evidence of the new ethnocentrism's popularity was the rise of organizations like the Ancient Order of Hibernians and the Clan Na Gael. The AOH's vigorous attack on every suspected enemy of the Irish won it hosts of new members in the late 1890s. Between 1896 and 1901, six new divisions of the AOH appeared in Worcester, and the combined membership of the order rose from five hundred to over two thousand five hundred. The Clan, a secret society devoted to the violent overthrow of British rule in Ireland, also prospered in the late 1890s. Both organizations labored to preserve or revive Irish culture in Worcester. In 1898, for example, they helped organize a branch of the Gaelic League in the city. The AOH also sponsored numerous Gaelic football clubs and embarked on a long campaign beginning in the 1890s to force Irish history into the curriculum of the city's public schools.[20]

By the end of the twentieth century's first decade this Irish ethnocentric revival had begun to peter out. In part its decline was due to simple demographics. Immigrant, lower class Irishmen had been its strongest supporters but their proportionate strength in the city's Irish population was steadily shrinking. Second generation Irishmen, meanwhile, grew restless with the AOH's myopic focus on Ireland and the past. Changes in the local environment also doomed the narrow, belligerent ethnocentrism of the 1890s and early 1900s. The most important new trend was the immigration of new ethnic groups, particularly the French Canadians, Italians, Poles, and Lithuanians. Worcester's Irish Catholics realized that their continued ethnocentric isolation in the face of this new immigration might seriously weaken their Church, deprive their institutions of rich client and financial bases, and undermine almost all of the political gains they had so recently won.[21]

In the 1910s, then, the Irish began to fashion a new conception of themselves and their place in the city's society. They called themselves militant American Catholics. As militant Catholics they were suspicious of their Protestant neighbors and ready to battle their Church's enemies in Worcester and around the world. Their fear of non-Catholic organizations—even the Boy Scouts and Protestant run boardinghouses were suspect—provided a renewed impetus for Irish Catholics to build up their own network of institutions and societies. Thus in the 1910s and 1920s, for the first time in the history of Worcester's Irish community, parochial schools began to attract popular support. Five Irish parishes opened their own schools in those two decades.

Nevertheless, the Worcester Irish were militant *Catholics* and American Catholics at that, not Irishmen. Second generation, upwardly mobile Irishmen were particularly interested in emphasizing their Catholic and American rather than Irish allegiances. They therefore flocked to the Knights of Columbus, an organization devoted not just to resolute defense of the faith but to the celebration of American patriotism as well. Between the early 1900s and 1920s the Knights' membership in the city increased from only a few hundred to over five thousand.

The Knights and similar organizations popular in the 1910s did more than satisfy the new generation's hunger for a conception of identity which would reconcile their American allegiances to their fidelity to Catholicism. By emphasizing Catholic and American loyalties over narrowly Irish ones, the Knights and these other organizations also opened up the possibility of drawing all Catholics, of whatever nationality, into a single group under Irish leadership. The K. of C. and other Irish dominated associations like the Ladies Catholic Benevolent Association worked hard, for example, to recruit members from among the new Catholic immigrants. Organizations like the Irish led Federation of Catholic Societies, singlemindedly devoted to forging Catholics of diverse ethnic origins into a single powerful group, also cropped up in the 1910s. Worcester's Irishmen proclaimed that not only Celts but French Canadians, Italians, Poles, and Lithuanians could also become proper Catholic Americans. United behind Irish leadership, the Irish weekly, the *Catholic Messenger,* boasted that Catholics could exert an influence and power "beyond calculation."[22]

In the 1910s this dream of American Catholic unity was still new, and given the entrenched national loyalties of most Worcester ethnics, still far from realization. Many Italians, Poles, Lithuanians, and especially French Canadians reacted savagely to what they perceived as Irish attempts to make them over in an Irish-American image. In 1911 the local French newspaper, *L'Opinion Publique,* for example, assailed the Irish for trying to "tear from us piece by piece the last vestiges of our national heritage." More important, perhaps, the Irish themselves were only tentatively committed to the new American Catholic identity. Overt Irish nationalist sentiment seemed dead or dying as late as the summer of 1916, when the *Catholic Messenger* replied to critics by stating that it had little interest in (Irish) "racial" issues. Yet loyalties to the old country were only submerged; they had not been erased, even among the American born Irish. When prospects for Irish independence brightened following the First World War, and Woodrow Wilson provided a patriotic rationale for supporting Irish nationalism through his speeches on self determination for small nations, Worcester's Irish community exploded in a frenzy of nationalist activity. The scale and breadth of this postwar nationalist outburst, which swept up even the most convinced proponents of the new American Catholic identity, testified but once again to the continuing volatility of the search by Worcester's Irish Americans for a proper conception of their identity.[23]

Nevertheless the Irish conception of themselves as American Catholics and leaders of a new group of diverse Catholic ethnics proved exceedingly durable. Irish nationalist fever faded once again in the early 1920s, and over the course of the next thirty years the trend toward unity among Catholic ethnics gathered increasing momentum. By 1947, two-thirds of the marriages in the oldest Irish parish in the city included non-Irish partners, and in the city's peripheral parishes Catholics of various nationalities mingled freely. Catholic devotion to the United States, if anything, became even more intense in the 1950s as Irish and other Catholics mobilized against atheistic and un-American communism. Meanwhile the barriers which separated Irish Catholics from their Protestant neighbors in Worcester remained as formidable as ever. A Unitarian minister remembered in a 1981 interview that when he first came to Worcester in the 1950s "Protestants feared the Catholics, and Catholics feared the Protestants."[24]

In the 1910s, then, the Worcester Irish had finally defined an identity and a role for themselves in their city's society which proved more or less enduring for the next four decades. To the question of who they were or what kind of Americans they were, they had ultimately answered militant American Catholics. In response to the dilemma of whether they should try to join the "ins" or become champions of the "outs," they projected themselves as leaders of a host of Catholic outs, a group of diverse Catholic ethnics welded together under Irish direction.

They did not arrive at these solutions easily. Though the more permanent circumstances of their environment may have hinted that such responses were predetermined, there was enough play in the conditions of that environment and sufficient significant change within their own population to suggest other plausible solutions such as accommodation or ethnocentric isolation to the questions of their identity and role. Thus the powerful constraints they confronted, constraints which their cousins further west apparently did not encounter, did not prevent them from changing. Indeed their entire history in the turn of the century era was marked by persistent attempts to make sense of the ever shifting balance of change and tradition which shaped their lives.

NOTES

1. Vincent Powers, "Invisible Immigrants: The Pioneer Irish of Worcester, Massachusetts, 1826–1860," (Ph.D. dissertation: Clark University, 1976), pp. 94–124.

2. Robert A. Roberge, "The Three Decker, A Structural Correlate of Worcester's Industrial Revolution," (M.A. thesis: Clark University, 1965), p. 50; Franklin Rice, ed., *The Worcester of Eighteen Hundred and Ninety Eight* (Worcester, Mass.: F. S. Blanchard, 1899), p. 455; Charles Washburn, *Industrial Worcester* (Worcester, Mass., 1917), pp. 49–52, pp. 292–299.

3. U.S. Census Office, *Statistics of the Population of the United States at the Tenth Census* "Population," (Washington, D.C.: 1882), p. 677; *Fourteenth Census of the United States Taken in the Year 1920* Vol. II, "Population: General Report and Analytical Tables" (Washington, D.C.: 1922) p. 729; *Census of the Commonwealth of Massachusetts 1905* Vol. I "Population and Social Statistics," (Boston: Wright and Potter, 1909), p. 445; Charles Nutt *History of Worcester* (New York: Lewis Historical Publishing Co., 1919), Vol. II pp. 947, 953, 963, 783–784. Study of members of Worcester's elite Worcester Club based on 82 of 142 members names drawn from *Dau's Blue Book and Elite Directory* (New York, 1905) indicates overlapping memberships in other elite clubs. Rev. A. Z. Conrad "Protestant Churches" in Rice, ed., *The Worcester of Eighteen Hundred and Ninety Eight,* pp. 289–291; *Twelfth Census of the United States Taken in the Year 1900* Vol. I, "Population," Washington U.S. Census Office 1901 p. 802; *1920 U.S. Census* Vol. II, "Population: Composition and Character of the Population by States," (Washington, D.C.: G.P.O., 1922) p. 470.

4. V. Powers, "Invisible Immigrants," pp. 96–122, 150–205, 240–286; U.S. Census Office *Statistics of the Population of the United States at the Tenth Census,* June 1, 1880, "Population," (Washington, D.C.: 1882) p. 677; *Twelfth Census of the United States Taken in the Year 1900* vol. I, "Population," (Washington, D.C.: 1901) p. 802. By 1900 the number of American born Irish over age 18 had risen to about 9,500, while the number of immigrants over age 18 that year was about 11,000. Based on samples of 1,218 immigrant

men and women over age 18 (one of every nine) and 797 second generation Irish over age 18 (one of every twelve) taken from the Manuscript Schedules of the 1900 U.S. Census.

5. *Catholic Messenger* January 21, 1910; Lawrence J. McCaffrey, *The Irish Diaspora in America* (Bloomington, Ind.: Indiana University Press, 1971), pp. 77–79.

6. William Shannon, *The American Irish: A Political and Social Portrait* (New York: Collier McMillan, 1970), pp. 131–136.

7. John F. O'Connor, "Address to the St. John's Temperance Society," clipping, no citation, March 18, 1899, Richard O'Flynn papers, Holy Cross College Treasure Room, Worcester, Mass.

8. *Catholic Messenger* July 23, 1912, July 25, 1913; *Messenger* May 3, 1905. Men and women listed in Nutt's *History of Worcester* Volumes III and IV who were born in Ireland or parents born in Ireland and men and women listed who were born in Sweden or their parents were born in Sweden.

9. Immigrant samples: 1900 U.S. Census Manuscript schedules.

10. *Eighteenth Annual Report of the Massachusetts Bureau of Labor Statistics, December 1887,* p. 215; Report on the Population of the United States at the Eleventh Census, 1890 Part II (Washington, D.C.: G.P.O., 1897) p. 743. By 1900 only 2.2% of Irish immigrant males were boot and shoe workers. Immigrant sample: 1900 U.S. Census. Washburn, *Industrial Worcester* p. 313; *Worcester Daily Times* April 29, 1886.

11. O'Connor address to St. John's Temperance Society March 18, 1899, F. Flynn papers; Gearoid O'Tuathaigh, *Ireland before the Famine 1798–1848* (Dublin: Gill) pp. 117–126; Joseph Lee, *The Modernization of Ireland 1848–1917* (Dublin: Gill) pp. 16–17; Rev. John J. McCoy, "Christmas Sermon," Rev. John J. McCoy papers, Holy Cross Treasure Room; *Catholic Messenger* August 26, 1915; *Worcester Evening Post* March 18, 1903; Rev. John J. McCoy, *History of the Diocese of Springfield* (Boston: Hurd and Everts, 1900); p. 32 *Messenger* September 29, 1902.

12. Second Generation Samples: 1900 U.S. Census Manuscript Schedules.

13. Immigrant Samples: 1880 U.S. Census Manuscript Schedules; *Worcester Telegram* December 13, 1893; Rice, ed., *The Worcester of Eighteen Hundred and Ninety Eight*, pp. 495, 497, 499, 508, 523, 524; *Worcester Telegram* December 6, 1893.

14. *Catholic Messenger* August 11, 1911; November 17, 1916; June 24, 1926. Harold Creveling, "A Cultural Geography of Worcester, Massachusetts" (Ph.D. dissertation, Clark University, 1953) p. 39.

15. *Worcester Daily Times* November 26, 1881; *Catholic Messenger* March 20, 1915; St. John's Temperance and Literary Guild Records Vol. I, April 4, 1884, St. John's Parish Archives, Worcester, Mass.; *Messenger* July 29, 1893; *Worcester Spy* April 4, 1887; *Catholic Messenger* October 7, 1915, April 31,

1915. Timothy J. Meagher "'Why Should We Care for a Little Trouble or a Walk Through the Mud': St. Patrick and Columbus Day Parades in Worcester, Massachusetts, 1845–1915," *New England Quarterly* Vol. LVIII no. 1 (March: 1985) pp. 17–18. Statistics on marriage ages and fertility taken from second generation and Immigrant samples: 1900 U.S. Census Manuscript Schedules. In 1900 8.3% of Irish immigrant and 7.0% of second generation Irish wives over age 45, married ten to twenty years, had no children; 83.5% of the immigrant and 80.7% of the second generation wives had three or more children. By contrast, 23.7% of the native stock women married eleven to twenty years had no children and only 34% had three or more children. Statistics taken from a one in twenty sample of all native stock residents of Worcester from 1900 U.S. Census Manuscript.

16. See Timothy J. Meagher, "'Irish All the Time': Ethnic Consciousness among the Irish in Worcester, Massachusetts, 1880–1905," *Journal of Social History* (Winter 1985, Vol. XIX) for a full discussion. On schools see John J. McGratty, *The Life of Very Rev. John J. Power* (Worcester, Mass.: 1902), pp. 10–11, 21–26, 72–81, 104; *Alumna* May 1886 p. 4; January 1887 p. 2; *Messenger* July 7, 1894. On cooperation see Donna Merwick, *Boston Priests: A Study of Social and Intellectual Change* (Cambridge, Mass.: Harvard University Press, 1973), p. 156; *Messenger* January 28, 1893. On temperance see *Messenger* July 7, 1888; *Worcester Daily Times* January 13, 1883; and Meagher, "What Should We Care." On nationalism see *Worcester Daily Times* October 14, 1881, January 13, 1882; *Worcester Evening Spy* March 1, 1886. Worcester's Yankees contributed $922 or 39 percent of the funds collected for the Parnell parliamentary fund in 1886: Folio I, p. 173, O'Flynn papers, Holy Cross College.

17. See Meagher, "Irish All the Time," *Journal of Social History* (Winter 1985, Vol. XIX). On Civil War see *Celebration of the 200th Anniversary of Worcester: October 14 and 15, 1884* (Worcester: 1885) pp. 68–75. On economy see Roy Rosenzweig, *Eight Hours for What We Will: Workers and Leisure in an Industrial City, 1870–1920* (New York: Cambridge University Press, 1983), pp. 16–26; *Worcester Daily Times* January 17, 1883. On local politics see *Worcester Evening Gazette* December 7, 1877; December 10, 1879; *Worcester Telegram* December 25, 1887; *Worcester Daily Times* December 5, 1883.

18. On Parnell's fall and its effect on the Worcester Irish see *Messenger* February 28, 1891, March 21, 1891, March 4, 1893. On liberal Catholicism's new disrepute see *Messenger* February 9, 1901, February 10, 1903. On nativist revolt see *American* January 23, 1894; *Worcester Evening Spy* December 14, 1893, December 6, 1896; *Worcester Evening Post* November 13, 1899. On Irish isolation see *Worcester Telegram* November 27, 28, 1899; *Messenger* December 12, 1903.

19. *Messenger* March 18, 1899; *Worcester Labor* October 5, 1895; *Messenger* October 24, 1903, November 7, 1903.

20. On AOH see *Messenger* August 23, 1902; October 22, 1898; November 19, 1908; January 1, 1904; *Catholic Messenger* March 1, 1907. On Clan see *Messenger* June 8, 1895; November 30, 1895; April 18, 1899; June 3, 1904; November 30, 1905.

21. On immigrant lower class participation in the ethnocentric revival see Meagher, "What Should We Care," pp. 16–21 and Meagher, "Irish All the Time," *Journal of Social History*. On new immigrants and Irish perception of their potential power see *U.S. Census 1920* Vol. II, "General Report," p. 949; *Messenger* October 10, 1903, April 1, 1899; *Catholic Messenger* November 5, 1909.

22. On non-Catholic institutions see *Messenger* July 5, 1902; *Catholic Messenger* August 11, 1911; September 20, 1912; August 5, 1915. On schools see Timothy J. Meagher, "'The Grand Privilege of Our Public Schools': The Delayed Development of Parochial Education among Irish Catholics in Worcester," *Historical Journal of Massachusetts* Vol. XII, no. 1 (January 1984) pp. 53–55. On K of C growth see Historian's Report Alhambra Council no. 88, 1943, Alhambra Council Archives, Worcester, Massachusetts; *Catholic Messenger* June 24, 1915. Between 1903 and 1915 over 62.7% of the Worcester Knights were white-collar workers, Minutes of the Meetings, 1903 to 1915, Alhambra Council Archives. On Knights American patriotism see *Catholic Messenger* January 20, 1916; April 10, 1918. On efforts to reach out to new groups see *Catholic Messenger* April 22, 1910; September 30, 1913; March 9, 1916.

23. *L'Opinion Publique* August 27, 1911; *Catholic Messenger* June 8, 1916; *Catholic Messenger* December 13, 1918; March 21, 1919; April 4, 1919; November 4, 1920.

24. *Catholic Messenger* February 25, 1926. Parish announcements, St. John's Parish, St. John's Parish Archives; *Catholic Free Press* June 10, 1955, April 11, 1955, January 21, 1955; March 11, 1955. *Worcester Sunday Telegram* 1981.

intrepið men: three philaðelphia irish leaders, 1880 to 1920

As the decade of the 1880s opened in Philadelphia the city was in its greatest industrial period. America's most historic city, cradle of the republic, was surging with industrial energy. Its 129 square miles were overlaid with thousands of mills and factories and laced with 350 miles of street railways. Third largest city of the nation, its coal, iron, steel, and textile production were massive, and it was the chief railroad nexus of the east and also a port where five full miles of wharves imported sixty-seven million dollars of materials. The city had 847,000 inhabitants in 1890, about one-fifth of them immigrants. Among the armies of workers that trooped to their labor daily in the foundries, the port, the rail yards, and the businesses in 1900 were 98,000 Irish born and 123,000 American born of Irish parentage. Together with tens of thousands of third and fourth generation Irish they were a powerful emerging resource in the city's economic, educational, political, and cultural life.[1]

William V. Shannon has characterized the Irish-American social situation in this period as one of "unstable, unformulated compromise between the neighborly code of the old country village and the individualistic code of the open American society."[2] Philadelphia is a good context in which to examine and test this judgement. As a leading industrial city, increasingly diverse in population, with a tradition of exclusion and unfair discrimination practiced against the Irish by its upper class Anglo leaders and their civic allies, the city was a social arena that certainly challenged the Irish. Did the Irish leaders, those who set the model for imitation by others, respond with irresolution and instability, with inchoate compromise, or did they respond with assured activism and determined achievement? What kind of a social compact did they fashion in this richly varied industrial mecca?

So extensive was the Irish social structure in the city by the 1880s that some delimitation has to be made to frame a representation of leadership that is practical to examine in a brief essay. Dale Light has shown in his study of Philadelphia Irish organizations in the 1880s how diverse they were and what a veritable hive of activity and promotion they constituted.[3] As the Irish had moved up the scale of social and economic betterment since the Civil War they had elaborated their ethnic identity and made it into a complex instrument for urban interaction. By 1880 over half of the Irish born and over two-thirds of their children were working as artisans, skilled or white-collar workers. Their neighborhoods were largely stable workingmen's areas of decent housing.[4] There were leaders and leaders, scores of them, and choosing among their interesting ranks is not easy. Leaders named Dougherty could be chosen, and orator-lawyers, a budding Cardinal, and a dozen successful businessmen plus many worthy Donegal Doughertys could be highlighted. The name Donnelly would call up several generations of medical distinction. Sullivan would identify bankers, manufacturers, and educators. Kelleys would tax the ability to transcribe. For this examination, however, I would choose men named Ryan to illustrate the leadership disposition of the Philadelphia Irish at the time and simply defer exposition about the wide range of others in the interests of a sharper, more immediate focus.

The first Ryan to consider is James J. Ryan, building contractor born in Kilkenny in 1848 when the stench of potato blight and Famine disaster still hung in the air. He emigrated to the United States in his youth. A hardy lad, he became one of the multitudes of Irish in the different gangs excavating and laying track for the railroads, a brutal laboring life. Organizing his own work force, Ryan began to "hire out" his cohort for small contracting jobs. By the 1870s he was laying track for branch lines for those economic empires, the railroads, that controlled whole cities, owned state legislatures, and ruled in untrammeled sovereignty over the economies of regions bigger than most European countries.

By 1900 there were fifty-two construction contractors listed in the Philadelphia city's business directory and a score of others unlisted. They ranged from small firms confined to neighborhood work to major companies. Daniel Brogan sold building materials, as did P. J. Foley, but they also constructed all kinds of buildings. Charles Lafferty built extensively in South Philadelphia, and P. J. McManus erected buildings and did railroad work all the way to Atlantic City. Daniel and Patrick McNichol did road work and excavating, sometimes competing with their brother, James P. McNichol. Most of these contractors were intensely competitive, quick mobilizers of Irish skilled and unskilled labor, and all were beneficiaries of the huge ongoing process by which the city extended its urban infrastructure, and rebuilt its facilities and spread outward across its generous endowment of open land. Some of the contractors, most notably James P. McNichol, entered politics and benefited greatly by securing municipal public works contracts. Others specialized in railroad, commercial, industrial, and residential building where political influence was less significant. All of them represented an energetic contribution to the expansion of the metropolitan framework of the city.[5]

In the 1880s James Ryan's work crews were part of this Irish construction network in Pennsylvania, New Jersey, and Delaware. His company laid the track that brought the Baltimore and Ohio Railroad into the center of Philadelphia to challenge the Pennsylvania Railroad. One thing led to another, and the construction work embraced all kinds of basic facilities and buildings. James Ryan was one of the leading contractors in the city by 1880. His business was so large that he felt no need to go into politics as other builders did to add to their contracting prospects, although he did maintain ties to the Democrats.[6]

The great landmark east of the new, extravagantly ornate City Hall in Philadelphia that would symbolize Ryan's building career was the Reading Terminal Building. Attached to a vast cavern of an iron and steel train shed, the pink tinted brick railroad headquarters rose twelve stories above Market Street. Full of Italian Renaissance flourishes in its facade, it had cream-colored terra cotta details and a heavy copper cornice. It was a monument to the power of the Reading Railroad, the line that controlled the richest coal deposits in America in the age when coal was the nation's chief fuel. The Reading controlled thousands of square miles of forest, canal systems, port facilities, massive real estate holdings, and financial resources, and legions of middle men and legal firms. Through the building each day passed throngs of Philadelphia bourgeois who came from the stately outlying areas that the railroad had developed. Pennsylvania Dutch farmers brought splendid produce for the city's tables from their green acres beyond the city's suburbs, and they sold their bounty in a bustling market under the train shed. In the panelled executive offices of the Terminal Building the brokers, lawyers, and managers of the rail empire plotted endlessly to garner even more wealth from the smoking industrial hinterland that stretched away as far as the eye could see.

James Ryan built that building in a mighty race to meet the tight construction schedule, and he met all the deadlines. It was dedicated with all due pomposity and civic salutation in 1893. Ryan and all his workmen knew well that the building was a monument to the railroad that had been headed by Franklin Gowen, one of the most vicious foes the Irish ever had in America. Gowen had repeatedly broken every labor organization he could attack in his role as monarch of the Reading. It was he who used provocateurs, paid informants, assassins and perversion of the courts to accomplish judicial murder, all to eliminate the Mollie Maguires and any other resistance to his regime in the coal fields in the 1870s. James Ryan and his colleagues were, in their own way, as calculating as their enemies. They needed work and money. They would sup with the devil, long spoon or no. They would live off the corporate enemy that had persecuted them. Ryan was not a man to let passions divert him from lucrative enterprise. He built the Reading Railroad's monument and in the process brought still more Irish to the city after each of his trips to recruit workers from Ireland.

James Ryan's renown grew. He was not only a member of the Catholic Club and the Friendly Sons of St. Patrick, which were a whole web of business interconnections in themselves, but he was one of the few Irish Catholics in the stolidly WASP Racquet Club. In 1903 he was president of the Master Builders Exchange. He retained membership in the Irish nationalist Sheares Club and was on the board of St. Joseph's Hospital and the Catholic Protectory. He gave generously to Catholic causes, including a gift of $50,000 to the Catholic University of America for a chair in biblical studies, for he was a man interested in books and scholarship. Thus, James Ryan rose to business eminence from the lowly status of an impoverished track-layer's helper. His success as a builder starting from poor beginnings testifies to qualities of immigrant ambition and adaptability. His capacity to remain at the top of a keenly competitive field evidences a shrewd character. The support he gave to Catholic causes and institutions shows the way in which his personal life and civic interests were integrated with the complex of Irish-American social and religious organizations that were a potent force in the life of the city.

Another Ryan of much wider renown was John Patrick Ryan, orator, intellectual, bishop, and a churchman of notable achievement. Born in Tipperary in 1831, his talents were evident early. One of the few roads to education then was study for the priesthood, and this boy entered the seminary. In 1844 he was chosen from among the youthful rhetoricians in Ireland to deliver a speech in Dublin on the subject of Daniel O'Connell's imprisonment after the nationalist hero had been seized by the British. America was crying out for priests to serve its swiftly growing churches, and in 1852 young John Ryan was posted to St. Louis where the Irish born Peter Kenrick was Archbishop. In 1853 Ryan was ordained for the priesthood and began a period of tutelage under the influential Kenrick. In 1872 Ryan was made a bishop and became coadjutor for his failing mentor. His reputation as an orator grew, so that at the Second Plenary Council in Baltimore in 1866 he had been invited to deliver one of the major sermons to the assembled bishops. In 1879 he addressed the congregation at the dedication of St. Patrick's Cathedral in New York, that edifice of Gothic grandeur built on Fifth Avenue by immigrants who only a generation before were hardly permitted access to that fashionable thoroughfare.

Appointed Archbishop of Philadelphia in 1884, John Ryan was already widely known as a distinguished Catholic leader. One of his addresses, "What Catholics Do Not Believe," had been distributed in tens of thousands of copies as a response to militant Protestant distortions of Catholic doctrines and practices. In Philadelphia Archbishop Ryan had an energetic Catholic population with a vigorous middle class and a broad array of committed and diligent parishioners and priests. The Archdiocese, however, extended far into the mountains and farmlands of Northern and Central Pennsylvania. In the 1880s both Philadelphia and the upstate coal regions were drawing a new tide of immigrants from Eastern Europe. Poles, Estonians, Lithuanians, Slovaks, Croatians, and Italians poured into the towns and cities of the state, and the Irish kept coming as well. Ryan responded positively by erecting an astonishing array of sixty ethnic parishes plus other institutions. He argued with other bishops that ethnic identity plus civic participation must guide Catholic relations, and this was his version of the Americanization process that was such a controversial issue in the 1890s. Still, he faced intimidating problems. Labor unrest, poverty, and the need for orphanages, hospitals, schools, and churches challenged John Ryan wherever he turned.[7]

In the next twenty-five years Archbishop John Ryan erected a massive addition to the institutional structure to the Archdiocese he had inherited from his predecessors. In 1884 there were fifty-eight Catholic schools under his care. By 1903 there were over a hundred in Philadelphia alone. To the old Irish parishes in South Philadelphia and the mill districts and warehouse areas, he added fifteen largely Irish parishes in new, clean, row house neighborhoods that ringed the historic older areas of the city. And, in a course of administrative and cultural advocacy hardly thinkable anywhere but in America, he oversaw the building of scores of ethnic parishes for Germans, Italians, and an extraordinary panorama of East European congregations.

Archbishop Ryan was the embodiment of that archetypal American Catholic phenomenon, the building bishop. But, he was also keenly interested in education and pressed for the education of women in a time when that was not especially popular. Handsome, urbane, eloquent, and powerfully committed to the welfare of his congregation, he was a confident exponent of his views, the views of his church, and the needs of the immigrant poor. As editor of the *American Catholic Quarterly Review,* patron of the American Catholic Historical Society, and author of numerous articles against the exploitation of labor, he added intellectual talent to moral fervor. He was not as liberal as his friend, James Cardinal Gibbons of Baltimore, but he agreed with Gibbons that any church condemnation of the Knights of Labor or other legitimate union organizations would be folly. He worked at conciliating the views of Gibbons and the conservative Archbishop of New York, Michael Corrigan.[8] When Charles Stuart Parnell visited Philadelphia, he supported him. When a cargo of relief supplies for persecuted Jews in Russia was loaded, he joined a rabbi and a Protestant minister at the wharf to bless the ship. When transit magnates locked out their workers, the Archbishop had the parishes feed the wageless families while he strove to settle the strike. John Patrick Ryan was as much a civic figure as he was a church administrator, "eloquent of speech, kind of heart and wise in action" as the *Jewish Exponent* said. This was quite a departure from the mid nineteenth century, when Catholic leaders were deeply suspect in a city where religious riots had torn the social fabric. More than his predecessors or successors he set the tone and cast the educational and institutional mold for the kind of urban Catholicism that Irish Americans would practice for four generations in Philadelphia and its related areas.

A review of the life of a third Philadelphia Irish leader further illustrates the temper and aspirations of the Irish community in the city in the late nineteenth century, and this man's life is especially revealing of the dynamics of leadership. Michael J. Ryan was born in Philadelphia in 1862. He attended St. Augustine's parish school in the oldest section of the city. Ryan's father had a bootmaking shop, and he employed a number of Irish born bootmakers. Some of these men could not read. Some were Gaelic speakers and were attuned to a rich oral tradition. While these men trimmed soles, sewed leather uppers, and worked at their lasts, they enjoyed a daily discourse that dealt with affairs of moment and enlivened their labor. On his return from school each day young Michael Ryan was required to read to these bootmakers the accounts from the Irish and American newspapers of reports and debates about current affairs. The press at this time frequently carried extensive verbatim accounts of speeches in the British Parliament and in the American Congress, and also speeches by leading figures of the day. The addresses of Irish Parliamentarians could be analyzed and assessed by the bootmakers as they discussed tenant rights, the drive to relieve Irish Catholics from the tithes they paid to the Protestant Church of Ireland, and the agitation to free Irish men imprisoned as Fenian rebels. For Ryan this discourse was an early training in the art of argument, and in his later years he attributed his oratorical prowess to the reading of speeches in his father's shop. During his studies at LaSalle College, he continued his interest in rhetoric and oratory. Michael Ryan thus had early ties to the vigorous nationalist constitutionalist tradition that would prevail in Irish life after the failure of the radical Fenian Brotherhood leadership in the 1860s.[9]

Ryan's career is significant because it spanned three major phases of Irish-American nationalism, a whole lifetime of organizational leadership when the Irish were not only a powerful force in American life, but a critical influence in the animation of political drives of nationalism in Ireland. Ryan was deeply involved as a young man in the Land League activities that sought to redeem landholdings in Ireland from the grip of the English landlord class. In his middle years he was the national head of the United Irish League, the chief American supporting group for the Irish Parliamentary Party which sought Home Rule for Ireland within a British constitutional framework. When the Rising of

1916 in Dublin ignited the drive for an independent Irish state, Ryan was a mature and experienced figure, widely known in Ireland and America, and able to participate in efforts to secure a just solution to the Irish guerrilla campaign after World War I.

In 1884 at the age of twenty-two Ryan was admitted to the Philadelphia Bar after reading for the law in the office of George H. Earle and Richard P. White. He was tall, highly articulate, and robust. He made his first foray into local politics by working in the mayoralty campaign of 1884 for the Democrats. In Philadelphia the Democrats were a party foredoomed to go down in defeat before the all powerful Republican machine that reigned over the city's politics from one generation to the next. This distinctive long-term exile of a major Irish urban population in the political wilderness produced in the group a certain self-reliance, a go-it-alone mentality that induced in them a pragmatic preference for limited goals and self-sufficiency. In Philadelphia the Irish were not so much machine politicians as they were organic politicians, growing themselves into whatever soil and electorate available. Still, the Irish Democrats conducted intermittent wars of harassment and electoral challenges for individual offices whenever the Republicans made a miscalculation or put up a vulnerable candidate in the Irish wards in North and South Philadelphia. In 1881 the city had elected a Democrat, reformer Samuel King, to the mayor's office in a rare spasm of public protest under a bipartisan "Committee of 100." He was driven from office in the 1884 campaign in which Ryan worked, partly because he had appointed the first blacks to the police force. Ryan continued his political activities, running for a Congressional nomination in the heavily Irish First District in North Philadelphia in 1886, and won a surprisingly heavy vote while losing the nomination.[10]

It was not possible for a man to be in politics in the Irish neighborhoods of the city in the 1880s without making known his views on a wide range of Irish issues. Ireland's affairs extended right into the wards of Philadelphia, and candidates were expected to know and discuss tenant rights, no-rent manifestos, boycotts, Parliamentary participation, and other concerns about life in Ireland debated in the Irish newspapers in America. In addition, the rights of labor, problems of anti-Catholic discrimination, and the relations of the United States with England were also keen political topics. Michael Ryan tutored himself in such issues and developed an increasing facility to discuss them. He became a lecturer for the Irish National League and gave addresses in the meetings that were held by the twenty-four branches of the Land League in Philadelphia. The Land League activities gradually merged with those of the Irish National League, and Ryan became a state delegate from Pennsylvania in the latter organization, making his first entry into the shifting currents of the national Irish-American leadership stream.

As a young orator Ryan was not only an expression of a long Irish tradition of oral facility with such legendary exponents as Henry Grattan, Daniel O'Connell, and the Irish Parliamentarians who followed Charles Stuart Parnell, he was also part of a Philadelphia succession of orators who arose from the Irish community. These orator advocates included Father Patrick Moriarty, a fiery Augustinian priest who defended the Irish Catholics in the turbulent period after the Famine influx from 1846 to 1860, and Daniel Dougherty, a lawyer famous for his speeches in defense of the cause of the Union.[11] Audiences of thousands gathered to hear them, encouraging public debate and providing diversion. Speeches were often reprinted as pamphlets. Michael Ryan was part of this tradition whose devotees studied Cicero and Edmund Burke, competed keenly in local debating societies, and advanced their careers by extensive public speaking. It was in campaigning for the Land League and later for the Irish National League that Ryan developed his own oratorical skills as part of his nationalist endeavors.

Ryan's profile was sharpening when in 1886 Charles Stuart Parnell and William E. Gladstone's Liberal Party launched a campaign for Home Rule for Ireland, a bid for limited Irish self-government under the British Crown. As a sequel to the continuing campaign to secure land for the Irish people, Home Rule had a strong appeal for the American Irish. Ryan could enter into support for Home Rule with fully developed talents as an orator, as a man of political promise, and as a man with extensive local connections and growing national ties. His constituents in the area where he was politically active included the population around the Church of the Gesu, a huge Jesuit edifice that was the focus of a big Catholic area where successful Irish businessmen lived in spacious brownstone homes on Girard Avenue or in white-lintel, three story row houses with ornate Victorian interiors on adjacent streets. Ryan courted the support of one of the city's most upwardly mobile groups, for the "lace curtain" Irish were intent upon respectability, creating an image of competence, and expressing their Irish Catholic ethos through work on behalf of Irish undertakings and Catholic growth. The constituency Ryan sought to represent was conservative and even bourgeois. Dale Light has shown that the Irish National League, which Ryan headed, was more than two-thirds composed of members who were in the white-collar and proprietary classes. Ryan's support for Home Rule was a moderate position appropriate to his moderate "lace curtain" acquaintances. Light found that "Irish nationalist associations showed extremely high levels of wealth among their memberships," while as early as 1880 they joined together "laborers, artisans, merchants, and capitalists mixed, without discrimination."[12] The Irish leader William A. O'Brien, who had extensive firsthand contacts with the Irish-American network, recalled that the group as a whole, supposed by the British to be implacable, was moderate and had to be patiently persuaded to more aggressive viewpoints.[13]

By 1890 there were twenty-three Councils of the Irish National League in the city. At a single meeting they voted to forward $2,150 to Ireland to relieve hunger among families evicted by landlords. Ryan believed the British could delay Irish Home Rule but could not in the end defeat it, and he retained this belief for years.[14] The attempts of the British to turn back Home Rule agitation by coercion and to frame Parnell with forged documents implicating him with violence merely spurred Irish-American enthusiasm. When Parnell's colleagues William O'Brien and John Dillon visited America in November 1890, Ryan organized a spectacular center city rally for them. Fifteen hundred people welcomed the Parliamentary leaders at City Hall. They were escorted that night from the Bellevue Stratford Hotel through files of an honor guard holding torches aloft as bands played Irish martial music. At the Academy of Music Ryan chaired a meeting where O'Brien told the packed audience, "We come from a country that has had five thousand political prisoners in the last few years." To resounding cheers he and Dillon were given a check for $13,000 to aid the Home Rule drive. The next night at another rally in Ryan's home area, another $3,000 was contributed.[15]

The great drama of the Parnell years ended in 1890 in the tragedy of the O'Shea-Parnell divorce case scandal that caused religious support to fall and smashed Parnell's career. It left his followers bitterly divided as they fought for leadership of the wrecked Irish party. Opinion in Ireland and America was either alienated or deeply confused. A rump organization, the Irish National Federation was set up in December 1890 to rival the Irish National League. A year later the League was dead.[16] Michael Davitt, perhaps the most popular Irish leader after Parnell, said in 1896,

"I am convinced that unless there is reunion (of the Irish Parliamentary Party) no future of the constitutional movement here in Ireland will obtain sanction of support from the Irish race abroad."[17] After some years of disillusionment, the Irish Parliamentary Nationalists pulled themselves together, and in 1898 William O'Brien formed the United Irish League (UIL). Its branches spread swiftly in Ireland. The goal remained what it had been in 1886, Home Rule, but the UIL branches also became involved in local boycotts and pressure campaigns against landlords. Ryan was to be a key figure in the UIL. He threw himself into the work of reorganizing Irish Americans to follow the lead of John Redmond, who had assumed direction of the Irish Parliamentary Party with the backing of John Dillon and William O'Brien. By 1904 the UIL convention in New York drew delegates from thirty-three states which were part of the League's network.

Writing from Philadelphia to John Redmond in 1906, Richard Harleton reported,

> Ryan is a marvel. His heart is in the work and his energy is overpowering. He has launched a scheme for setting 25 men to subscribe $1000 each, 50 to subscribe $100. He seems very confident of big results and hopes $10,000 is reached. . . . The Clan crowd are very bitter towards him, but that is because they are mortally afraid of him. They have not ventured any open opposition anywhere even to the extent of a solitary interruptor at a meeting, although the *Gaelic American,* Devoy's sheet, has, of course, been nasty.[18]

In 1908 Michael Ryan was elected president of the UIL. The organization was directed by the Parliamentary executive committee in Ireland, but there was still great scope for American leadership. Effecting collaboration among Irish-American groups was a continuous process. Large organizations like the Ancient Order of Hibernians, headed by Ryan's fellow Philadelphian Maurice Wilhere, were not always easy to maneuver behind the Parliamentary strategy. The Home Rule goal was still there, however, a familiar Grail to be sought by sheer persistence against the intransigence of the reactionaries of the British political parties. In the kind of patronizing statement that infuriated the Irish, Lord Grey said, "Ireland may still redeem her past by providing the excuse for Imperial Federation."[19] Indeed, much of the problem of Home Rule was that it would provide a model for Imperial devolution. Nevertheless, it was a familiar goal, a peaceful goal, and one that most Irish Americans thought reasonable.

Under Ryan the UIL stepped up organizing work, especially among the white-collar, shopkeeper, and business class that he knew well. By 1910 John Redmond would write him after a visit to America of his gratitude, and, "What struck me more than it ever did before was the widespread interest taken in the present phase of the Irish movement by business and professional men." Redmond expressed his conviction that "the Irish in America will not allow the Irish Party to be beaten."[20] This had to be Redmond's hope, for the Irish Parliamentary party had that year contested seats in eighty-two districts in Ireland at an estimated cost of $100,000. Ryan's aide in the UIL, Secretary John O'Callaghan, had sent a fifth installment of $50,000 to the Irish political leaders in November 1910.[21] American money was fueling Irish Parliamentary pressure in a continuation of that extraordinary trans-Atlantic influence on Irish affairs that had become traditional for the Irish Americans.

It is pertinent to note that Ryan's moderate nationalist outlook emerged gradually. As a young man he was president of the Irish-American Club in Philadelphia for three years. This Club was controlled by the Clan na Gael secret society, and Ryan actually attended a national convention of the latter group in Chicago in 1888. Whatever his earlier sentiments, by World War I Ryan had for years been a backer of solutions to Ireland's problems sought through the British Parliament. The old revolutionary agitator Dr. William Carroll wrote to the arch-rebel John Devoy in 1910 that Ryan and Redmond betrayed the nationalist cause. Ryan's political aspirations would not permit him to identify with the physical force advocates as his career advanced. He condemned those "who talk of revolution and do nothing else." His appeal was to the Irish bourgeoisie and the steady workmen in the decent Irish parishes across the city.

In 1910 in the *Philadelphia Public Ledger* Ryan explained in a long article why American aid was needed to propel the Home Rule movement. The poverty of Ireland, the extra expenses of Irish members of Parliament who had to travel to and live in London, the enormous resources of the English ruling class working against Home Rule were all reasons. Ryan noted that the goal of a republic advocated by Irish militants would be rejected completely and bitterly opposed by Irish Protestants loyal to the Crown if Home Rule were granted.[22] In 1911 following a meeting of the National Directory of the UIL, Ryan issued a statement saying that, thanks to the overseas Irish, "the UIL is the only national organization since the Act of Union (1800) which can boast of having brought the cause of Irish self-government to the threshold of assured and final success.''[23] In 1914 Parliament did at last pass a Home Rule bill with a clause permitting Ulster's exclusion. The confrontation with Ulster, however, was postponed by the outbreak of World War I. Up to this time Ryan's chief, John Redmond, had held his political supporters together, but the prospect of Irish nationalists fighting a war at England's side split the Irish Volunteer militia leaders. Redmond had promised Irish collaboration in the war effort, and the more militant nationalists refused to follow his lead.

The tension in Ireland had its reflection in America. Militant nationalists led by wealthy Philadelphian Joseph McGarrity repudiated any Home Rule scheme that would permit Ulster to exclude itself. McGarrity headed efforts to gather funds to arm the Irish Volunteers, the militant nationalists who were imitating the Ulster Volunteer Force in preparing to fight for their point of view. He was a key figure in the Clan na Gael, the secret organization seeking full Irish independence.

The more radical faction in the city's Irish leadership led by Joseph McGarrity and Dennyman William Bradley were allied with the remnants of the old Fenian physical force movement and the emerging visionaries of the Gaelic League and Sinn Fein who would be led by Patrick Pearse. Visiting the city in 1915 Pearse collected funds for his Irish-speaking school, for his propaganda work, and for the militia groups whose organization would lead to the 1916 rebellion. Some small businessmen contributed to such work, but the fund raising for Pearse was tiny compared with the extensive efforts that Ryan headed. The Clan na Gael had a core of several hundred devotees and was able to produce several thousand adherents at rallies, but Michael Ryan's contributors in the city numbered tens of thousands.[24]

In 1914 McGarrity called on Redmond to renounce any Home Rule enactment and to insist that the nationalists be allowed to import arms to Ireland just as the Ulster loyalists were doing. McGarrity's group assailed Ryan and the United Irish League for refusing to help raise funds for arms. Ryan had previously attacked McGarrity's fund raising committee. Ryan as a constitutionalist and a moderate could not countenance the commitment of McGarrity and his colleagues to physical force and revolution in behalf of an Irish republic. McGarrity, General Dennis Collins, Denis Spellissy, and Patrick Griffin headed a network that had cells in major Eastern cities, Western cities like San Francisco and Butte, Montana, as well as St. Louis and New Orleans.[25] In July

1914 Ryan launched a major effort to support Redmond's militia which was pledged to collaborate with Britain. Ten thousand dollars was raised immediately, toward a one million dollar goal, which McGarrity charged would not buy arms for Irish liberty but would go to political funds for the Irish Parliamentary Party. For Ryan to break openly with McGarrity's adherents was a step that would have notable adverse effects on his career and leadership. But, as he was fond of repeating, he believed that England could delay but could not defeat the drive for Home Rule.[26]

In addition to his very active role in Irish-American affairs, Ryan did not neglect his local political involvements. In 1914 he ran for the Democratic nomination for Governor of Pennsylvania; he was opposed by Congressman A. Mitchell Palmer and lost his bid. In 1915 he campaigned against Philadelphia's servile political status under the Republicans and called for a new Pennsylvania Constitution that would break the fetters that controlled the city, a far-sighted proposal that would not be enacted for another thirty-five years.[27] In his work as City Solicitor he had seen the legal limitations that were a permanent constraint on the city's government. Ryan's nationalist ties were clearly an asset to his political ambitions, and in 1916 he was elected president of the oldest Irish organization in Philadelphia, The Society of the Friendly Sons of St. Patrick, founded in 1771, a charitable and interreligious fraternity. With his increasingly reenforcing connections he was able to mount a strong campaign for Public Service Commissioner of Pennsylvania, and in 1916 he was chosen for that position.

But the armed rebellion in Dublin in 1916 changed Ryan's status swiftly. The Easter Rising had been aided by his enemy Joseph McGarrity. The incredible daring of the rebellion and the execution of its leaders drew youthful opinion in Ireland to the cause of a Republic, and Home Rule was cast into the dustbin. In October 1914 Ryan already had believed that the United Irish League was dead when Home Rule was placed on the statute books. Redmond's support for Britain's war effort gave Ryan the excuse he needed to break with the Parliamentary Party leader, which he did, but the redirection of his nationalism was not easily accomplished. Home Rule was forgotten as the new Grail of the Republic was exalted. John Redmond sealed his own doom by backing conscription in Ireland to aid England's military needs. The Sinn Fein (Ourselves Alone) movement that had sponsored the 1916 rebellion swept aside the Parliamentary Party with its old Home Rule goal.

Ireland moved toward a war of independence in 1917, and Ryan's attachment to constitutional nationalism after decades of work was transformed into a liability in the face of the swelling prestige of the rebel martyrs of 1916 and their dynamic Sinn Fein followers. He quickly perceived this and made numerous pro-German statements at Irish meetings, urging Americans not to aid England in the European war. After American entry into World War I, he artfully downplayed such sentiments as the tide of American patriotism rose. The stimulus of the 1916 Rising was altering Irish-American opinion as well. Ryan smoothly identified the Irish fight for independence with the superpatriotic American commitment to liberty for small nations. As an artist of rhetorical methods this was no difficult feat for him. By 1918 he had reconciled these differences and was moving closer to the McGarrity bloc of militant Irish nationalism. By 1918 he had successfully maneuvered himself into position so that he was chosen to make a major address at the Irish Race Convention in New York, although the Convention had been organized by the physical force advocates.[28]

Ryan's experience in Irish-American affairs, his great power as a speaker, and even his image as a moderate made him useful to the militants, as well as to moderates who, though they might be stirred by the drama of the growing Irish revolution, were not comfortable with the radical and youthful Sinn Fein partisans. Ryan served as an intermediary in various situations. The fact that there was rancor between him and other leaders was neither extraordinary nor a bar to joint efforts in a time of crisis. In the United Irish League Ryan had always been a proponent of surmounting factionalism, and his political skill held together coalitions of vigorously dissenting personalities. His adroitness and conservative reputation made him uniquely valuable in 1919 during the frenetic period of the Irish independence drive when the battle against England involved not only guerrilla war in Ireland, but a struggle to win world opinion and American sympathy for the emerging Irish state. The opportunity for Ryan to exercise his talents on a larger stage than ever before arose in 1919 when Irish-American leaders sought to induce Woodrow Wilson to press for Irish independence at the Versailles peace conference.

As the Sinn Fein rebels extended their efforts to mobilize American opinion in behalf of an Irish republic, their representative, Dr. Patrick McCartan, was conferring in the United States with Ryan and other leaders. McCartan and Dr. W. J. Moloney of Boston took a more moderate position in the discussions than the fiery old John Devoy, Judge Daniel Cohalan, and Joseph McGarrity. As World War I closed, and the Versailles peace conference was being planned, Woodrow Wilson's peace plans and his doctrine of "self-determination" for small nations became intensely interesting to the Irish. Devoy said, "If Wilson leaves Ireland out [of peace conference consideration], I'm afraid he will not live long enough to live it down." In the winter of 1919 it was decided by the Irish-American leaders that a delegation should be sent to Paris to urge Wilson to include Ireland's case in the post-war discussions of the status of European nations. The delegation was to represent the American Committee for Irish Independence, a broadly representative organization. The Commissioners chosen were Frank P. Walsh, a prominent labor lawyer, Edward F. Dunne, former mayor of Chicago, and Michael J. Ryan. Although Ryan was believed to be close to the militant wing by this time, he assured Senator David Walsh, a powerful Democratic party leader, that he believed the delegation should accommodate itself to President Wilson's position at Versailles.[29]

None of the delegates had been associated with anti-Wilson elements in the Democratic party, but Wilson knew of Ryan's pro-German statements prior to American entry into World War I. At a rally in New York's Metropolitan Opera House attended by Wilson, his aide Joseph Tumulty urged Wilson to meet the Irish delegates. Wilson was reported to have responded that Tumulty could tell them "to go to hell."[30] On March 31, 1919, before leaving for Ireland on the journey to Paris, Ryan expressed the hope of the delegation, Wilson's truculent position toward Irish issues notwithstanding.

America is our home and we proceed with the hope that the blessings of civil and religious liberty under which our Republic has grown great will be extended to Ireland. . . . Our President has declared in favor of the freedom of small nationalities and for the right of the governed to determine the form under which they should live. The claim which we shall urge on behalf of Ireland in cooperation with Ireland's representatives is just this.[31]

The journey to Paris was to no avail, and the Irish were coldly shut out of all discussions despite their pleas.

Ryan's speeches on the conditions in Ireland on his return from Europe were influential in mobilizing still further support for the Irish cause. Early training in the classics and constant practice in rhetoric, long platform experience, a familiarity with Irish issues, and the atmosphere of high emotion attending the Irish freedom drive gave his speeches a notable power. On March 13, 1919, at the Philadelphia Academy of Music, Ryan addressed the traditional martyr's celebration in memory of Robert Emmet sponsored by the militant Clan na Gael. England sought a "super-sovereignty," he told the huge audience. "England's overlordship means that her ships continue to carry our goods and her merchant marine shall dominate the seas," he said. He recited England's exploitations of Ireland and decried those who contended Ulster was opposed to Irish independence. "For thirty years prior to this year the majority of the elected representatives from Ulster were nationalists. . . . Ulster is part of Ireland's heart, and while Ireland lives can never be torn from her." The speech attacked the League of Nations proposals of Woodrow Wilson "savagely" as the *Evening Bulletin* said, with Ryan characterizing the peace conference as a gathering of birds of prey.[32] His appearance at the big annual Clan na Gael rally testified to the emotional solidarity among the Irish in the city wrought by the momentous events in Ireland since 1916.

At an overflow meeting of the Philadelphia Irish at the city's Metropolitan Opera House on June 8, 1919, Ryan thundered forth the determination of the Irish to win their liberty:

There is a unanimity of opinion in Ireland that is past all understanding. The desire for freedom permeates the very thought and atmosphere of Ireland. Those men over there are determined to win their freedom even if they have to go— more and more and more of them—to the dungeon and the scaffold. The same spirit exists among the women of Ireland, too, and even from the children comes the inevitable cry "up the Republic!"

Referring to Lloyd George and the hope of Ireland for a "degree of self-government unparalleled by any past offers made," Ryan said "abominable censorship" was keeping the truth about the Paris peace sessions secret. "Danger is menacing the world, and instead of making a peace of justice and a peace that will stop forever the death and destruction of wars, our President, M. Clemenceau and Lloyd George, speaking for Robert Cecil, are merely allotting the earth, parcelling out this section and that of one country and another." So great was the audience for this speech that overflow crowds had to be accommodated in street meetings near the Opera House. The wildly cheering crowds roared approval of Ryan's report of Ireland's struggle and his attacks on Wilson and England.[33]

During this period Ryan worked feverishly to obtain funds for the Irish independence campaign which had set a goal of $150,000 for Philadelphia. He addressed audiences tirelessly. After the peace treaty of 1921 between England and Ireland that granted a measure of Irish independence, the mass enthusiasm of Irish America faded, however, and with it Ryan's national prominence. He continued to give ceremonial addresses through the 1920s, but advancing age and the growth of the mass media and more commercial diversions reduced the appeal of the kinds of speeches for which Ryan was noted. During the Depression of the 1930s Ryan organized a soup kitchen to help feed the unemployed. He continued to associate with churchmen and Irish leaders, but his political career declined as did the bank that he had founded, the Girard Avenue Title and Trust Company.

The career of Michael J. Ryan is a prototype of thousands of Irish-American careers of the period from the Civil War to the 1920s. The Irish-American network provided a vehicle for personal development and also opportunity to reach national prominence. Michael Ryan exemplifies the gifts involved with mobility in such a network. His intelligence, political aptitude, and oratorical skill combined to promote his ambitions in organizational activities. Sean T. O'Kelly, later President of the Republic of Ireland, who had met Ryan in Paris in 1919, considered him one of the most able Irish Americans of his generation, but "tremendously vain."[34] For a bootmaker's son to be in a position to pressure the heads of nations at Versailles was occasion for some ego satisfaction, and Ryan may have inflated himself for the occasion. His career had taken him from local politics to the heights of a climactic struggle for Irish freedom, and this provided a role model dear to the hearts of Irish Americans. He represented the socially mobile generation, the "Parnellian" generation, of Irish America, educated, ambitious and widely connected. Locally it included such men as William Harrity, member of the Democratic National Committee, and Michael Francis Doyle, noted international lawyer, like Ryan, graduates of local colleges. Nationally their ranks included men as diverse as war hero "Wild Bill" Donovan and a phalanx of Senators from various states of the Union.

Such a man as Ryan was especially adapted to the role of mobilizer and mediator in behalf of Irish nationalism in his time. The elaborate Irish organizational network of the United States required men with sufficient breadth of ambition and experience to assume national positions and to manage the complex and often contradictory personal, regional, and organizational interests involved in Irish affairs around the turn of the century. Ryan's tutelage in the 1880s and 1890s among Philadelphia's widely connected and varied Irish community permitted him to master the art of balancing local political, nationalist, fraternal, and religious elements in behalf of the Land League, the Irish National League, and his own career.[35] His adeptness and oratorical ability led to his recognition by Irish-American leaders and visiting leaders of the Irish Parliamentary Party as a man of notable abilities. Ryan was able to comprehend the far-flung extent of Irish-American ties and to oversee an extraordinary system of voluntary financial contributions that funneled hundreds of thousands of dollars to the Irish nationalist politicians in Ireland.

Ryan's role as a mediator extended beyond America to Ireland. As head of the United Irish League he tried to warn John Redmond about the decline of the organization. When the Sinn Fein movement gained dominance in Ireland, he was astute enough to position himself so that he became one of the bridges between the moderates and the militants in the United States, and in doing so he enhanced his significance in the eyes of leaders in Ireland. When it came to a choice of delegates to seek some accommodation with Woodrow Wilson at Versailles, Ryan had sufficient credibility with both Sinn Fein leaders and the Irish-American network to be selected as one of the members of the commission. He was one of those personalities whose emotional and organizational ties to Ireland were the basis for the Irish-American connection that profoundly influenced Ireland's affairs from 1880 to 1921.

Both in his national and international role, Ryan's career was evidence of the fact that the Philadelphia Irish community was closely linked to the broad constellation of Irish concentrations and organizations that were part of a trans-Atlantic ethnic tradition. As an orator Ryan was a tribune of this tradition, and his speeches expounded its views and history both to non-Irish Americans and to leaders in Ireland. The capacity of Irish-American communities to produce such spokesmen with their blend of personal political ambitions and Irish organizational attachments manifested the educational, political, and cultural identification that the Irish Americans had been able to perpetuate for themselves. In his long and active life from 1862 to 1943 Michael J. Ryan saw an amazing revolution in Irish life from the post-Famine period to the establishment of an independent Irish state, and one of the most dynamic influences in that revolution of Irish life was the contribution of men like himself.

It might be argued that these three men because of their prominence were singular leaders, untypical, different from their Irish-American compatriots. This is hardly sustainable in view of the close relationships each had with the working class and small business constituencies that were the basis of their power. Rather, they were exponents of the energy, aspirations, and social motivations that were widespread in those constituencies. It is apropos also to note that they were complemented in their roles by dozens of other Irish-American figures of similar mettle in the same city's life. They were expressive not only of the spirit of their times, but of certain timeless qualities that have been assets in the Irish tradition over the generations.

The three men whose careers are summarized here are examples of leadership styles produced by the urban community when the Irish were at the height of their local power numerically. Contractor, churchman, and organization leader, they functioned at sophisticated levels of power and had the capacity to pursue their own courses even against formidable opposition. They were each competitive and unlikely to yield to intimidation, and this style accorded with values among their followers. Their positions did reflect the community out of which their power arose. James Ryan was one among the many contractors whose access to Irish labor and construction trade skills made them key figures in an ethnic community intent upon steady work. Archbishop Ryan was both a symbolic representative of that same community and also a figure whose activities epitomized the striving of the group toward stability, social acceptance, education, and civic leadership. Michael Ryan, by virtue of his articulation of Irish nationalist aspirations, spoke for his ethnic community and in his career exemplified the advancement and political interests of a broad segment of the Irish-American population. Each was a mobilizer not only of men and of commitment, but of money. In an America that was intensely proud of its constructions, its proclamations of fellowship, and its wealth, they fitted into the social landscape admirably.

It is significant that none of these men was for any long period of his career confused about what role to play. They did not compromise easily, nor is there evidence of notable instability in their lives. Rather, they pressed toward their goals with a remarkable energy. While Ireland and its problems remained prominent in their attachments, they were fully dedicated to American careers and institutions. Their relation to Ireland was not one of ineffectual nostalgia but was marked by practical efforts to secure livelihoods for emigrants and political liberty for that country. The careers of these leaders express determination, assurance, and a swift adaptation to the needs and opportunities of America.

The process by which these men rose to their representative status was not electoral, though Michael Ryan did hold public offices. It was part of a larger adaptation. A working class identity had enabled many men to make a satisfactory adjustment of their urban roles. A common language with the host society, freedom to associate, effective ties to the homeland, and a growth of social and economic opportunities made for a general *modus vivendi* with their urban situation. For Ireland's "neighborly village code," a code that in reality was often laced with antagonism, they substituted their own local ethnic code, one of complex urban self-interest and affinity. They accepted the American individualist work ethic but tempered it with a powerful commitment to social and educational goals for families and religious groups. As leaders their influence was in part based on their command of important streams of information about jobs, education, and Irish affairs. They had control of resources of money and contacts, and control over their own status as symbols and experts. These factors sustained their careers. As a result of the social compact in which they figured, the Irish became conscious of their own ethnic status in a new way, with a new and broadened communal and historical sense of their own achievements. The process was complex, as David Doyle and John Higham have emphasized, and it took place at various levels of society and included contradictions, but it did promote a fairly clear procession of leadership advancement that was not a confused and disorderly casting up of weak and unprepared men, but rather a process that was part of the economic, religious, and political pluralism of the city.[36]

NOTES

1. Theodore Hershberg, ed., *Philadelphia: Work, Space, Family and Group Experience in a 19th Century Community* (New York: Oxford University Press, 1981), p. 471. *U.S. Census of 1900* Vol. I, Part I, pp. 798 and 877.

2. William V. Shannon, *The American Irish* (New York: The Macmillan Co., 1963), pp. 33–34.

3. Dale Light, "Ethnicity and Urban Ecology in a Nineteenth Century City: Philadelphia's Irish, 1840–90," Ph.D. thesis, University of Pennsylvania, 1979.

4. Nathaniel Burt and Wallace E. Davies, "The Iron Age, 1876–1905," Russell Weighley, ed., *Philadelphia: A 300 Year History* (New York: W. W. Norton, 1982), pp. 471–523. Dennis Clark, *The Irish in Philadelphia: Ten Generations of Urban Experience* (Philadelphia: Temple University Press, 1973), pp. 166–67.

5. Daniel J. Dougherty, *History of the Friendly Sons of St. Patrick* (Philadelphia: Society of the Friendly Sons of St. Patrick, 1952), p. 380. *Boyd's Business Directory of Philadelphia, 1900* (Philadelphia: C. E. Howe Co., 1900), pp. 923–24, 1022.

6. Dennis Clark, *The Irish Relations: Trials of an Immigrant Tradition* (East Brunswick, N.J.: Fairleigh Dickinson University Press, 1982), pp. 86–100.

7. Sister Mary Consuela, IHM, "The Church in Philadelphia, 1884–1918," James F. Connelly, ed., *The History of the Archdiocese of Philadelphia* (Philadelphia: The Archdiocese of Philadelphia, 1976), pp. 271–338.

8. John Tracy Ellis, *The Life of James Cardinal Gibbons* (Milwaukee, Wis.: Bruce Publishing Co., 1963), p. 115. *The Episcopal Silver Jubilee of the Most Reverend Patrick John Ryan, D.D.* (Philadelphia: St. Dominic Rectory, 1897), p. 234.

9. The Philadelphia North American, *Philadelphia and Popular Philadelphians* (Philadelphia: The North American, 1891), p. 58.

10. Interview with John J. Reilly, January 28, 1982, Philadelphia. Tape in the files of the Clark Collection, Balch Institute for Ethnic Studies, Philadelphia.

11. References to Moriarty and Dougherty are in Clark, *The Irish in Philadelphia*, op. cit., pp. 96 and 121.

12. Light, "Ethnicity and Urban Ecology," op. cit., pp. 109–112.

13. William A. O'Brien, *Recollections* (London: The Macmillan Co., 1905), p. 411.

14. *The Irish World* (New York), October 18, 1890. *The Evening Bulletin* (Philadelphia), January 17, 1914.

15. *The Irish World* (New York), November 15, 1890.

16. F. S. L. Lyons, *Ireland Since the Famine* (London: Weidenfeld and Nicholson, 1971), p. 177.

17. *The Irish World* (New York), February 1, 1896.

18. Carl Wittke, *The Irish in America* (Baton Rouge, La.: Louisiana State University Press, 1956), p. 168.

19. J. E. Kendle, "The Round Table Movement and 'Home Rule All Round,'" *The Historical Journal* XI, No. 2 (1968), 332–353.

20. *The Irish World* (New York), December 3, 1910.

21. *The Irish World* (New York), November 3, 1910.

22. *Philadelphia Public Ledger,* December 11, 1910.

23. *The Irish World* (New York), February 4, 1911.

24. Dennis Clark, "Eireannach Eigin: William J. Bradley (1892–1981), Sinn Fein Advocate," *Eire-Ireland* XVIII, 2 (Summer 1983), 116–26.

25. *The Evening Bulletin* (Philadelphia), June 6, 1914.

26. *The Evening Bulletin* (Philadelphia), January 17, 1913. F. M. Carroll, *American Opinion and the Irish Question: 1910–1923* (Dublin: Gill and Macmillan, 1978), p. 33.

27. *The Evening Bulletin* (Philadelphia), March 12, 1918. Carroll, *American Opinion and the Irish Question,* op. cit., p. 27. Ryan's early ties to the Clan na Gael are made clear in minutes of the Irish American Club, May 26, 1889, Balch Institute for Ethnic Studies, Clark Collection, Philadelphia, and the Letterbook of Henri Le Caron, July 18, 1888, Balch Institute, Philadelphia.

28. Carroll, *American Opinion and the Irish Question,* op. cit., pp. 38, 127. *The Evening Bulletin* (Philadelphia), May 12, 13, 1919.

29. John B. Duff, "The Versailles Treaty and Irish-Americans," *Journal of American History,* LV, No. 4 (December 1968), 582–89.

30. Duff, "The Versailles Treaty," p. 589.

31. *The Evening Bulletin* (Philadelphia), March 31, 1919.

32. *The Evening Bulletin* (Philadelphia), March 14, 1919.

33. *The Evening Bulletin* (Philadelphia), June 9, 1919.

34. Interview with John J. Reilly, January 28, 1982, Philadelphia, Balch Institute for Ethnic Studies, op. cit. Reilly knew Ryan well. Clark, *The Irish Relations,* op. cit., pp. 126–40.

35. Ryan's attempt in 1910 to overcome factionalism in Irish circles by federation plans is one example of his mediating role. Carroll, *American Opinion and the Irish Question,* p. 15.

36. Eric Foner makes clear that assimilation could mean assimilation within working class settings, as was true for the great majority of the Irish in Philadelphia. Eric Foner, "Radicalism in the Gilded Age: The Land League and Irish-America," *Marxist Perspectives* (Summer 1978), pp. 6–55. Social factors in the Irish accommodation are cited as general pre-conditions in Margaret M. Wood, *The Stranger: A Study in Social Relationships* (New York: Columbia University Press, 1934), pp. 137–54. The bases of leadership power are analyzed in Barry Collins, *Social Psychology* (Reading, Mass: Addison Wesley Publishing Co., 1970) passim; Robert Dudley Edwards, *A New History of Ireland* (Toronto: University of Toronto Press, 1972), p. 257, explains the growing historical consciousness of the Irish Americans at the end of the nineteenth century.

ellen skerrett

the development of catholic identity among irish americans in chicago, 1880 to 1920

After years of poverty and fragmentation, Chicago's Irish emerged in the 1880s as the city's most powerful political and religious group. Since refugees of the Great Famine overwhelmed Chicago in the 1840s, the Irish had been among the city's poorest residents. Their shantytowns along the Chicago River constituted the city's first slums, familiar to newspaper readers as the scene of violent crimes. Although the Irish had become voters in significant numbers, their involvement in the political process was decried by nativists as a threat to American democratic institutions. Despite the fact that a large segment of the Chicago Irish population was only nominally Catholic, they were popularly regarded as the backbone of the Catholic Church. Throughout the 1850s and 1860s, for example, the Republican Chicago *Tribune* devoted many of its editorials to the Irish problem. In addition to characterizing Irish immigrants as criminally prone, the *Tribune* charged that they were taught to obey ecclesiastical rulers first. Because of their loyalty to the Church, Irish Catholics were incapable of performing their duties as United States citizens. As the *Tribune* saw it, "the laws of [America] must hold a secondary place in their allegiance."[1]

Many leaders in Chicago's early Irish community agreed that the future of their group looked bleak indeed. Beyond establishing organizations such as the Hibernian Benevolent Association and Total Abstinence societies, men such as William J. Onahan promoted schemes to relocate Irish families on farms in the West. If immigration from Ireland could not be halted, then at least the Irish would be directed away from cities such as Chicago where men, women, and children eked out an existence in industrial slums.

Parish priests tended to be more optimistic about the future of the Chicago Irish. Already by the 1870s, the Irish parish system had become firmly entrenched in the city. Although poverty hampered institutional development, the Chicago Irish had made significant gains in terms of building churches and establishing schools. The process of parish-building not only strengthened Catholic identity but also established the Chicago Irish as stout supporters of America's tradition of voluntary church contributions.

Chicago's early Irish parishes were located in the "waste places of the city . . . where . . . the populace are humbly and poorly housed."[2] However unimpressive the pioneer church and school buildings, the fact remains that parishes were the Chicago Irish's major institution. With their emphasis on respectability and conformity, Irish parishes were important forces in transforming immigrants into law-abiding urban dwellers. As the Irish prospered economically they invested more money in their parishes and schools. While their primary purpose was to reinforce Catholic identity, these institutions accelerated Irish integration into the larger society. Though local parishes and schools were predominantly working-class institutions, they nevertheless fostered middle class aspirations.

The Chicago Fire of 1871 which began in the rear of Patrick and Catherine O'Leary's barn on DeKoven Street had long-term consequences for the city's Irish, then estimated at more than forty thousand. With nearly four square miles of the city leveled, the demand for Irish labor was unprecedented. By the mid-1870s, Irish contractors were making fortunes as a new modern city rose from the ashes of the fire. While the Irish were outnumbered by Swedish carpenters and German craftsmen, there was steady work for laborers, including newly arrived immigrants who swelled the ranks of Chicago's Irish community. Although the period of heavy immigration was just about over, children of the city's early Irish settlers began to enter the labor force in the late 1870s and 1880s.[3]

In addition to the erection of a new business district, Chicago was expanding outward. By the 1880s, streetcar lines criss-crossed the city providing the Irish with yet another source of employment. New residential sections required sidewalks, sewers, gas, electric, and telephone lines, endeavors in which the Irish were conspicuous. As the city's population increased to more than a million in 1890 so did the demand for policemen and firemen. The Irish dominated both departments and for most of the next century, the Chicago Police Force and Fire Department remained largely Irish institutions.

The Chicago Irish had much to gain as the city's economy expanded. Unlike New England towns and cities, Chicago had a diverse economic base. Irish workers were not concentrated in a single field such as meatpacking or steelmaking but were found in a variety of occupations. One result of this diversity was that the Irish as a group were better able to weather depressions in the national economy. Steady paychecks eased the burden of domestic life, diminishing much of the violence that had been associated with Irish families in the 1850s and 1860s. Then too, Irish prosperity enabled hundreds of families to move out of slum districts into decent housing. Although limited, upward social mobility among the Irish was evident in the 1870s and it gained momentum during the next four decades.

By 1920, the Chicago Irish were no longer industrial slum dwellers. Paralleling their advance up the economic ladder, they had moved outward in the city into apartment house districts and bungalow belts. While Catholic immigrants from Southern and Eastern Europe remained behind in industrial areas, transforming them into liveable neighborhoods, the Chicago Irish cast their lot with the city's native born Protestants. This preference was ironic, for as leaders of the Democratic Party and the Catholic Church, the Irish practiced cultural pluralism. Irish politicians established ethnically based tickets, and Irish churchmen presided over a parochial system that met the needs of more than ten national groups. Their reputation as ethnic brokers notwithstanding, the Chicago Irish preferred to live as outsiders in largely Protestant areas rather than to remain in heavily Catholic ethnic neighborhoods.

In the 1920s, the Chicago Irish were well on their way to becoming middle class in terms of aspirations if not economics. More American than Irish, the community was also intensely Catholic. Indeed to a large extent Irish identity had been transformed into a strictly Catholic identity, one which was consistent with the special needs of Catholic Chicago's largest English-speaking group. Although Irish identity did not disappear completely, it was not reinforced at the parish level or in the Catholic educational system. To understand why Chicago Irish readily accepted an identity that was nearly devoid of Irish content it is necessary to examine three major forces which shaped the Irish community in the 1880s: Catholicism, politics, and nationalism. In this analysis, special attention will be paid to the way in which politics and nationalism affected the Catholicism of the Chicago Irish.

By the 1880s, the Catholic Church in Chicago had weathered nativist attacks and internal strife to become the largest denomination in the city. Although in terms of membership the Catholic Church was ethnically diverse, it was Irish-dominated. Five of Chicago's six bishops between 1834 and 1880 were Irish and they appointed priests of Irish birth and descent to important positions in the Church hierarchy. Nativist attacks in the 1850s and 1860s had the effect of strengthening Catholic identity, especially among the Irish who were the most visible Catholics in the city. As victims of nativist propaganda, the Chicago Irish were particularly conscious of how undemocratic their Church appeared. Disregarding criticism of externals such as the use of Latin in the Mass and sacraments, many Irish Catholics were nonetheless uncomfortable about the near absolute authority of American bishops.

Since the early days of the Church in Chicago, Irish priests had wielded enormous control over congregations. As controversies in the 1850s and 1860s made clear, Chicago's Irish Catholics preferred strong pastors to powerful bishops. When Bishops Anthony O'Regan and James Duggan attempted to limit the power of Irish priests, they were confronted by angry parishioners. At issue was the bishops' arbitrary dismissal of diocesan clergy. In their fight with Chicago bishops, Irish parishioners and priests revealed just how American they had become. Again and again they argued the issue of priests' rights in strictly American terms. Just as Chicago Fenians asserted that "America herself was free and it was her holy duty to assist other nations to gain the same God-given right," so too Irish Catholics argued that they merely wanted to see "the checks and balances of constitutional freedom" applied to their Church.[4]

Although Irish Catholics were unsuccessful in the battle over priests' rights, to a certain extent they discouraged bishops from interfering unnecessarily in the affairs of local parishes. Until the administration of Archbishop George W. Mundelein (1916–1939), pastors of all ethnic backgrounds were given a wide berth in running their parishes.[5] While Lithuanian, Polish, and German laymen on occasion fought for the right to be involved in parochial matters, especially finances, Irish Catholics by and large were content to let pastors make decisions about buildings, schools, personnel, and money.

A continual stream of priests from Ireland since the 1850s had made possible the expansion of Chicago's English-speaking system. Because of the greater availability of Irish priests, Chicago bishops readily established new territorial parishes with as few as fifty families. This was no inconsequential matter because after 1880, the territorial parishes spread outward forming the nucleus of Catholic communities throughout Chicago.[6] While pastors of foreign-language (national) parishes were loath to have their parishes divided, Irish pastors had few qualms. They saw the creation of new parishes as a way to extend Catholic power and influence in the city as a whole. As the drive for national parishes intensified among Germans, Poles, Lithuanians, and Slavs, the Irish by default gained control of English-speaking parishes, thereby dominating the institutional Church from below as well as from above. Not only did the expansion of the English-speaking parish system keep pace with Irish mobility in the 1880s and 1890s, but the parishes themselves reflected the needs and aspirations of Chicago's largest contingent of English-speaking Catholics.

Often overlooked in discussions of the nineteenth century Chicago Irish is the great diversity which existed in their parishes in terms of structure, personnel, and orientation. The largest and most well known Irish parish was Holy Family, established by the Jesuits on the Near West Side in 1857. Despite divisions of its territory, Holy Family still claimed more than twenty thousand members in 1881. In addition to a massive Gothic church, the parish complex embraced four grammar schools, a convent academy, and St. Ignatius College, the forerunner of Loyola University. Although in many respects Holy Family fulfilled James Sanders' description as "the single great Irish workingman's parish," it was not an intensely ethnic community.[7] While pastors such as Arnold J. Damen did not denigrate Irish identity, neither were they interested in promoting it through parish groups or in the parochial schools. As a result, social and religious organizations in Holy Family parish were overwhelmingly Catholic in nature, from sodalities to reading circles and groups such as the Catholic Order of Foresters.

Unlike the Jesuits, Chicago's diocesan clergy shared no common training or ideas about parochial life. Depending on their own backgrounds and orientation, Irish pastors enjoyed enormous freedom in establishing parishes that were ethnic, Catholic, or a combination of the two. Some pastors encouraged their parishioners' involvement in the cause of Irish freedom. For example during his twenty-seven-year tenure as pastor of St. John's Church, Rev. John Waldron was an enthusiastic supporter of the nationalist cause. Not only did he proudly display two pikes from the 1798 rebellion in Ireland, but he invited such groups as the Fenians, Irish Rifles, Clan na Gael Guards, and Ancient Order of Hibernians to participate in parish celebrations.

For every Waldron, however, there was a Chicago Irish priest like Rev. Daniel J. Riordan who was intent on creating parochial structures that were strictly Catholic and American in outlook. In 1881 he established St. Elizabeth parish on the South Side just a mile east of the Union Stock Yards. The new parish included the notorious Federal Street slum as well as fashionable Michigan and Wabash avenues. Although Riordan himself was a director of the Irish Catholic Colonization Society, he did little to promote St. Elizabeth's as an Irish parish. During his forty-one-year tenure as pastor he forged a Catholic community that bridged the gap between railroad workers, office workers, and professionals.

While the congregation drew its numerical strength from laborers who lived in frame shanties, St. Elizabeth parish was a model of middle class respectability. It was no coincidence that the French Romanesque church and brick school buildings were located in the wealthy part of the parish. Nor was it an accident that the parish supported elaborate musical programs. However uncomfortable poor Irish men and women may have felt in the parish, their children were exposed to a Catholicism that was decidedly middle class, nearly "high church." Beyond a grammar school, St. Elizabeth parish also included a high school which gained a reputation as a training ground for girls who wished to pursue careers as teachers in the city's public schools.

New territorial parishes such as St. Elizabeth's generally reached a peak population of a few hundred families. In contrast to older parishes such as St. Patrick's, Holy Family, or Holy Name, which served thousands of Irish immigrants in the 1860s and 1870s, English-speaking parishes established in the 1880s and 1890s were smaller in terms of territory and population. Yet smallness did not retard the church-building process nor did it affect the development of cohesive communities. On the contrary, the two processes were interrelated. In building permanent churches and schools, Irish pastors found a cause that cut across class lines, uniting Irish congregations and diminishing old county factionalisms. Like their counterparts in ward politics, Irish pastors were known as pragmatists, men of action who had little time for intellectualizing or preaching. In contrast with Protestant clergymen who delivered elaborate sermons Sunday after Sunday, Chicago's Irish priests concentrated on pastoral activity rather than scholarship.

Irish priests and congregations were well aware of the tensions which existed between American and Catholic identities, and they were conscious that the larger American society often regarded the Catholic Church as an alien institution. Since the 1850s, Chicago newspapers regularly debated issues such as the temporal authority of the Pope, papal infallibility, church-state relations, and the appropriateness of Catholic schools. As a result, brick-and-mortar Catholicism had a special appeal for the city's Irish. The building of the churches and schools was pragmatic, it involved fund raising and planning, and it left a permanent mark on city neighborhoods.

Although Catholics were regularly criticized for spending money on churches instead of orphan asylums and reformatories, by 1875 Chicago newspapers were forced to concede that the construction of Catholic churches "improves and helps to fill up the surrounding neighborhood and swells and enhances the value of property."[8] While questions about the Catholic Church's compatibility with American institutions remained unresolved, the existence of new parish complexes offered tangible proof that Chicago's Irish were becoming stable urban dwellers.

The policy of parish formation with its emphasis on permanent church buildings and schools was not unique to Chicago's Catholics. German and Swedish Lutherans also built massive churches and established schools where their children could receive bi-lingual instruction. English-speaking Protestants, however, favored the establishment of missions in poor areas of the city. Funded by prosperous parent churches, these missions were modest affairs housed in simple frame or brick buildings. From an economic point of view, missions were a sensible solution because they relieved poor families of financial obligations. In contrast, Catholic church-building demanded ambitious fund raising programs which often extended over a period of ten or fifteen years. Because there were few wealthy Catholics in Chicago, brick-and-mortar Catholicism was wholly dependent on individual congregations.

In Irish parishes, fund raising schemes were a constant part of parochial life, and they combined religious fervor with political acumen. In addition to regular Sunday contributions of nickels and dimes, Irish parishioners raised money through bazaars. Far from being New England clambakes or ice cream socials, these events were lively affairs made more festive by the availability of liquor. Although special booths and concessions did a steady business, the main attraction was the popular voting contest. In parish after parish, Irish pastors pitted prominent citizens against one another in contests for gold-headed canes. Opponents might be railroad or meatpacking executives or union leaders, Irish nationalists or political candidates. In 1896, for example, St. Vincent de Paul parishioners overwhelmingly "elected" Governor John Peter Altgeld against his Republican contender John R. Tanner to raise funds for a $150,000 church. While popular voting contests raised the hackles of some Irish Catholics, they were effective means of enriching parish coffers. Although this process of church-building often seemed interminable, it played a crucial role in the creation of cohesive communities, something Protestant missions rarely accomplished.

Irish control of the Catholic Church in the 1880s was matched only by the success of the Irish in Democratic party politics. As early as the 1840s, the Chicago Irish gained a reputation for their political skills. Their command of English coupled with a talent for organization gave them a lead over other ethnic groups as well as the city's native born Protestants who generally disdained politics in favor of "respectable" employment. Although the Irish were outnumbered by the Germans in the 1860s and never regained their status as the city's most numerous ethnic group, they constituted the largest segment of Chicago's Democratic voters. Whereas the German vote was split between Republicans and Democrats, the Irish remained solidly in the Democratic camp. By 1885, the Irish dominated the Democratic Central Committee, and in 1890 they accounted for at least twenty-three of the city's sixty-eight aldermen.[9]

Chicago's Democratic politics in the nineteenth century was far from being issue oriented. Aldermen built up large ward organizations by dispensing patronage jobs as well as distributing food and coal to the poor. Although Irish aldermen provided much needed social welfare services for their constituents, they regarded politics primarily as a means of personal and financial gain. Like their diocesan counterparts, Irish politicians did not come from similar backgrounds. Some like "Foxy Ed" Cullerton (1842–1920) were Chicago born, men who literally grew up with the city. Others such as Johnny Powers (1852–1930) emigrated from Ireland as young men. Powers forsook a career as a small grocery store owner in Chicago to become the saloonkeeping alderman of the old nineteenth ward, a position he held almost continuously from 1888 until 1927. In addition to "native sons" and immigrants, Chicago's Democratic politicians included men like Judge Edward F. Dunne, mayor of Chicago from 1905 to 1907. Dunne was born in Connecticut, grew up in Peoria, attended Trinity College in Dublin, and moved to Chicago in 1876 where he set up a law practice.

Chicago was one of the fastest-growing cities in the United States in the 1880s, and its physical expansion (aided by annexation) provided a steady source of income for Irish politicians.[10] Building contractors elected to the City Council found themselves in a unique position to aid their own businesses. Even more important, Irish politicians without sidelines benefited from the sale of public property to private companies. In return for payoffs or shares of stock, "boodle" aldermen passed ordinances and granted franchises to companies that laid streetcar lines and elevated railroad tracks throughout the city. They also guaranteed companies the right to lay sewer, gas, and electric lines in new residential subdivisions. In short, Chicago's Irish aldermen exerted enormous control over the expansion of the city, a process which affected rank-and-file Irish laborers.

While the Chicago Irish benefited economically from the skills of their aldermen, Irish political power did not improve the group's social standing. Far from conferring respectability, political power often reinforced negative images of the Chicago Irish. Nowhere was this more evident than in the Hamline controversy in 1888. The ordinance introduced into the City Council sought to prohibit new saloons from being established within 200 feet of schools, churches, hospitals, and colleges. Existing saloons in violation of the proposed ordinance would be refused licenses and phased out over a two-year period.[11]

Although Irish politicians were not the only aldermen to oppose the Hamline ordinance, the resulting conflict was cast in Irish-Catholic terms. Fueling the controversy was the Chicago *Tribune*'s charge that the ordinance was defeated because of the "solid Roman Catholic vote in the Council." Despite the efforts of City Controller William J. Onahan to promote the Hamline ordinance, nineteen Catholic aldermen voted it down. The reaction among Irish Catholics was swift. Twelve hundred Catholic laymen and clergy gathered in Holy Family Sodality Hall to call for the resignation of nineteenth ward aldermen Johnny Powers and John Sheridan and to assail charges that "the Catholics of this parish are ruled by the groggery influence." Prominent residents, including ex-alderman "Honest John" Comiskey, vigorously refuted the contention that Catholic aldermen had voted the interests of their constituents. The resolution adopted on behalf of "the respectable citizens of this parish and ward" called for a reconsideration of the Hamline ordinance.[12]

In nearby St. Pius parish, plans for a similar mass meeting prompted Alderman Cullerton to propose an abridgement of the saloon ordinance. While it is likely that the Chicago *Tribune* seized the opportunity to single out the Council's predominantly Irish Catholic aldermen, the newspaper was not alone in its criticism. Archbishop John Ireland, the liberal prelate from St. Paul, Minnesota, charged that in regard to the liquor question American Catholics had separated religion and morals from politics. Instead of using their political power to reinforce their convictions, Catholics had been "praying well and voting badly." Archbishop Ireland expressed his gratitude to the "so-called Catholic Aldermen of Chicago" for awakening the indignation of Catholics in Chicago and across the country.[13]

Eventually the City Council reached an agreement over the proximity of saloons to schools, churches, and hospitals. While the Hamline controversy did not result in defeat for any of the city's Catholic aldermen, it symbolized the increasing middle class orientation of Chicago's Irish. Far from being prohibitionists, Irish residents in the nineteenth ward nonetheless sought to limit the number of saloons which existed near Holy Family parish complex, the center of their community. Despite the fact that Holy Family parishioners were predominantly working class, they were intent on improving the quality of neighborhood life. Significantly, on this issue the Irish were in closer agreement with Protestants than with their Bohemian, German, or Polish co-religionists.

Beyond taking an interest in their parish-based communities, the Chicago Irish in the 1880s were active supporters in the cause of Irish freedom. The city's first nationalist group, a branch of Daniel O'Connell's Repeal Association, was established in 1842. Moderate in tone, the organization supported the repeal of the Union between Great Britain and Ireland. By the 1860s, Chicago's Irish were backing more radical solutions to the Irish problem. Despite condemnation by Bishop James Duggan, a large segment of the Chicago Irish supported the Fenians in their campaign to free Ireland through physical force. The first Fenian National Convention was held in Chicago in 1863, and in 1866, Irish Chicagoans joined "General" John O'Neil in the disastrous Fenian "invasion" of Canada. Although this military action did not succeed in provoking an international incident between Great Britain and America, the strategy was endorsed by Irish men who favored violent revolution over parliamentary solutions. For years after the abortive attempt, Chicago Fenians were regarded as folk heroes, contributing a mythic dimension to the nationalist campaign.

The nationalist cause had an enduring appeal, especially for first and second generation Irish who felt alienated from the larger society. In his classic study of Irish nationalism Thomas N. Brown notes that the movement derived its most distinctive features from life in America: "A pervasive sense of inferiority, intense longing for acceptance and respectability, and an acute sensitivity to criticism."[14] As in other American cities of the nineteenth century, large numbers of the Chicago Irish harbored a deep conviction that their inferior status in America was directly related to British oppression of their homeland. Many Chicago Irish subcribed to Michael Davitt's view that only when Ireland was a free and independent nation would they be accorded full status as Americans.[15] To this end, they supported a wide range of nationalist groups from the Clan na Gael to the Irish National Land League.

The Irish nationalist movement in Chicago included Irish immigrants as well as upwardly mobile second generation Irish. Just as the city's Irish community encompassed many factions so did the nationalist cause. The Clan na Gael, for example, was a secret extremist group dedicated to financing the activities of the Irish Republican Brotherhood in Ireland and keeping alive the nationalist cause in Irish–American communities. In 1884, members of the Clan enthusiastically supported the Dynamite Campaign in England. They greeted bombings at Whitehall, Victoria Station, Scotland Yard, and the Tower of London as blows struck for Irish independence.

One of the reasons why the Clan remained so powerful in Chicago was its ties to the city's Democratic political machine. According to Michael F. Funchion, in no other American city was the Clan na Gael so deeply involved in machine politics. In their capacity as Democratic politicians, Clansmen were able to secure patronage jobs "from lofty judicial chambers to the city sewer system," thereby strengthening the nationalist cause at the same time they extended their political power.[16]

Throughout the 1880s, Chicago's most well–known Clansman was Alexander H. Sullivan, a lawyer credited with masterminding the Dynamite Campaign. As chairman of the national executive committee, Sullivan was one of the Clan na Gael's three top men (often referred to as "the Triangle"). His popularity in Chicago remained strong despite attempts by Edward Dunne and Dr. Patrick Cronin to remove him from office because of questionable financial dealings. Indeed, Sullivan counted among his closest friends Archbishop Patrick A. Feehan and Rev. Maurice J. Dorney, pastor of St. Gabriel parish on the South Side.

Although Chicago's Irish priests generally supported the nationalist movement, clerical approval did not render the cause wholly respectable. To many Anglo–Americans, the involvement of the Catholic clergy in the nationalist movement was yet another example of Irish Catholic power. Formerly attacked for their allegiance to Rome, Irish Catholics now smarted under criticism that they were hyphenated Americans. Especially during the Dynamite Campaign of 1883–1885, Irish nationalists were regarded as subversive rather than patriots interested in freeing Ireland. The rise of Charles Stuart Parnell and his Irish parliamentary party in the mid-1880s did much to redeem the nationalist cause.

While the Clan continued to exert tremendous influence in Chicago Irish nationalist politics, the Irish National Land League of America emerged as a powerful group after 1880. Its goal of abolishing the landlord system in Ireland through protest and parliamentary reform appealed to many Irish Americans who disdained the Clan's philosophy of violent revolution. In Chicago, Irish Catholics established branches of the Land League in their parishes and wards. This method of organization drew on the strengths of the city's Irish community. Unlike the Clan with its secret cells and camps, Land League branches operated as local groups, and they were effective in bringing Parnell's message to the wider Chicago Irish community. Priests from Ireland made the rounds, commending Irish Americans for their generous donations which enabled "Irish tenant farmers to hold out against eviction."[17]

Although many Irish-American nationalists were intent upon extending the values and political freedoms they enjoyed as Americans to their Irish relatives, others were motivated by deep hatred of England. One of the ironies of the Irish nationalist movement is that its members endorsed violent revolution in Ireland yet remained among the most loyal "law and order" supporters in American society. As events in Haymarket Square in 1886 revealed, Chicago's Irish might finance armed revolution in Ireland but they were less than enthusiastic when workers threatened Irish policemen.

More than any other event, the Haymarket Massacre cast light on the fragile nature of Irish-American identity and respectability. In 1886, Chicago was the center of agitation for the eight-hour day. On May 4, 1886, a group of angry workers gathered in Haymarket Square to protest the killing of a striker by police. The peaceful meeting ended in tragedy when a bomb exploded killing seven Chicago policemen, four civilians, and injuring nearly seventy-five patrolmen in addition to scores of workers. Five of the seven dead officers were Irish, a figure consistent with the ethnic make-up of the police force in the 1880s. Although inquiries into the affair disputed the need for a police guard of 176 men, the predominantly Irish force was praised for its steadfastness in the face of grave danger. As far as the *Tribune* was concerned, the performance of Chicago Irish police officers laid to rest doubts about their loyalties as officers of the law.[18]

While a few Irish labor leaders viewed the Haymarket affair as a classic confrontation between workers and police, by and large the Irish community shared the *Tribune*'s judgment that the policemen were victims of anarchy. However sympathetic they were to the cause espoused by striking workers, Irish men and women found it impossible to condone the killing of policemen. Whereas large segments of the city's German community championed the cause of Haymarket defendants, the more conservative Irish lined up on the side of the policemen. For many Irish in the city, Haymarket was a turning point in their battle for acceptance in the larger society.

Just as the public image of the Chicago Irish seemed to be improving, disaster struck. The brutal slaying of Dr. Patrick Cronin on May 4, 1889 split Chicago's Irish nationalists into two warring factions, and it focused worldwide attention on the nationalist movement in Chicago. It also called into question the conduct of Chicago Irish policemen who belonged to Camp 20 of the Clan na Gael Guard. Just three years after Haymarket, the loyalty of Irish and Irish-American policemen was once again suspect. Chicago's Irish community as well as the larger public was shocked to discover that Sergeant Daniel Coughlin, one of the officers in charge of the original murder investigation, was involved in Cronin's slaying. Although convicted of murder and sentenced to prison for life, Coughlin was granted a new trial by the Illinois Supreme Court and later acquitted.

No sooner had the Chicago Irish recovered from the first Coughlin trial with its sordid disclosures about the Clan na Gael than a second scandal rocked the nationalist cause. In December 1889, Charles Stuart

Parnell was cited as a co-defendant in a divorce suit brought by Captain William O'Shea. Popular support for the Protestant parlimentary leader diminished, and Chicago newspapers once again were filled with stories critical of the Irish cause. By the time Parnell died in 1891, Irish nationalism as a powerful force in Chicago was all but extinguished.

In the 1890s, the Chicago Irish increasingly turned their attention away from the nationalist cause. While the issue of Ireland's freedom remained alive, a large proportion of the Irish community no longer saw the movement as a viable means of attaining respect and acceptance in the larger society. Groups such as the Ancient Order of Hibernians and the Irish Rifles continued in existence but they began to operate in closer connection with local Catholic parishes. Much of the energy formerly directed to the nationalist cause was now channeled into parish-building and the expanding network of Catholic schools.

The shift in focus from nationalism to religion was not a sudden one. Since the 1870s, Chicago's Irish Catholics had formed fairly cohesive communities around their parishes and schools. Although the building of permanent churches was the primary concern, Catholic schools had also made headway in Irish parishes. Because they spoke English and had no ancestral language to preserve, Irish Catholics had less need of parochial schools than their German or Polish co-religionists. Still, they aggressively supported the cause of parochial education because it reinforced their identity as Catholics.

Throughout the 1890s, Chicago's public schools remained largely Protestant-dominated institutions. Although the reading of the King James version of the Bible had been outlawed in 1875, the schools were hardly pluralistic. Textbooks contained glaring examples of anti-Catholic and anti-Irish bigotry, and in newly annexed sections of the city, old New England traditions persisted. In Englewood, for example, holidays such as Decoration Day were still celebrated in the area's Protestant churches. While Catholic children were excused from attending, they keenly felt their status as second class citizens. For upwardly mobile Irish Catholics who settled in Englewood, parochial schools were necessary to maintain Catholic identity.

Teachers such as the Jesuits, the Christian Brothers of De La Salle, the Sisters of Mercy, and the Sisters of Charity of the Blessed Virgin Mary seized the opportunity to establish Catholic schools where the children of Irish immigrants could learn their catechism as well as secular subjects. On May 20, 1889, the Chicago Irish turned out in large numbers for the cornerstone laying of De La Salle Institute. This new school at 35th and Wabash testified to the increasing commitment of Irish Catholics to higher education, and it was a visible sign of upward mobility as well. The old Christian Brothers' Academy in St. Patrick's parish had been a popular institution in the 1860s and 1870s. But as the Irish moved outward in the city, its student body declined. The site for the new commercial academy was located in a fashionable residential district on the South Side where Irish families had begun to settle in large numbers after the Chicago Fire. Financed by contributions from Catholic and Protestant businessmen, De La Salle aimed to prepare young Catholic men for commercial careers in downtown offices.

Contemporary newspaper accounts make it clear that Catholic leaders were acutely aware of the plight of the city's Irish. Not yet full fledged members of the larger society, Irish Catholics nonetheless were conscious of their image and eager to prove their loyalty as Americans. Archbishop Feehan, for example, expressly thanked Protestant benefactors for their liberality and assured them they "were not laboring among a people of ingrates, but among those who appreciate their efforts." The Archbishop emphasized that De La Salle would produce patriotic Americans, Catholic boys who would "raise this Republic to a higher standard and work to the best interests in our common country." The featured speaker of the day was none other than Father Dorney, the ardent Irish nationalist and friend of Alexander Sullivan. Dorney called De La Salle the beginning of a new era in the history of Chicago Catholicism, and he predicted that this school and others that might follow "would make us a better and a greater people."[19]

The Christian Brothers' pragmatic view of education was shared by the Sisters of Mercy who opened St. James and St. Elizabeth high schools on the South Side in 1890. Unlike convent academies and select schools where young women followed a course of studies that was primarily religious, with emphasis on the fine arts, St. James and St. Elizabeth prepared Catholic girls for the world of work.[20] In the Irish community, the most coveted female job was that of schoolteacher in the public school system. Women religious responded to this demand by structuring their curriculum after the local public high schools so that Catholic girls could compete on an equal basis with their public school counterparts. Before long, the Sisters' schools were sending record numbers of graduates to Chicago Normal College in Englewood. Although admission to the teachers' college was free, students had to pass a rigorous qualifying exam. Graduates of St. James compiled an impressive record, accounting for thirty-six of one hundred candidates admitted to the teachers' college in 1901.[21] So successful were Catholic graduates in gaining admission to Chicago Normal that in 1915, Schools Superintendent Ella Flagg Young tried to impose a quota system. It would have limited the number of students accepted at Chicago Normal from any one school.

The Archdiocesan newspaper, the *New World,* denounced the plan because it would have made religion "a qualification for office, a thing absolutely forbidden by the United States Constitution."[22] Significantly, in the past the Catholic newspaper had criticized the teachers' college. Now it agreed that the entrance requirements were fair because they admitted only the best-prepared candidates. The fact that so many Catholic students passed the test was simply proof of the efficiency of the Sisters' methods. Catholic attempts to defeat the quota system were successful, and by 1920, Archbishop Mundelein estimated that "70 per cent of the teachers in the public schools" were graduates of Chicago's Catholic high schools.[23]

Not only did Catholic high schools established in Chicago between 1890 and 1920 reflect the Irish community's preoccupation with their status as Americans, but they offered a solution to the longstanding conflict between religious and civic loyalty. Far from being Catholic ghetto institutions, schools such as De La Salle, St. Mary's, St. James, and St. Elizabeth's prepared students to compete in the larger world. These institutions sought to prove that sons and daughters of Irish immigrants could be Catholics as well as Americans. However much Catholic leaders argued that their churches were compatible with American institutions, it was the Catholic schools which finally settled the matter. As teachers and office workers, Catholic school graduates demonstrated that they could function in the larger society and that their religion did not affect their performance. Especially in the business community, Catholic high schools earned a reputation for producing disciplined, efficient workers.

Although Catholic high schools (like their public counterparts) enrolled only a small percentage of Chicago's adolescents between 1890 and 1920, they played a crucial role in fostering middle class attitudes in the larger Catholic community. Catholic boys who otherwise might have gone to work in factories or meatpacking plants now obtained jobs as typists, stenographers, and clerks in Chicago offices. To a certain extent, this process would have occurred naturally without the intervention of Catholic schools, especially considering the number of Irish men and women who attended public schools, by necessity or choice. However, the fact remains that Catholic nuns and priests used their influence to convince immigrant parents of the value of secondary education. They discouraged parents from sending children to work after grammar school, arguing that the family's standard of living would be greatly improved by sons and daughters who secured white-collar jobs. This campaign, begun by the Irish religious, was later adopted by Polish nuns and priests who were distressed over the high percentage of their own group's children who left school after the sixth grade.

The push for Catholic education occurred at a significant point in the history of Chicago's Irish community. By 1890, the Irish population had ceased to be predominantly foreign born. Not only did the second generation outnumber immigrants (113,816 to 70,028), but a third generation had come of age.[24] Whereas Irish immigrants were confined to manual labor jobs, the second and third generations had made steady gains. As Michael Funchion notes, between 1870 and 1890 about 85 percent of Irish immigrants were manual workers. By 1900, when second generation Irish were included for the first time in the federal census, the percentage of manual laborers had declined considerably. Although 70 percent of Chicago's 76,000 Irish males were manual workers, more than 25 percent held white-collar jobs, owned businesses, or were professionals. While the female Irish workforce was smaller (25,000), nearly 40 percent held white-collar jobs or were business proprietors. Indeed, the percentage of Irish women professionals was double that for Irish men.[25] Not counted in the federal statistics as Irish were third generation Irish men and women who swelled the ranks of white-collar workers.

By the turn of the century, Irish Americans were beginning to enjoy their status as a valuable commodity in an increasingly ethnic city. Widespread immigration from Southern and Eastern Europe had several beneficial effects on the Chicago Irish. Not only did new immigrants push the Irish up the economic ladder, but by comparison, they made the Irish appear more American and less foreign. Moreover, the new immigrants from Southern and Eastern Europe enhanced Irish political and religious power in the city. Changing ethnic neighborhoods meant new constituencies for Irish politicians such as Johnny Powers and Edward Cullerton, and new Catholic parishes extended the Church's influence throughout Chicago. While the Irish community's quest for respectability was not yet over, conditions were far better than they had been during the turbulent 1880s when thousands of Chicago Irish placed their hopes for acceptance in the nationalist cause.

As we have seen, Catholic schools play a significant role in the changing character of Irish-American Catholicism. With their emphasis on discipline and pragmatism, these institutions accelerated the integration of Irish Catholics into larger society. Schools staffed by predominantly Irish religious orders consciously avoided ethnic identity, seeking instead to foster a supra Catholic identity. According to Lawrence J. McCaffrey, Catholic education severed the American Irish from their historical roots by emphasizing "Catholic, Continental, and Anglo-Saxon histories at the expense of Irish culture."[26] While this decision had long-term consequences for the Chicago Irish, in the early years of the twentieth century it provided them with an acceptable means of proving their dual loyalties as Catholics and Americans. As the Irish entered the ranks of the middle class they continued to support Catholic schools at all levels, thereby strengthening the bonds of the Chicago Irish community.

Although Chicago's Irish population was widely dispersed by 1920, it continued to be parish-centered. Far from diminishing in influence, the parish became even more important as Irish families improved their economic and social status and moved to outlying areas of the city. In neighborhood after neighborhood, English-speaking territorial parishes formed the basis of emerging middle class Catholic communities. Many, like St. Anselm's (1909), were established in the wake of Chicago's apartment building and bungalow boom which transformed prairies into urban neighborhoods. Unlike the old immigrant parishes, these newer institutions continued the trend to smaller parochial communities begun in the 1880s.

One of the most accurate portrayals of Chicago Irish parochial life in the 1910s occurs in James T. Farrell's famous trilogy, *Studs Lonigan*. Based on his boyhood parish of St. Anselm's, the novel documents just how American the Chicago Irish had become on the eve of World War I. Like many of St. Anselm's founding parishioners, Patrick Lonigan was born in Ireland but raised in an immigrant Chicago neighborhood. By dint of hard work he established his family in a "steam heat" apartment in the new Washington Park subdivision just west of the University of Chicago. Located in the midst of a white middle class neighborhood, the parish forms the center of community life for the Irish. Yet it is not an ethnically oriented institution. Indeed, the foreign born Irish pastor's attempts to promote Irish history in the school carry little weight with either Lonigan or his son, Studs.

For the elder Lonigan, the boulevard and the tree-shaded streets of Washington Park are a world away from the stockyards neighborhood of his youth, and St. Patrick's (Anselm's) parish is a fitting symbol of his newfound respectability. As the novel opens, Lonigan reflects that he had set the right example for his children, "sent them to Catholic schools to be educated, seen that they performed their religious duties, hustled them off to confession regularly, given them money for the collection, never allowed them to miss mass, even in winter."[27] To Studs, the parish is simply part of his familiar middle class world. Like most of his friends, Studs attends the parish school and, before joining his father in the painting business, spends a lackluster year in a Jesuit high school.

What becomes increasingly clear in the Lonigan trilogy is the extent to which Catholic parish life has taken root among the Chicago Irish. With its emphasis on respectability and adherence to strict religious observance, St. Patrick's is a model middle class parish. When the Washington Park neighborhood is threatened by racial change in 1919, the pastor convinces his parishioners that the construction of a new Gothic church will keep the neighborhood white and increase property values as well. In the face of large-scale black immigration from the South, Father Gilhooley's scheme is destined for failure. Yet so powerful is the concept of parish community that the Lonigans and others contribute eagerly to the building of a $350,000 church in 1925. When the neighborhood becomes black not long after the new church is dedicated, the Lonigans move, reluctantly, to the next neighborhood beyond, South Shore. As Lonigan explains to Studs on moving day, he and his wife regarded St. Patrick's parish and the Washington Park neighborhood "kind of like home. We sort of felt about it the same way I feel about Ireland, where I was born."[28] Displaced by racial change, the Lonigans once again become newcomers in another middle class neighborhood and they never wholly adjust.

Farrell's portrayal of the Lonigans and the breakup of St. Patrick's parish tells an important part of the Chicago Irish story.[29] While several thousand Irish Chicagoans shared the Lonigans' feelings about racial change in the 1920s, the experience did not alter their view of urban

life. Not unexpectedly, they looked to the parish in their new neighborhoods as the means by which they could re-establish a sense of
community. St. Philip Neri parish in South Shore, for example, grew
tremendously during the 1920s, due in part to the racial resegregation of
Washington Park. The prosperous congregation financed a massive
$600,000 church in 1928 and expanded the parish high school to ac-
commodate eight hundred students.[30] Like other parishes established on
Chicago's North, West, and South sides in the 1910s and 1920s, St.
Philip Neri remained a flourishing center of Irish-American community
life well into the 1960s.

Of all the forces that shaped the Irish community in Chicago during
1880 to 1920, Catholicism had the most pervasive influence. While the
Irish exerted political power in the city out of all proportion to their
numbers, politics did not confer respectability. Indeed, in the case of
the Chicago Irish it reinforced some of the worst stereotypes about the
group. However much the Chicago Irish benefited from political power,
they remained uncomfortable about the public image of Irish politicians. Although the rank and file Irish remained loyal to the Democratic
Party, increasing numbers of upwardly mobile Irish became Republicans in the 1920s. While they remained a small minority, Irish
Catholic Republicans effectively separated themselves from the city's
ethnically oriented and Catholic-dominated Democratic Party.

As the Chicago experience makes clear, the Irish nationalist cause
failed in its attempt to bridge the gap between Irish and American
identities. While the movement succeeded in raising enormous amounts
of money, it fell far short of achieving respectability for the American
Irish. The Cronin murder and the Parnell divorce suit were bitter chap-
ters in the cause for the Irish freedom, and only the deeply committed
could ignore the rising tide of anti-Irish feeling in the 1890s. Rather
than sacrifice the gains they had made economically and politically, the
Irish withdrew their support from the nationalist cause.

After the collapse of the Irish nationalist movement, the Catholic
Church played a larger role in the life of the Chicago Irish community.
Through its system of parishes and parochial schools, the Church was
the most viable Irish institution from the 1880s on. Flexible enough to
meet the needs and aspirations of both working class and middle class
Catholics, its parishes and schools played a crucial role in the integration of Irish Catholics into the larger society. Between 1830 and 1890,
the Chicago Irish became the most devout, disciplined, Catholic urban
dwellers in the city. No longer nominal Catholics, they emerged as

Chicago's most important group of English-speaking Catholics. In their attempts to create American parishes and Catholic schools, the Irish downplayed ethnic identity and tried to force other Catholic immigrants to do the same.

For the most part, the Chicago Irish story is a successful one. After 1900, Irish Catholics entered the middle class in increasing numbers. Just as the Irish had been the pioneers of the urban ghetto in nineteenth century America, they began the move to suburban communities in the 1920s. In their trek from urban immigrant neighborhoods to outlying areas, the Irish continued to use their parishes and schools to create cohesive communities. More American than Irish, these communities reflected the changing nature of Irish Catholicism. Unlike politics or nationalism, the institutional Church permitted Irish Catholics freedom to develop an identity that was as American as it was Catholic.

NOTES

1. Chicago *Tribune,* Dec. 23, 1853.

2. Chicago *Times,* August 21, 1876.

3. Chicago's foreign born population increased from 19,889 in 1860 to 39,988 in 1870. Although census figures reveal a marked increase in the number of foreign born Irish in Chicago between 1880 and 1890, from 44,411 to 70,028, it is likely that a sizeable proportion was due to annexation rather than immigration. Using parish statistics as a guide it is clear that the towns of Lake and Hyde Park had substantial Irish populations which supported 16 English-speaking parishes in the period 1857–1890. In an interview with the Chicago *Times,* June 3, 1888, William J. Onahan estimated the Chicago Irish community at 300,000 persons, of Irish birth and descent. Based on *The People of Chicago: Who We Are and Who We Have Been* (Chicago: City of Chicago Department of Planning, 1976) and Rev. Msgr. Harry C. Koenig, ed., *A History of the Parishes of the Archdiocese of Chicago,* 2 vols., (Chicago: The Archdiocese of Chicago, 1980).

4. Chicago *Times,* November 5, 1866 and September 28, 1868.

5. For a full treatment of Chicago Catholic parishes and bishops see Charles Shannabruch, *Chicago's Catholics: The Evolution of an American Identity* (Notre Dame, Ind.: University of Notre Dame Press, 1981) and Edward Kantowicz, *Corporation Sole: Cardinal Mundelein and Chicago Catholicism* (Notre Dame, Ind.: University of Notre Dame Press, 1983).

6. Between 1844 and 1900, 61 English-speaking parishes and 67 national parishes were formed in Chicago. Of the 61 territorial parishes, 37 were organized after 1880. Based on *A History of the Parishes.*

7. James W. Sanders, *The Education of an Urban Minority: Catholics in Chicago 1833–1965* (New York: Oxford University Press, 1977), p. 91.

8. Newspaper article, "Our Religious Orders, the Jesuits in Chicago," March 27, 1875, St. Ignatius College Prep. Archives.

9. The Chicago *Inter-Ocean*, September 26, 1890.

10. For background information on the Chicago Irish community see Charles Fanning, Ellen Skerrett, and John Corrigan, *Nineteenth Century Chicago Irish: A Social and Political Portrait* (Chicago: Center for Urban Policy, Loyola University of Chicago, 1980).

11. Chicago *Sunday Herald*, April 22, 1888.

12. Chicago *Tribune*, May 21, 1888.

13. Chicago *Tribune*, May 22, 1888.

14. Thomas N. Brown, *Irish-American Nationalism, 1870–1890 (Philadelphia: J. B. Lippincott Co., 1966), p. 23.*

15. *Irish World*, November 13, 1880.

16. Michael F. Funchion, "Irish Chicago: Church, Homeland, Politics, and Class—The Shaping of an Ethnic Group, 1870–1900," *Ethnic Chicago*, eds., Peter d'A. Jones and Melvin G. Holli (Grand Rapids, Mich.: William B. Erdmans Publishing Co., 1981), p. 25. For a full treatment of the Irish nationalist movement in Chicago see Funchion, *Chicago's Irish Nationalists, 1881–1890* (New York: Arno Press, 1976).

17. Lawrence J. McCaffrey, *The Irish Diaspora in America* (Bloomington, Ind.: Indiana University Press, 1976), p. 130.

18. "Haymarket a Tribute to Early Irish Policemen," *Sceal* (the newsletter of the Chicago Irish Folklife Society), Vol. 2 No. 2 (1981).

19. Chicago *Tribune*, May 20, 1889.

20. See Eileen M. Brewer, "Beyond Utility: The Role of the Nuns in the Education of American Catholic Girls, 1860–1920," (Ph.D. dissertation, University of Chicago, 1984).

21. *The New World*, August 31, 1901.

22. *The New World*, August 13, 1915.

23. *The New World*, June 25, 1920.

24. Based on U.S. Bureau of the Census, *Eleventh Census of the United States: 1890*, "Population," Part I (Washington, D.C.: Government Printing Office, 1895), pp. 671, 708, 714, 720, 726, 728.

25. Funchion, "Irish Chicago," pp. 26–27.

26. McCaffrey, *Irish Diaspora*, p. 175–176.

27. James T. Farrell, *Studs Lonigan* (New York: The Modern Library, 1938), p. 21.

28. Farrell, *Studs Lonigan*, p. 373.

29. See Charles Fanning and Ellen Skerrett, "James T. Farrell and Washington Park," *Chicago History* 7:2 (Summer, 1979), pp. 80–91.

30. Koenig, *A History of the Parishes*, pp. 788–792.

keRRy patch RevisiteƊ: IRish ameRicans in st. louis in the tuRn of the centuRy eRa

A newspaper editorial of 1880 described St. Louis as "still divided, like all Gaul into three parts, disputed by Ireland, Germany, and aboriginal America."[1] This statement summed up the history of one of the most cosmopolitan cities in the United States. Frenchmen founded St. Louis in a Spanish province in 1764. The French dominated until the early years of the nineteenth century when American emigration overwhelmed them. A flood of foreign immigration caught St. Louis in its tide by the later 1840s. By 1850 native born Americans were outnumbered by foreign born citizens, the majority of these being from Germany. Second only to the Germans were the Irish, numbering approximately eleven thousand in 1850. Although Irish surnames played a prominent part in the earlier history of the city, the bulk of the St. Louis Irish arrived in the later 1840s and early 1850s. Impoverished refugees from famine, they squatted on a wooded common located in a wide trough on the northern fringes of the city. Their dilapidated shanties and crowded hovels formed an irregular patchwork between the middle class neighborhoods occupying the nearby north and south running ridges. Soon boundaries shifted slightly westward and substantial brick buildings appeared as the inhabitants moved from "shanty" to "lace curtain" and even to "stone front" Irish.[2]

By 1900 the Irish had passed the stage of strangers huddling together for mutual companionship, aid, and protection. The Irish had grown in wealth, prestige, and acceptance. Older Americans no longer damned or scorned later Irish immigrants and isolated them. The Irish mingled freely with the older Americans in the social, business, and civic life of the community. The explanation for this transformation in attitude might serve to shed light on the situation of the Irish throughout the nation at the turn of the century.

The classic study of the Irish in America sprang from their experience in Boston. In the years immediately following World War II, Oscar Handlin set the scholarly tone for the treatment of the Irish for several decades. Handlin found the Irish trapped in Boston's slums, limited to the working class, and bitter at their treatment on both sides of the Atlantic. The progressive, enlightened Anglo-Bostonians disdained the priest-ridden people who were not likely to reap the benefits of American life. Not a pretty picture, nonetheless it was Boston's immigrants.[3]

With Irish-American scholars investigating their own heritage during the past decade, the picture has been changing. Revisionism has been especially strong from the opposite side of the country. James P. Walsh has found the San Francisco Irish experience to be radically different from that of Boston. Thus he theorizes that the Irish experience improves as one moves away from the industrial northeast. The further from Boston the better for the Irish.[4]

St. Louis sits astride the nation, a border city between the north and south that is as much the gateway to the east as to the west. If the Walsh hypothesis is correct, the Irish experience in St. Louis should be somewhere between the Boston and San Francisco experiences. It is not. If anything, the St. Louis experience is more akin to that of San Francisco. The Irish, considering their impoverished economic status and lack of skills upon arrival, fared well in St. Louis. A number of factors, other than geography, may explain this situation. Whereas the Irish came to a heavily Anglo-American city in Boston, St. Louis was, like San Francisco, multi-ethnic. St. Louis, also similar to San Francisco, had a strong Catholic foundation, and the Irish met much less religious prejudice than in other major cities. In summary, geography does not seem to play as much a part as the general social and ethnic atmosphere and the general level of tolerance of the receiving city.

An examination of the Irish experience within the framework of St. Louis history bears this out. St. Louis, founded as a French fur-trading post in 1764, remained essentially a French village until the 1820s. Its founding fathers, its pioneers in the Rocky Mountain fur trade, its men of social standing and economic wealth, and even its black servants were French-speaking Catholics. Even though this small group, numbering perhaps no more than two thousand, was later deluged by American settlers, the city never lost its thin-edged veneer of Catholic aristocracy.

Even before the coming of the Americans, the acceptance of things Catholic was reinforced by the arrival of about one hundred Irishmen. Well educated professional men or substantial merchants, many of them veterans of French military service, these newcomers quickly established a tradition of Irish acceptance. While some were Protestant, most were Catholics who worshipped at the St. Louis Cathedral where they sparked a twenty-year quarrel over the proper language for the sermon.[5]

"The Irish Crowd," as these early nineteenth century immigrants were called, also established precedents for Irish acceptance and public service. John Mullamphy of County Fermanagh, a close friend of Bishop John Carroll, was not only the city's first millionaire but also provided the funding and guidance for the establishment of the city's first hospital, plus many other forms of philanthrophy. His son, Bryan, was mayor and also introduced the St. Vincent dePaul Society to respond to the charitable needs of the city. Joseph Charles from Westmeath, Ireland, was its first newspaper editor, and Jeremiah Connor formerly of County Roscommon served as its first sheriff and later as collector and treasurer. Men such as John McKnight, Thomas Brady, William Shannon, Patrick Killon, William O'Hara, and John and Edward Walsh helped supply the growing community with mercantile skills. Three-hundred-pound William Sullivan not only operated a very popular tavern along the riverfront but also served as the city's first constable and coroner. Even the city's roster of early justices of the peace include names such as Patrick Walsh and Thomas McGuire.[6]

The solid foundation of respectability laid by these men survived even the coming of the Famine Irish. As elsewhere, these Irish were of a different sort. Poor, at best semi-literate and suffering from the degradation of the past, they settled in the city's poorer districts or congregated in Kerry Patch, a shanty town on the outskirts of the growing city. They quickly filled the lowest ranks of the working class and strained the city's charity institutions to their limits.

Yet, St. Louis' Famine Irish found themselves moving into an urban situation which differed substantially from the seaboard experience. First they found Catholicism not only firmly established but flourishing. Once reinforced by the Irish Crowd and twice by the Famine Irish, the Church was again bolstered by the arrival of a strong German Catholic contingent. As in other cities, the problem of Catholic multi-ethnicity was solved by Cahenslyism in practice if not in theory. In 1843, four new churches were established to care for the town's growing Catholic population; two English speaking and two German speaking.[7]

Second, the St. Louis Irish were not, as in the case of Boston and other east coast cities, "The Immigrants." As the history of the city continued to unfold, they found themselves in a progressive, more cosmopolitan rather than a provincially Anglo-Saxon milieu. In the 1820s and 1830s two diverse streams of Americans poured into the French-Irish-Black village, Yankees from New England and would-be plantation aristocrats from the upper south. Then, as the growing town became the booming river city of the west, immigrants swelled its population still further.

Holding down one corner of the German Triangle, St. Louis' Germans outnumbered the Irish by three to one. In fact, by 1850 the German population slightly outnumbered Missouri born St. Louisians. A decade later, St. Louis was the most foreign born city in the nation, with almost 60 percent of its inhabitants born abroad and the Germans still maintaining their three to one ratio over the Irish. In stark contrast to the Famine Irish, the Germans arrived with educational backgrounds and skills that placed them solidly in the ranks of the middle class and, in the more respectable neighborhoods on the city's north and especially the south sides.[8]

Yet despite the city's multi-ethnic complexities, the St. Louis Irish were not exactly in the same situation as their San Francisco brethren. There were no immigrants, such as the Chinese, even more lowly and despised. Despite St. Louis' southern characteristics during the antebellum period, the city's Black population declined steadily, shrinking to only 2 percent by 1860. As in Boston, the newly arrived Irish in St. Louis were in unquestioned possession of the lowest rungs of the socioeconomic ladder.[9]

Early Catholic and Irish respectability and multi-ethnicity paid real dividends for the St. Louis Irish, however, in terms of a lack of the overt, virulent hostility found elsewhere. First, it muted anti-Catholicism during the two periods of strong nativist feeling that surfaced in nineteenth century American history, the pre–Civil War Know Nothings and the late century American Protective Association. St. Louis nativists were slow to adopt an open anti-Catholic stance, and when they did, it cost them votes. Second, Civil War era nativism was directed locally against the German population.

Nativism began making ripples in the St. Louis political pond in 1840 with the formation of the Native American Association which endorsed second generation Edward Charles for mayor. Largely due to factional struggles within the Whig and Democratic Parties, the Association swept city-wide offices in 1845 and 1846. However, it quickly became very unpopular when Mayor Peter G. Camden stopped omnibus service on Sunday afternoons causing the Germans to complain that the measure was specifically designed to curtail their enjoyment of the sabbath. The Association, which generally avoided open anti-Catholic sentiment, disappeared the following year.[10]

The movement was revived by 1854 when four lodges of the Supreme Order of the Star Spangled Banner appeared in St. Louis. As before, the party which had been restrained in its anti-Catholic appeals gained a good deal of local success in the 1855 elections due to factionalism in the Democratic Party and the rapid disintegration of the Whigs. Their success spurred them to open anti-Catholic statements, but the move invited disaster. Despite continuing political chaos, the nativists lost all city-wide political offices the following year.[11]

The nativists' single gain in 1856, local support for their presidential candidate, Millard Fillmore, points to the complexities of St. Louis politics and the importance of the immigrant vote. Faced with a Democratic ticket led by pro-slavery James Buchanan and the failure of the newly formed Republican Party to qualify on the Missouri ballot, liberal German Americans wrote "Under Protest" across the ballots they cast for Fillmore. This quirk of local politics, which artificially kept the nativist movement alive locally in 1856, disappeared the following year as did the party.[12]

The final nativist attack on the St. Louis Irish Catholics took place during the decade of the 1890s with the emergence of a local chapter of the American Protective Association. While rhetoric remained the only arena of conflict, it was heated. Father David S. Phelan conducted a vigorous defense of the Irish Catholics in the pages of his *Western Watchman* throughout the decade. A subtle change in the nativist target was directed more at the Catholic Church than at the immigrant Irish.[13]

Besides softening the blow of anti-Catholic sentiment, St. Louis history conspired to draw much of the city's anti-immigrant feeling away from the Irish and toward the Germans. While Brahmin Boston's love of abolitionism put them in direct confrontation with Boston's Irish, who correctly perceived themselves as economically and socially inferior to Blacks, the situation was entirely different in St. Louis. The city's Anglo-American elite, with strong ties to Virginia and Kentucky, saw the liberal and exceedingly vocal segments of the newly arrived German community as "The Enemy."

The conflict between pro-southern elements in St. Louis and the pro-abolitionist Germans came to a head in an almost comic-opera affair known as the Battle of Camp Jackson. The stage was set when pro-Confederate Governor Claiborne Fox Jackson called the Missouri militia to muster at Camp Jackson in Lindell Grove on the western outskirts of the city. Republican politicians, notably Francis Preston Blair, and the commander of the St. Louis Arsenal, Captain Nathaniel Lyon, fearing this the first step in taking Missouri from the Union and seizing important facilities in St. Louis, turned to German-American politician Henry Boernstein and newspaper publisher Carl Danzer. Sworn into Federal service in the dead of night, members of the German Turn-vereine in St. Louis marched with regular army troops to demand the surrender of the militia on May 10, 1861.

The military maneuver went smoothly until pro-Union officials mulled over the previously neglected question of what to do with over six hundred prisoners. While the victors wallowed in indecision, a large pro-southern mob gathered and began pelting the newly recruited troops with stones. The troops fired into the crowd, giving rise to several days of skirmishes known as the Battle of Camp Jackson. While troops and civilians clashed on the streets, respectable Anglo-Americans fled the city in fear of being murdered in their beds by hostile Hessians. After armed patrols found Teutonic south St. Louis peacefully normal, tensions relaxed.[14]

The validity of German Missouri's fondest myth, that this action saved the state for the Union, is unimportant here. What is significant is that it deflected a good deal of anti-immigrant feeling from the Irish and fastened it on the German population. A popular ballad of the times summed up the sentiment. A few stanzas will suffice.

> Chorus:
> Oh! Oh! Oh! Oh! Oh! Oh! The time for glory is coming
> We yet shall see the time when all of us will shine
> And drive the Dutch from this happy Land of Canaan.
>
> Our men looked so neat when they forced upon the street
> You could tell that sauer kraut was not their feeding,

Our men were straight and tall, the Dutch were thin and small,
And a disgrace to this happy land of Canaan.

The people gave three cheers for Davis and the Volunteers
Which raised the Hessians's indignation
Who fired upon our brothers, killing sisters and mothers
But we'll avenge them in this happy land of Canaan.

Or, as one grande dame later remembered, it was an era when "goddamn dutch" was a single word in St. Louis.[15]

Looking at the St. Louis Irish within this context of the city's history, several things are immediately evident. Like Boston, the Irish in St. Louis became the lower class without an even more alien cushion beneath them on the socio-economic ladder. But St. Louis resembled San Francisco not only in the unusually high level of Catholic acceptability but in the fact that the Irish found themselves in a multi-ethnic situation in which they were a minority among immigrants. With these points in mind, the question of how the Irish fared in St. Louis can be examined. The more numerous and initially more affluent German population forms a convenient point for a comparative study. The complexities of such an investigation can probe economic, political, and social adjustment and advancement.

The Famine Irish began life in St. Louis at the very lowest economic level. At the mid-century point, there existed a close relationship between place of origin and occupation. The majority of the city's professional and affluent mercantile class were native born. Newly arrived Germans held a majority of the semi-skilled and craft positions which placed them firmly into the middle and lower-middle class. The Irish had a larger representation among the upper class than the Germans, 28 percent of the top levels versus only 7 percent, resulting from the presence of the old Irish Crowd, but the vast majority of the Irish, some 87 percent, fell into the lowest class. As a group, they were overwhelmingly unskilled laborers and servants.[16]

These socio-economic configurations stood firm for a generation. In 1880 the native born still dominated among the city's upper class; German craftsmen still clung tenaciously to the lower half of the middle class; and the Irish still swelled the ranks of the unskilled. Yet there were significant signs of Irish progress. In two central St. Louis wards, Irish born craftsmen narrowly outnumbered Irish born laborers. On the near north side, the unskilled Irish still dominated but not by the huge majorities of previous decades. There were also categories in which the Irish born were more greatly over-represented than among the unskilled, namely among policemen and firemen, 39 percent, and governmental officials 32 percent, a fact not unrelated to their prowess in the political arena.[17]

A major shift in occupational patterns occurred between 1890 and 1900, partially due to the nature of the data available. The figures for 1890, like those of the previous years, included only the foreign born. The figures for 1900 include all those of foreign born parents. Rather than invalidating their use, this enhances the study significantly. It sheds light on the intergenerational progress of both the Germans and the Irish. Additionally, by the turn of the century both communities were primarily second generation. No true picture of ethnic progress can therefore emerge for 1900 without their inclusion.[18]

In half a century St. Louis shifted from a principal immigrant entrepôt to one of the most native born cities in the nation. As its economy failed to keep pace with such burgeoning industrial giants as Chicago or Detroit, St. Louis lost its attractiveness for the immigrant. The trend toward second generation became apparent by 1870 when only 2 percent of the city's public school children were German born while 44 percent of their parents were. In 1900 only 19 percent of all St. Louisans were foreign born but fully 62 percent of its white inhabitants had foreign born parents. If the third generation could be added, the number of white ethnics would have undoubtedly been more considerable. Germans still accounted for the majority of first and second generation ethnics classified as a single group, 56 percent, while the Irish trailed behind with 16 percent, 19,421 Irish born and 41,972 second generation.[19]

The occupational position for those of German parentage in 1900 is strikingly similar to those born in Germany in 1890 and even to the 1850 figures. Germans were still heavily over-represented among the city's craftsmen, making up a substantial portion, as indicated in the following table, of the city's bakers, stone cutters and masons, coopers, cabinet makers, harness and saddle makers, gunsmiths, clockmakers, and the like. There was some advance. Those of German parentage in 1900 made strides among merchants, clerks and copyists. Thus, it can be maintained that Germans held their initial lower middle class, skilled position and improved it by moving into the lower echelons of the white-collar world and small mercantile enterprises.[20]

Those of Irish parentage in 1900, on the other hand, gained parity with the Germans as they moved a step ahead of the Famine Irish. For the first time, the Irish were under-represented among police, firemen, and other governmental officials, and they had strongly entered the skilled building trades as plumbers, electricians, and steamfitters. This was not a trend restricted to the second generation but reinforced a trend first evident among the Irish born of 1890. Similarly, the Irish were drawn to newer industries, making up more than their share of telephone and telegraph linemen and gas company employees. Overall, they were also over-represented among industrial foremen, clerks and copyists, salesmen, teachers and clergymen, bankers and brokers, at the upper end of the occupational scale.[21]

Similar trends were evident among women. A comparison of German born women in 1890 with those of German parentage in 1900 indicates an unexpected preponderance in skilled and white-collar areas. Irish born women of 1890, like those of an earlier era, were greatly over-represented among servants and laundresses. But in 1900 women of Irish parentage were under-represented among these same categories and far above their expected numbers among telephone and telegraph operators, teachers, stenographers, typists, bookkeepers, accountants, clerks and copyists. Since this rapid movement from lower to middle class positions was in no way indicated in the 1890 figures, it can be viewed as a largely generational change dependent upon improved education and skills.[22]

Table 7.1 reflects the occupational status of immigrant and first generation German and Irish men and women in 1900.[23]

In an overall comparison between the Germans and the Irish, the Germans grasped lower-middle class skilled positions upon their arrival in St. Louis. During the following half century they made some progress as white-collar workers and small businessmen but essentially remained in the middle and lower-middle class. The Irish, on the other hand, began as the poorest of the poor and in half a century moved, in steady progression, to solid middle and lower-middle class and parity with the Germans. While their progress was not spectacular, it indicated economic accommodation, adjustment, and a measure of acceptance.

Residential mobility, used as another economic barometer, corroborates occupational progress. Better housing, especially in the absence of pressure from large scale migration of other incoming groups, was the usual reason for residential movement. Again, Germans began with the

Table 7.1
St. Louis Occupational Statistics: 1900 Census

Occupation	Total Employed	German		Irish	
Men					
Bakers	1,619	1,204	74%	49	3%
Bankers & Brokers	677	127	19%	130	19%
Cabinet Makers	996	769	77%	10	1%
Clergymen	562	150	27%	83	15%
Clerks & Copyists	12,600	3,593	28%	1,942	16%
Clockmakers	175	98	56%	3	2%
Coopers	1,005	654	65%	72	7%
Electricians	1,084	288	26%	160	15%
Gas Workers	109	14	13%	53	47%
Governmental Officials	749	272	36%	96	13%
Gunsmiths	145	93	64%	5	3%
Harness & Saddle	572	371	65%	44	8%
Industrial Foremen	481	126	26%	85	18%
Masons	2,184	949	43%	400	18%
Members	9,022	4,658	52%	699	8%

Plumbers	1,558	447	29%	570	37%
Police & Firemen	3,199	902	28%	1,169	37%
Salesmen	8,951	3,768	42%	862	10%
Steamfitters	410	78	19%	189	46%
Stonecutters	632	272	43%	135	21%
Teachers	537	177	33%	63	12%
Telephone & Telegraph Linemen	212	37	17%	52	25%
Women					
Bookkeepers & Accountants	920	228	25%	155	17%
Clerks & Copyists	944	247	26%	158	17%
Stenographers & Typists	2,319	494	21%	434	19%
Teachers	2,403	561	23%	577	24%
Telephone & Telegraph Operators	350	61	17%	119	34%
White Collar Workers	8,761	2,622	30%	1,572	18%

advantage. While the Irish of 1850 crowded into the poorest sections of the central river wards or the shanties of Kerry Patch on the city's outskirts, the Germans settled in the lower-middle class neighborhoods north and south along the Mississippi River.

Initially stretched out along the banks of the river, St. Louis grew in radial fashion away from the river, always about three times as long north to south parallel to the waterway, as wide, east to west. Its inhabitants generally moved southwestward, westward, or northwestward as if along the spokes of a wheel. Rarely did St. Louisans cross these invisible boundaries, remaining within north, central-west, and south corridors. Thus, the city's ethnic patterns, set in the mid-nineteenth century, spread westward as the city grew.

While the overall pattern is interesting, the task is to confirm occupational-economic patterns. Definite economic neighborhoods emerged by 1887. The city's poorest housing lay along the central river wards and moved westward along the city's main railroad links to the west. This corridor stretched from just south of the city's downtown mercantile and business district to its western limits. Meanwhile, the wealthy congregated in private places, islands of exclusivity in the west end, which were surrounded by middle class and upper-middle class housing. Substantial brick dwellings, housing various gradations of the middle class, covered vast stretches of north and south St. Louis.

As expected, the Germans moved southwest and northwest from their areas of original inhabitance into better, more substantial neighborhoods. By 1890 the Census reported, "Germans of good class" living in two of the city's finer south side wards.[24] Another study found substantial numbers of Germans moving into solidly upper-middle class private places on the south side and into better neighborhoods west of Grand Boulevard, a popularly designated north-south axis delineating upward socio-economic mobility.[25]

The Irish too were moving west of Grand Boulevard. From the central river wards, the Irish were moving along their own corridor of residential advancement in an ever widening triangle to the northwest. By 1900, of the Irish in this area, fully 71 percent were west of Grand Boulevard. Again, residential mobility clearly indicated Irish progress, reaching a rough parity with the Germans.[26]

Political involvement is another measure of adjustment and accommodation. Again, St. Louis differed in significant ways from the Boston model. The Irish Crowd set an early example not only of Irish acceptance but of Irish public service. Later, the crucible of the Civil War politics, which realigned St. Louis politics, brought the lowly Irish and the native born upper class together rather than placing them in a confrontational position. Prior to the Civil War, St. Louis' upper class tended toward the Whig Party, while the Germans initially joined the Democratic Party on arrival and stayed there. During the war, the Democratic Party became a coalition of the wealthy native born, the poor Irish, and a residue of German Catholics and Lutherans, while the majority of the Germans formed the backbone of the Republican Party. The latter also attracted St. Louis' small Black population.[27]

While the state of Missouri was heavily Democratic, St. Louis was narrowly divided with the balance of power see-sawing back and forth between the two major parties. No group could be ignored, denied, or scorned without courting political disaster at the polls. In such a situation the politics of confrontation, pitting one ethnic group against another as happened in Boston, simply did not develop.

This is not to say that ethnic rivalries did not spill over into St. Louis politics. Indeed there was clear conflict between the Irish Democrats and the German Republicans. The *Westliche-Post* called a conservative slate headed by John Finn in 1867 an "Irish Ticket,"[28] while a contest between Henry Overstoltz, John McGuire, and Arthur B. Barret in 1875 was largely an ethnic contest.[29] Shortly thereafter, the *Missouri Republican* satirically advertised for a mayoralty candidate who "in addition to speaking the English language must be able to handle the sweet German accent as well as command the Irish brogue."[30] In that same year, of the twenty-five members of the Democratic Central Committee, sixteen were Irish, including Thomas L. O'Sullivan, chairman; John W. McGrath, secretary; John Sheehan, treasurer; and Patrick J. Byron, sergeant-at-arms.[31]

Within the context of St. Louis politics, the Irish did quite well, matching the numerically superior Germans in the political arena. The city's first foreign born mayor, George Maguire, was born in Ireland in 1796 and came to the United States as a child. Midway between the Irish Crowd and the Famine Irish, he arrived in St. Louis in 1826 and was spiritually more akin to the latter in making politics, rather than business, his primary interest and serving the city in various capacities before becoming mayor in 1842. Despite their superior numbers and early entrance into politics during the turmoil of the 1850s and 1860s, the Germans did not elect one of their own as mayor until 1875. Henry

Overstoltz, who served two terms as mayor, was born in Muenster, Westphalia, and made fortunes in merchandizing lumber, banking, and insurance before entering politics in 1849 as a member of the city council.[32]

The Irish also did well on a lesser scale. With the parties narrowly divided, ticket balancing was an important consideration in St. Louis politics. Between 1867 and 1869, for example, twenty-five Americans, twenty-five Germans, twenty Irishmen, one Scot, one Canadian, and one Frenchman held city offices.[33]

For the last three decades of the nineteenth century, St. Louis politics was dominated by what the local press referred to as the "Combine." This highly centralized political machine had the unique trait of serving both the Democratic and Republican Parties, whichever suited its purposes best at the time. The man who directed both the electioneering and the boodling was an Irish immigrant blacksmith, Edward Butler, always referred to as "The Colonel." Colonel Butler's regulars who carried out the more rowdy assignments were known as "Indians."[34] The other half of the Combine was known as the "Big Cinch," whose membership comprised the city's social and financial oligarchy. Until 1902 this Combine enjoyed a comfortable arrangement which gave them virtual unchallenged control of the city's administration.[35] Throughout its existence, descendents of the Irish Old Crowd figured prominently in the Big Cinch. In 1901, of the sixty-six members believed to represent the group, 18 percent were Irish Americans. Two grandsons of Dr. William Maffitt and Julia Chouteau were William Maffitt, president of Mercantile Bank and Trust Company and chairman of the Democratic State Committee in the early 1890s, and his brother, Thomas Skinker Maffitt, a director of State National Bank. Other direct decendents of the Old Crowd involved in the Big Cinch were Julius Walsh, son of Edward Walsh, a lawyer prominent in banking, railroads, and public utilities, and James Harrison's son, Edwin, Democratic nominee for mayor in 1897 and involved in street railways and banking.[36]

Irish Americans continued to be over-represented in elected city offices throughout the last three decades of the nineteenth century. In 1880 they held 29 percent of city-wide offices, 23 percent of the Council, and 28 percent of the House of Delegates.[37] In 1890 they held 57 percent of city-wide elected offices including Edward A. Noonan as mayor, 46 percent of the Council, and 36 percent of the seats in the

House of Delegates.[38] In 1900, with a Republican sweep, they dropped to 14 percent of city-wide offices, 15 percent of the Council, and 25 percent of the House of Delegates.[39]

Using these figures as a narrow gauge, the Irish, who did well everywhere in large measure due to their familiarity with Anglo-Saxon governmental principles and instruments, did better politically in St. Louis than their numbers would imply. The Germans did worse.

Social acceptance, a nebulous thing, can be used as another gauge of adjustment and accommodation. Accurate measurement is difficult in this area. Glimpses can be seen in a number of things, newspaper attitudes and acceptance of ethnic elites and upwardly mobile members into the clubs and business organizations of the host society. Again, comparison with German immigrants and their children gives a sense of perspective and the unfailing conclusion that St. Louis was more akin to the San Francisco experience than that of Boston.

A study of early twentieth century newspaper opinion finds easy acceptance of all immigrant groups but especially the Germans and the Irish. This is hardly surprising in a primarily second generation city in which the Germans were the dominant group followed by the Irish. The activities of both groups were reported faithfully, factually, and respectfully without the slightest hint that their existence or functions were anything but normal. In the case of the Germans, there was little or no editorial comment for two reasons. One was that readership had to be heavily German American, and two, prior to 1914 the activities of the community were non-controversial as far as the general public was concerned. In the case of the intra-communal squabbling, the press could only lose readership by taking any sides, and the main thrust of German-American political activity, fighting proposed prohibition legislation, was in accord with the city's majority opinion.

The same can be said for the Irish, with one exception. The Irish community had a cause, Irish freedom. In the pre–World War I years when peaceful, parliamentary means of obtaining that goal were in the ascendancy, there was total agreement in the daily press that the cause of Irish freedom was just. The *Globe-Democrat* thought Ireland deserved home rule as a matter of simple justice and equated continued English domination with calamity.[40] The *Post-Dispatch* spoke of the "rank injustices" of the landlord system and thought the nation merited home rule with the "fundamental principle of democracy."[41] The *Times* thought the political and economic aspects of the pre-war Sinn

Fein movement "admirable" and "appealing."[42] The *Republic* defended the Irish Parliamentary Party and its leader, John Redmond, against any and all criticism.[43] Between 1900 and 1914, there was no deviation from such acceptance of Irish and Irish-American aims.

Acceptance of the German and Irish upper-middle classes and elites mirrored the newspaper attitudes. Turn of the century biographies in popular city histories confirm the general impressions of late nineteenth century history in St. Louis. Both the Irish and the Germans maintained ties with their own communities as well as the host society. In spite of individual cases of exclusion, foreign born Irish and Germans, under the right circumstances, could and did belong.[44]

At first glance there is a wide area of dissimilarity between the Irish and the Germans. The biographies indicate that while 64 percent of the successful German born affiliated with some German-American organization, less than 1 percent of the Irish born affiliated with an Irish-American one. This pattern was reflected in the general weakness of exclusively Irish organizations in St. Louis as well. For example, the Ancient Order of Hibernians, founded in 1855 in the city, by 1900 had only ten divisions with less than one thousand members.[45] This startling difference has several root causes. First, the second and third generation Irish Americans in St. Louis seemed to identify themselves more as Catholics rather than exclusively with their ethnic heritage. This can be seen in the relatively small membership in purely Irish organizations as opposed to the rather large percentage of Irish-American membership in such Catholic organizations as the Knights of Father Mathew and the Knights of Columbus. Another example would be William Igoe, second generation Irish American, who entered political life shortly after the turn of the century and served two terms in the United States Congress. Although his roots were Irish and that heritage constituted much of his political base, Igoe always identified himself more as a Catholic leader and politician than as an Irish American.[46]

A second root cause has to do with the nature of Irish organizations in the city and the time at which the biographies were compiled. The Germans had an elite organization which drew heavily from the ranks of successful Germans. The Liederkranz, founded by successful business and professional men in 1870, maintained an elaborate club house and an extensive social season designed to include all members of the family. It served as a sign both of upward mobility to both German and

American communities while serving as a highly acceptable vehicle of ethnic attachment.[47]

The Irish also had such an organization, in fact they had two in 1900. The old line Knights of St. Patrick, also founded in 1870, and the Irish-American Society, founded in 1900 expressly for the American born, also served as highly selective and prestige giving links to the Irish community. But these organizations had only a single elaborate function, impressive St. Patrick's Day banquets at the city's leading hotels.[48] Perhaps because of the single purpose nature of these societies, they were not listed in the biographies, even when their subjects were known to belong to them. It is interesting to note, however, that the same individuals prominently listed their membership in the Catholic Church, usually the specific parish.

Nationalistic organizations promoting Irish freedom did draw prominent Irish Americans to their own community. A study of officers and committee chairmen of such organizations between 1900 and 1921 showed that fully 96 percent were either business owners and/or executives or professional men. But at the same time these biographies were gathered, shortly before the turn of the century, there was a lull in nationalistic activities both in Ireland and America. So these, like the two elite organizations, were not reflected in the biographies.

A third root cause radically changes the seeming disparity between the Germans and the Irish. Irish history welded nationalism and religion to such a degree that many students of Irish-Americanism simply refer to Irish Americans as people of the parish. Yet, whereas maintenance of religious-ethnic ties for Germans indicated fellowship in foreign language and hence, ethnic churches, the English-speaking Irish belonged to English language Catholic parishes and parish organizations. If one considers Catholic as ethnic for the Irish, as one would a German-speaking church for German Americans, then the ethnic affiliation for the Irish rises a few percentage points above the German born ethnic affiliation. Thus, when this and the nature of some Irish organizations is considered, there really is little difference between the two groups in maintaining ethnic identification. This evidence would also point to the fact that second and third generation Irish Americans were identifying themselves more as Catholic Americans than as Irish Americans.

While this throws some light on the differing nature of the two communities and establishes high degrees of ethnic attachment on the part of the more successful members of the two ethnic American communities, the major question here is how many of these people also indicated non-ethnic affiliations. Again, both the German and the Irish samples exhibit roughly the same trends. Fifty-eight percent of successful German immigrants had non-ethnic social and fraternal affiliations while 54 percent of the Irish did. It is also significant to note that those with ethnic and non-ethnic affiliations were not mutually exclusive groups. Thirty-nine percent of the Germans indicated simultaneous ethnic and non-ethnic affiliations while 43 percent of the Irish did the same. Concluding that although these are minorities in both cases, there is an element of choice in the matter. With such a large minority having both sorts of ties, and over half of each community having non-ethnic ties, the fact is that the whole question was open to individual preference without any pervasive or large scale bar to either ethnic group in their social relations.[49]

Another approach to the problem of social acceptance is found in the St. Louis *Blue Book* whose exclusivity was somewhat marred by commercialism. A glimpse into the city's social organizations also indicates German and Irish acceptance. The newly formed Missouri Athletic Club was the most ethnically cosmopolitan organization listed, probably reflecting the aspiring upward mobility of both Germans and the Irish. But even among the country clubs listed, there is a wide sprinkling of German and Irish surnames, such as Busch, Neidringhaus, Noonan, Walsh, Griesedieck, Lemp, Dolan, and Leahy. Very successful immigrants even invaded the most exclusive St. Louis Country Club as in the case of Richard C. Kerens, an Irishman who made a fortune in railroading, and Oscar Neidringhaus, the German born founder of Granite City Steel Corporation.[50]

Looking at social mobility from another point of view, the sampling of 119 Irish Americans taken from turn of the century biographies indicates a tendency toward non-Irish fraternal organizations as a sign of upward mobility. Only one of the 119 belonged to the Ancient Order of Hibernians which required Irish blood rather than gentility for membership. However, 20 percent belonged to the Knights of Father Mathew, a temperance organization which was Irish only by implication and style but was more closely affiliated with the Catholic Church and required active church membership.[51] Thirty percent joined the Knights of Columbus, an organization founded especially for "Catholics regardless of race."[52]

An analysis of these three organizations confirms the upwardly mobile Irish-American propensity for Catholic rather than strictly Irish membership. A sampling taken from Hibernian leaders, those listed by newspapers as officers or chairmen of various committees, reveals 15 percent business or professional men, 47 percent as white-collar workers, and 38 percent as skilled or supervisory labor.[53] The Knights of Father Mathew, on the other hand, had 49 percent business and professional men, 25 percent white-collar workers, and another 25 percent skilled or supervisory labor.[54] The Knights of Columbus was the most socio-economically desirable with 46 percent business or professional men and 49 percent white-collar workers.[55]

The Irish in St. Louis began in as lowly a socio-economic position as their compatriots in Boston. Their rise was not sudden or unduly rapid. But they made steady progress, particularly in comparison with the more numerous and initially more prosperous Germans. In this they were more akin to their San Francisco cousins.

The reason for the Irish success in St. Louis was not geographical but lay within the nature of the city. Like San Francisco, St. Louis had a high degree of Catholic acceptance and a cosmopolitan make-up which led to tolerance. Given an opportunity in St. Louis and San Francisco, the Irish did well, as well as other ethnic groups. Atmosphere and history, not geography, were the crucial factors.

NOTES

1. St. Louis *Globe-Democrat,* March 17, 1907, p. 7.

2. General histories of St. Louis for the nineteenth century are J. Thomas Scharf, *The History of St. Louis City and County* (Philadelphia: Louis H. Everts and Co., 1883) and Walter B. Stevens, *St. Louis, The Fourth City, 1764–1909* (St. Louis: S. J. Clarke Publishing Co., 1901).

3. Oscar Handlin, *Boston's Immigrants, 1790–1865: A Study in Acculturation* (Cambridge: Harvard University Press, 1941).

4. James P. Walsh, *Ethnic Militancy: An Irish Catholic Prototype* (San Francisco: R. & E. Research Associates, 1972).

5. Ellen Meara Dolan, *The St. Louis Irish* (St. Louis: No Publisher Given, 1967).

6. Marie Felicite Hanratty, "A Study of Early Irish Contributions to the Growth of St. Louis, 1804–1840," (M. A. thesis, St. Louis University, 1933) and Sister Mary Hayes, "Politics and Government in Colonial St. Louis: A

Study on the Growth of Political Awareness,'' (Ph.D. dissertation, St. Louis University, 1972).

7. William B. Faherty, S. J., *The Catholic Ancestry of St. Louis* (St. Louis: Bureau of Information, Archdiocese of St. Louis, 1965).

8. William Hyde and Howard L. Conrad, *Encyclopedia of the History of St. Louis* (St. Louis: Southern Publishing Co., 1899), p. 397.

9. Frederick Hodes, "The Urbanization of St. Louis: A Study in Urban Residential Patterns in the Nineteenth Century," (Ph.D. dissertation, St. Louis University, 1973).

10. James N. Primm, *Lion of the Valley* (Boulder, Colorado: Pruett Publishing Co., 1981), p. 171.

11. Primm, *Lion of the Valley,* pp. 177–79.

12. Primm, *Lion of the Valley,* p. 180.

13. Lawrence E. Walsh, S. J., "Father David S. Phelan Versus the American Protection Association," (M. A. thesis, St. Louis University, 1966).

14. Scharf, *History of St. Louis,* pp. 457–458 and 483–513.

15. Scharf, *History of St. Louis,* p. 510.

16. Dolan, *St. Louis Irish,* pp. 25–30.

17. Julian S. Rammelkamp, "St. Louis in the Early Eighties," *Bulletin of the Missouri Historical Society* XIX, July, 1963, pp. 328–339.

18. U.S., Bureau of the Census, *Twelfth Census of the United States: 1900, Abstract.*

19. U.S., Bureau of the Census, *Twelfth Census of the United States: 1900, Occupations,* pp. xxx–xxxi and 706–711.

20. *Twelfth Census: 1900, Occupations,* pp. xxx–xxxi and 706–711.

21. *Twelfth Census: 1900, Occupations,* pp. xxx–xxxi and 706–711.

22. *Twelfth Census: 1900, Occupations,* pp. xxx–xxxi and 706–711.

23. *Twelfth Census: 1900, Occupations,* pp. xxx–xxxi and 706–711.

24. U.S., Bureau of the Census, *Eleventh Census of the United States: 1890. Vital and Social Statistics.* Part II, p. 322.

25. Ruth Crawford, *The Immigrant in St. Louis* (St. Louis: No Publisher Given, 1916), p. 13.

26. Margaret LoPiccolo Sullivan, "St. Louis' Ethnic Neighborhoods, An Overview," *Bulletin of the Missouri Historical Society* XXXIV, January, 1977, pp. 64–76.

27. Scharf, *History of St. Louis,* pp. 687–694.

28. St. Louis *Westliche-Post,* October 8, 1867, p. 8.

29. Scharf, *History of St. Louis,* pp. 699–700.

30. St. Louis *Republic,* January 12, 1876, p. 3.

31. St. Louis *Globe-Democrat,* February 23, 1875, p. 1.

32. Hyde and Conrad, *Encyclopedia,* p. 841.

33. Scharf, *History of St. Louis,* p. 723.

34. Ann Harrison, "Edward Butler," (M.A. thesis, Washington University, 1968).

35. Alexander S. McConachie, "The Big Cinch," (Ph.D. dissertation, Washington University, 1976).

36. John W. Leonard, *The Book of St. Louisans* (St. Louis: St. Louis Republic, 1906).

37. *Gould's St. Louis Directory for 1880* (St. Louis: Gould Directory Co., 1880), pp. 1255–1256.

38. *Gould's St. Louis Directory for 1890* (St. Louis: Gould Directory Co., 1890), pp. 1723–1728.

39. *Gould's St. Louis Directory for 1900* (St. Louis: Gould Directory Co., 1900), pp. 2370–2374.

40. St. Louis *Globe-Democrat*, April 13, 1902, p. 4 and September 14, 1902, p. 4.

41. St. Louis *Post-Dispatch*, August 14, 1903, p. 4.

42. St. Louis *Times*, August 28, 1908, p. 8.

43. St. Louis *Republic*, September 19, 1910, p. 1; September 2, 1910, p. 9; September 23, 1910, p. 7; October 4, 1910, p. 9; October 13, 1910, p. 4; October 16, 1910, p. 9; October 19, 1910, p. 10; October 20, 1910, p. 1.

44. Hyde and Conrad contains biographies, gathered during the latter part of the 1890s, of numerous St. Louisans.

45. Hyde and Conrad, *Encyclopedia*, pp. 25–26.

46. Alice Thompson, "William Igoe: The Quiet Boss," (Ph.D. dissertation, St. Louis University, 1981).

47. St. Louis *Republic*, November 4, 1900, p. 3; *Globe-Democrat*, December 15, 1907, p. 8; February 1, 1914, p. 12; *Republic*, October 18, 1905, p. 1; October 29, 1905, p. 6.

48. St. Louis *Republic*, March 18, 1900, p. 3; *Post-Dispatch*, March 18, 1903, p. 1; *Globe-Democrat*, January 3, 1902, p. 5.

49. Hyde and Conrad, *Encyclopedia*.

50. Leonard, *Book of St. Louisans*.

51. Martin G. Towey and Margaret LoPiccolo Sullivan, "The Knights of Father Mathew; Parallel Ethnic Reform," *Missouri Historical Review* LXXV, January, 1981, pp. 168–183.

52. *Western Watchman*, (St. Louis) October 8, 1914; John J. Glennon Council, *Golden Jubilee Booklet*, (St. Louis, 1953), Knights of Columbus, *National Convention Souvenir Program*, (St. Louis, 1908).

53. *Western Watchman*, December 1, 1904; January 21, 1904; February 4, 1904; May 26, 1904; August 4, 1904; August 11, 1904; and September 1, 1904.

54. Towey and Sullivan, "Knights of Father Mathew," pp. 168–183.

55. *Western Watchman*, October 8, 1914; Knights of Columbus, *National Convention Souvenir Program*, (St. Louis, 1908).

exiles of confidence: the irish-american community of san francisco, 1880 to 1920

In 1963 William Shannon wrote: "The Irish, in short, stood at the opening of the 20th century with a foot in each world. The desire to join the 'ins' conflicted with the desire to lead the 'outs'."[1] Shannon suggested then that the Irish process of adjustment had only two possible outcomes: either total absorption by the host culture or retreat into a defensive ghetto. This analysis, however, does not apply to the Irish Americans of San Francisco between 1880–1920. The slight, almost negligible, degree of discrimination, alienation, and dislocation Irish Americans experienced in San Francisco did not engender a traumatic ethnic transition for the Irish of that city. They did not journey from Paddy to Studs; social, economic, and psychological adjustment did not create any lasting scars or an inferiority complex.

Ease in assimilation meant that the Irish thrived in San Francisco. As Shannon himself noted:

At a time when hundreds of thousands of Irish were packed in the slums of Boston's North End and New York's East side and were looked upon as laborers and kitchen help, other Irish of identical background were amassing millions from the Comstock Lode, running the governments of Nevada and California, and setting the social tone of San Francisco's Nob Hill.[2]

Such success produced exiles of confidence who developed a community that was unique in all of Irish America. Essentially, this Irish community found a group identity in a positive, not defensive, attachment to the Catholic Church and Irish republican nationalism during this forty-year period.

From the city's founding, the "Gold Coast" Irish were successful, economically, socially, and politically. In 1852, the Irish shared representation among San Francisco's high status occupations with a total of ten doctors and twenty merchants. Twenty years later, the San Francisco Irish occupied far more high status positions than their fellow Irish in Philadelphia or Boston. There were twenty-seven Irish born bankers and brokers in San Francisco, while Philadelphia had eighteen and Boston but four.[3] John McKay, James Flood, William O'Brien, James Phelan, Jasper O'Farrell, the Donahue brothers, Colonel Thomas Hayes, and the Tobin family were worth millions and set the social style of the elite in San Francisco.[4]

This pattern of Irish American achievement, set in San Francisco's formative years, did not cease as the city grew to become a major American metropolis. In 1880 the city's Irish immigrants alone could boast of forty-one lawyers, thirty-two doctors, and seventy-one bankers and brokers. Among the middle class occupations, they comprised almost five hundred clerks and salesmen and nine hundred traders and dealers.[5] Twenty years later in 1900, there were more first and second generation Irish lawyers in San Francisco than in Boston, over three times as many bankers and brokers, and about two-thirds as many salesmen, even though Boston's Irish population was much larger than San Francisco's.[6]

Irish political success in San Francisco matched their economic and social achievements. During California's first decade of existence, the Irish found themselves in high city, state, and federal offices, "preceding their cousins on the East coast by two generations."[7] In 1856, David Broderick of Irish parentage became a United States Senator from California. In 1862, John Downey, an Irish Catholic from Roscommon County, became the first Irish governor of the state. Five years later Frank McCoppin became the first Irish Catholic mayor of San Francisco, eighteen years before Hugh O'Brien became mayor of Boston and thirteen years before William Grace became mayor of New York.[8]

The Irish continued to dominate the city's politics in the 1880s with Christopher Buckley, the "Blind Boss," at the helm. James Phelan emerged as the reform mayor of the 1890s, and during the first decade of the 20th century, Patrick H. McCarthy was a major political figure. After 1912, James Rolph Jr. was mayor of the city until 1931, nevertheless, as one historian noted, "The Irish had the most significant part in running the city."[9]

In addition to their early success, Irish politicians of San Francisco were unique in another way when compared to their counterparts in the Midwest and East Coast. Usually well-educated and middle class, "Irish-American politicians in San Francisco acted as individuals for the most part before and after the turn of the century."[10] They never built a machine, and "there was no Tammany Hall West."[11] Irish participation in San Francisco politics was not organized around nor centered upon ethnicity. Not defensive reaction but confidence was the main impetus to Irish political activity. In the end, "politics for the Irish had never become an obsession. Here they always enjoyed politics but their collective well-being never depended upon it and contemporary San Francisco politics reflects the same lack of concern by the Irish."[12]

Over the years, several reasons have been given for the success of the Irish. John F. Maguire in his work *The Irish in America* (1868) concluded that in California "these men and women of Irish race soon caught the spirit of the American—the right spirit for a new country, the genuine 'Go Ahead'—that which always looks forward and never looks back."[13] Hugh Quigley's *The Irish Race in California and on the Pacific Coast* (1878) simply observed that in California the Irish had found a paradise where "the Celtic-Roman" spirit had prevailed.[14]

Maguire's American spirit and Quigley's promised land serve only as partial explanations at best. A more practical reason was the type and numbers of Irish immigrants that arrived in California after the discovery of gold in 1848. One historian noted: "In San Francisco during the 1850s everyone was uprooted, Americans and foreigners alike. The Irish, however, enjoyed the distinct advantage of having had experience in that condition. Most had not arrived directly from Ireland and their intervening experience had been urban, a characteristic not shared by older Americans."[15] The San Francisco Irish had first resided in the eastern cities of New York, New Orleans, Boston, and Philadelphia, while others came from Sydney, Australia. Most of them had also made their westward trek in family units. Stabilized and experienced, the Irish—numerous, urbanized immigrant families—competed well in an early San Francisco that was dominated by young and single males without urban experience.[16]

Perhaps, the personality of the Irish immigrant who made the long journey to San Francisco was another important factor. These Irish immigrants were probably the kind who were willing to take risks, who were more adventurous, and who were possibly even the most talented of the American Irish.[17] Lastly, the great material abundance and dynamic economy that existed in the state also contributed greatly to the success of the risk-taking Irish. The discovery of gold in 1848 and of silver in 1859 immensely expanded opportunities and precipitated social and economic upward mobility.[18]

As James Walsh has observed, the most important element in this explanation of Irish good fortune "was the lack of an established elite capable, by virtue of prior arrival and control of local resources, of ascribing inferior places to subsequent immigrants. The Irish arrived before any establishment was created and competed upon a more equal basis in multi-ethnic San Francisco than in the East".[19]

San Francisco was an "instant city" and California was an "instant state." Both initially lacked an established elite that could dominate economically, politically, or culturally. As late as 1880, San Francisco's population was still equally divided between native and foreign born. Not until 1920, when the city had become industrialized and sophisticated and when its total population had surpassed the 500,000 mark, did the native born outnumber the foreign born. The small number of native stock Protestants in San Francisco's population from the city's inception thus virtually ensured that the Irish and other ethnics could find places in the city's elite.[20]

The Irish were the largest ethnic group in San Francisco, but by no means the only one. In 1880 there were 75,000 first and second generation Irish in the city, and by 1900 95,000.[21] Yet the Irish numerical advantage over other groups was small. By 1920 the foreign stock Irish made up only one-fifth of the city's population, less than 3 percent more than proportion of first and second generation Germans and only 5 percent more than the percentage of the recently arrived Italians.[22]

With no one ethnic group dominating the city, each nationality felt the need to keep competition open and maintain the mutual tolerance which became characteristic of San Francisco. There was one exception, of course, Asian Americans. Even the virulent hostility to Chinese and Japanese immigrants, however, seemed to help the Irish and other European immigrants. Whatever anti-immigrant sentiment existed in San Francisco was largely directed at the Asians, not at Irishmen as in East Coast cities. Irishmen and other European immigrants thus largely escaped the role of nativist scapegoat, while the division between whites and Asians eclipsed more subtle differences within the white community.[23]

This atmosphere of mutual tolerance (at least for whites) and Irish economic, political, and social success bred feelings of "psychological contentment and emotional ease" among them.[24] The Irish on the West Coast thus never developed the defensive ghetto mentality so pervasive among the eastern Irish. On the contrary, a positive Irish identity thrived within the city's cultural pluralism. As James Walsh concluded: "The California experience was not that of the rest of Irish-America in the years 1848–1920. It was closer to what is now the experience of that community generally, affluence, opportunity, individualism, and diversity. In short, California offered both a special variety of Americanization and a foretaste of the general future."[25]

Although successful in political and occupational realms, the Irish of San Francisco did not perceive them as the binding ties of their community. The two intrinsic features of Irish cultural identity in San Francisco were Irish Catholicism and nationalism. Irish Catholics of San Francisco experienced toleration and not discrimination because of their religious belief. Nativists provided "only slight discomfort." In 1888 Archbishop Patrick Riordan reported to Rome "that though he had encountered some written and spoken hostility against the Church, his faithful enjoyed peace and were exposed to no form of persecution."[26] The U.S. Census at the turn of the century revealed that Protestants represented a minority of the city's population. According to its findings, there were 166,000 practicing Catholics and 22,000 practicing Protestants. Numbers alone, therefore, prohibited the practical effects of sectarianism, which relied upon religious hegemony.[27]

As a result of numbers, social diversity, and a spirit of toleration, the Catholic Church blossomed in the Irish community of San Francisco. As early as 1868, John Maguire wrote that there was no problem of "religious indifferentism" among the Irish.[28] The Irish provided the leadership of the Church. San Francisco had six Archbishops between 1853 and 1985; five out of the six Archbishops were Irish, Patrick W. Riordan, Edward J. Hanna, John J. Mitty, Joseph McGucken, and John Quinn.[29] The Irish represented the Church's first patrons which "helped give them their unshakeable hegemony within it."[30] They rebuilt the Church from its old Spanish structure and donated millions of dollars for the purchase of property. In the 1890s alone, 125 Catholic

Churches spent $2.5 million on physical expansion and $3 million on education. In short, at least outwardly, Catholicism seemed to be "the center of their being."[31]

Because of San Francisco's ethnic and religious toleration, the Church's major concern, unlike the Midwest and East, was not to wage battle against discrimination but to preserve and disseminate the faith among successful Americanized immigrants. The Church held a positive role which was reflected in the administration of Archbishop Riordan (1885–1914). A close friend of Archbishop John Ireland, Riordan was a liberal on religious issues and an "enlightened conservative" on secular ones.[32] To insure Catholic influence in all aspects of the city's life, Riordan approached his mission with reasonableness and not defensiveness. In the 1890s, a brief outburst of nativist wrath occurred and its source was the American Protective Association (APA). Archbishop Riordan appointed Father Peter Christopher Yorke to answer this bigotry in the pages of the diocesan newspaper, the San Francisco *Monitor*. Once the APA protest had subsided, however, Yorke continued to seek out anti-Catholic nativism, aggressively attacking fellow Catholics who befriended or worked along side suspected bigots. Displeased with Yorke's persistent and unreasonable accusations, Riordan accepted his resignation from his position as editor of the newspaper.[33]

Riordan sought Catholic penetration of San Francisco's secular world rather than Yorke's world of Catholic isolationism and defensiveness. At the turn of the century, he sponsored the construction of a Newman Hall on the Berkeley campus. After the earthquake of 1906, he became a very respected and distinguished civic leader because of his successful relief efforts to aid the victims and to rebuild the city.[34] Throughout his administration, Riordan seemed to seek a synthesis of Irish Catholic and American values which really reflected the positive vitality of the Irish, their taking advantage of urban life, their providing for the good life, and their "spirit of optimistic adjustment that led to the creation of a wide range of group activities in the city."[35]

Why did the Irish of San Francisco identify with the Catholic Church, especially if they did not possess a siege mentality and if they did not need the Church to fight battles against bigotry? In the early days of the city's existence, the Church was the only "institutional alternative" for Irish Catholics, not as a result of prejudice as in the rest of Irish America but as a result of necessity in a newly formed and disorganized society. There was simply nothing else for Irish Catholics to turn to as a social and psychological anchor in the midst of the chaos of the west. Later as success and stability began to characterize the Irish community of San Francisco, the Church served as the cultural reservoir of Irish cultural identity, providing the necessary link with the Old World in the Americanization process.

Irish republican nationalism was the second important force unifying the lower, middle, and upper classes of the San Francisco Irish. This was one wound that the cosmopolitan ethos and social diversity of San Francisco could not heal—that of an exiled group from a subjugated land. Most other activities of Irish Americans in the city were subordinated to Irish nationalism during the years 1880–1920. Nonetheless, historians of Irish nationalism have often ignored the West and failed to acknowledge the "Gold Coast" Irish for their role in the nationalist crusade.[36]

The roots of Irish nationalism in San Francisco extend back to the Gold Rush Days. R. A. Burchell has noted that "the political association that drew San Francisco Irishmen together at the end of the 1850s was, inevitably, the Fenians."[37] By 1871, three Circles had been formed, and a decade later, Irish nationalism centered upon the Ancient Order of Hibernians and the Land League, two organizations led by leaders sympathetic to the Clan-na-Gael. But not until the 1890s did Irish nationalism become a statewide movement under the guise of the Gaelic League and under the leadership of Father Peter Yorke.[38]

Father Yorke was born in County Galway in 1864. After studying for the priesthood at St. Patrick's College, Maynooth, he completed his education at St. Mary's Seminary in Baltimore and was ordained by Cardinal Gibbons in 1887. As already seen, the Church then assigned him to San Francisco under the authority of Archbishop Riordan. In addition to his active support of labor and Catholicism, Yorke was the main spokesman of Irish republicanism in California until his death in 1925. He was "the platform and mouthpiece of California Irish nationalism." Aided by T. J. Mellot, Yorke founded and edited the *Leader* in 1902, establishing the state's major Irish-American newspaper in San Francisco. At its inception, the *Leader* had five hundred subscribers. In 1910, it reached its peak of nearly twenty thousand and remained at that level until the 1920s. Weekly the *Leader* brought to its readership the political developments in Ireland and the details of the latest battle being waged against discrimination in the United States.[39]

During this century's first decade, Yorke publicly espoused the fundamentals of the Gaelic League. He contended that the League constituted the "true bedrock of Irish nationality." The Gaelic League's largest branch was in San Francisco. It sponsored classes in Irish history and the Gaelic language, held weekly dances, and periodically, organized Gaelic Athletic Field Days. Distinguished Gaelic League members of Ireland such as Douglas Hyde would also visit San Francisco.[40]

Due to events in Ireland the Gaelic League was replaced eventually by another organization. The Bachelor's Walk incident, the 1916 Easter Uprising, and the subsequent executions resulted in the first political activism of the city's Irish nationalists who espoused a revolutionary republicanism and who formed a new organization, the Friends of Irish Freedom (FOIF). Yorke once again was the state leader of this organization. To help advance the cause of Irish independence, Yorke and the FOIF held numerous public meetings, sent innumerable petitions to local, state, and national political leaders, and established an Irish Relief Fund which had collected forty thousand dollars by the end of 1916.[41]

The FOIF of San Francisco was less vociferous after the United States entered the war in April 1917 because its previous pro-German stance had made other Americans suspect them of treasonous activities. But to demonstrate their loyalty and their "100% Americanism," the Irish of San Francisco invested a great deal of time and money in the four Liberty Loan campaigns.[42] With the Armistice of 1918, a new outpouring of Irish nationalism occurred. The cry for Irish self-determination was heard throughout the city and state. Consequently, in the spring of 1919, the California State Assembly and Senate voted approval of the following resolution:

That at a critical time in the history of the human race, when idealism of America dominates the world throughout, we respectfully submit to our spokesman, the President of the United States, that in speaking for self-determination of all nations, small as well as great, he should not overlook the claims of the oldest nation of Western Europe, to wit, Ireland.[43]

When the elected candidates of the Sinn Fein party proclaimed on January 21, 1919 a Declaration of Independence and established a de facto Irish republic in the form of the Dail Eireann, Yorke and the Irish of San Francisco endorsed these actions and the FOIF began a new campaign for the recognition of the Irish republic by the United States.

To assist in this campaign, Eamon de Valera, president of the provisional Irish republic, visited San Francisco three times between 1919–1920.[44] As the *Monitor* accurately depicted, de Valera "conquered the hearts and minds of Irish-Americans."[45] At his request, the California Irish placed all of their efforts into the Irish Bond-Certificate campaign throughout the first half of 1920. The FOIF directed the campaign and established its state headquarters in San Francisco. The entire state was divided into twelve districts. San Francisco was responsible for collecting the highest sum of $500,000. "California Irish Bond Quota Has Been Over Subscribed!" headlined the *Leader* at the end of the drive. Most districts surpassed their quotas which caused one official at the time to comment, "The splendid cooperation throughout the whole state was unprecedented."[46]

The San Francisco as well as California Irish remained steadfastly loyal to de Valera. They supported him in his confrontation with certain leaders of the eastern establishment of the national FOIF, in particular Judge Cohalan. The dispute resulted in de Valera severing all ties with the FOIF and creating a new organization, the American Association for the Recognition of the Irish Republic (AARIR).[47] Yorke in the pages of the *Leader* approved of de Valera's actions and became the state director of the AARIR. The FOIF on November 28, 1921 held a state convention in Fresno to decide whether or not to merge their organization with the AARIR. The *Leader* of December 4 reported the decision of the convention: "FOIF with De Valera!"[48]

Solidly behind de Valera, Yorke and the AARIR instituted a recognition campaign throughout the state the following year. In April, Yorke had the privilege of presenting the keynote address at the first national convention of the AARIR in Chicago. By the end of the convention, the delegates had elected Edward Doheny as president and Joseph Scott as vice-president of the national organization, both representatives of the California Irish.[49] Departing the convention with recognition as the organization's goal, Yorke and other delegates from California eventually were overwhelmed by the transpiring of certain events in Ireland, which created confusion within the AARIR membership and which ultimately extinguished Irish republican nationalism as a cohesive element in the Irish-American community of San Francisco. The death knell was struck by the truce of July 1921, the Dail's passage of the London Treaty, the creation of the Irish Free State, and the commencement of the Irish Civil War.[50]

The reasons for the appeal of Irish nationalism in San Francisco were divergent and complex. Thomas N. Brown's assessment for the emergence of Irish-American nationalism adequately explains the rise of this movement in the East. Loneliness, poverty, and discrimination led to a search for respectability in the expression of Irish nationalism. A free and independent Ireland would lessen the hardships of assimilation and elevate the Irish in the eyes of Americans.[51] Brown's respectability thesis, however, does not account for San Francisco's fight for Irish freedom. San Francisco's Irish had respectability, economic success, and social status already, yet paradoxically they still became strong Irish nationalists. This paradox becomes comprehensible once the old and new world inspirations of San Francisco's Irish republicans are carefully scrutinized.

Father Yorke wrote in the early 1900s that the "Irish of California and Ireland are so closely knit together that whatever movements are in Ireland, are felt over here at once."[52] Yorke's observation was accurate because San Francisco's Irish nationalism was essentially a reaction to, and a byproduct of, events in Ireland, as the preceding short narrative demonstrated. San Francisco's fight for Irish freedom was provoked and influenced by Ireland's political turmoil and violence during the first two decades of the twentieth century. De Valera's visits to San Francisco served as another source of inspiration for Irish nationalism. His presence and speeches seemed to magnify the immediacy and urgency of Ireland's cause. P. T. Horan, an official of the state's Ancient Order of Hibernians, advised members of his organization after a de Valera speech that "this is a critical time in the history of our race and calls for a lively interest on the part of every Hibernian."[53] During de Valera's visit in San Francisco the *Monitor* compared him to St. Paul, a man "who fought and suffered for the sake of justice."[54] De Valera's influence was further evidenced by the state's successful Bond-Certificate drive and support of the AARIR.

Yorke was also influential. In the *Leader,* he weekly imposed his republican view upon the Irish community. His editorial concerning the Bachelor's Walk incident apprised readers that "perhaps Sunday's Baptism of Blood will be the regenerating Sacrament that will give life to Ireland a Nation."[55] In 1916, he headlined the paper with "Ireland Declares War on England!" and concluded in his story about the Easter Uprising that "to be free, one must fight!"[56] One could perhaps call Yorke the "Patrick Pearse of the West." His spoken and written word served as the most immediate and continuous catalyst of San Francisco's Irish republicanism for over two decades.

The Catholic Church of San Francisco contributed to this movement as well. Unlike some priests and bishops in the east, the clergy of San Francisco fully supported the cause of Irish independence.[57] Irish republicanism thrived in San Francisco because the Church prelates did not want to alienate loyal Catholics by imposing unpleasant strictures upon their political activities. As early as 1888 Archbishop Riordan had refused to denounce the Ancient Order of Hibernians for fear of alienating the militant Irish loyalists in his flock.[58]

Along with this self-imposed restraint, the Church of San Francisco actively supported and participated in the Irish nationalist movement. Yorke was the main statesman of the state's Irish republicanism. Archbishop Hanna, Riordan's successor, served as an honorary official for nationalistic organizations and fund drives. In November 1918, Archbishop Hanna, Bishop John J. Cantwell of Los Angeles, Bishop Thomas Grace of Sacramento, and numerous priests signed a resolution and sent it to President Wilson, beseeching him to seriously consider the cause of Irish independence at the Paris Peace Conference. This concerted effort of the clergy in California represented the first postwar promulgation for the cause of Ireland by the American Catholic Church.[59]

Events in Ireland, de Válera's visits, Yorke's editorials, and the Church's support account for the existence and republican nature of San Francisco's Irish nationalism. Together, they intensified the hate for Britain, fueled the "fanatic heart" of Irish immigrants, and nurtured a nationalism of hatred for Britain rather than love for Ireland. These four factors appealed primarily to the Irish part of the Irish-American identity, to the old world memories of injustice and suffering. On their own, however, they do not provide a sufficient explanation for the existence of Irish nationalism in the West. They do not fully explain why Ireland's woes found a receptive and concerned audience. The most important source of California's fervent nationalism was the Irish experience in the new world, the American side to the Irish-American psyche.

The Irish of the West were confident Americans. They had struggled and were successful. They had proven to themselves, despite all doubts that they might have carried with them from the old world, that they possessed talent, pride, and more important than respect from others, self-respect. Confident Irish Americans such as Joseph Scott and James Phelan made up the leadership of California's Irish nationalistic movement. Joseph Scott immigrated to the United States in 1899, worked as a laborer, teacher, and reporter in Philadelphia, and then made his way to Los Angeles three years later. Scott ended up becoming a successful attorney, was nominated for the United States Senate in 1910, and became a civic leader of his community so renowned that citizens of his city often referred to him as "Mr. Los Angeles."[60] James Phelan was born in San Francisco in 1861. His father had left Ireland in 1827, settled in New York, and finally moved to San Francisco in 1849. Owning a trading business, buying real estate, and establishing the First National Bank of San Francisco, Phelan's father was worth over two million dollars at his death. James Phelan expanded his father's fortune, became a major civic leader, and eventually became the reform mayor of San Francisco in the 1890s.[61]

Scott and Phelan were just two examples of Irish nationalists in California. The Tobin family, Andrew J. Gallagher, the Murray family, John Byrne, Edward Doheny, and a myriad of others could be enumerated. But the numbers were not as important as the quality. They had been successful and were considered among the best of the American citizenry. Their sensitivity to Irish nationalism sprang not from weakness but from strength, not from a posture of inferiority but from self-respect. Consequently they were convinced that Ireland should be given the same opportunities that they had been given in California. If this occurred, the result would be the same—a prosperous Ireland. Such a confident belief in Irish ability was expressed as early as 1870 in the San Francisco *Monitor*. It used this rationale to encourage Irish emigrants to move out West.

It is in our interest to have as many of our countrymen here as possible; and, moreover we honestly believe no other country holds out such advantages for their coming. They have not the prejudices of race or religious bigotry which exist in some parts of the East, to contend with. . . . We also feel a scruple about encouraging emigration from poor depopulated Ireland, where the fortunes of our race have yet to be retrieved. But in England and Scotland there are nearly a million Irishmen from whose ranks we could easily obtain an annual immigration of many thousands. . . . The Irish of California are wealthy and liberal. We hope our suggestions may turn the attention of some of them to the practical development of Irish immigration from England and Eastern cities.[62]

Tied to this tradition of self-respect to retrieve "the fortunes of our race" was the American political tradition. Emancipation from English oppression was an American right and Irish Americans of the West perceived it as their duty to support Ireland's fight for freedom. In numerous public settings, the Irish of California juxtaposed Irish independence to American political ideals. Joseph Scott called the executions after 1916 "unalterably stupid" and concluded that they represented the defamation of life and liberty according to American ideals.[63] James Phelan wrote that Lincoln's eradication of slavery was precisely the same thing that the Irish were attempting to do in Ireland and contended that "no man is a true American who does not sympathize with the struggles of weaker nations for justice and liberty."[64] During the recognition campaign, Yorke said that in order for Ireland to gain American recognition of the Irish republic "we must dust off the Declaration of Independence!"[65]

Irish nationalism in San Francisco was to some extent inspired by American political ideals and its republican creed. However, this conclusion does not suggest that the Irish of the West were ethereal idealists nor does it discount the favorable appeal such rhetoric would have to other Americans outside the Irish community. What it does suggest is that by translating Ireland's misfortune into American ideals, the Irish of San Francisco were expressing the American side of their personality. The United States had the answer for their individual success and certainly it must also have the answer for Ireland's redemption. Perhaps one could conclude, therefore, that the more Americanized the Irish community, the stronger the appeal of Irish nationalism, which was predicated upon ease and success and not conflict and crisis in the assimilation process.

Easy economic and social mobility, quick political success, Catholic vitality, and confident Irish republicanism characterized the Irish-American community of San Francisco between 1880 and 1920. They also distinguished that community very clearly from Celtic settlements further East. The key to understanding the differences is to examine the community's geographical location and condition, factors which ultimately shaped its psychology. On the Eastern seaboard, Irish Americans experienced nativist wrath and discrimination that inhibited economic and social mobility. Consequently the eastern Irish developed a defensive-ghetto mentality, dominated by an inferiority complex. As a result of their siege mentality, Irish Americans centered their community upon the Catholic Church, developed machine politics, and sought respectability in a free Ireland.

The Irish of San Francisco and the West inhabited an environment that was characterized by a cosmopolitan ethos, competition, and tolerance. In such a setting of opportunity and "healthy diversity," they experienced a "special variety of Americanization," a fine blending of American and Irish values, that engendered an Irish psychology of confidence and pride. These confident exiles were not Studs Lonigans. Ease in assimilation allowed a healthy Irish cultural identity to reside in the community's Catholicism and Irish nationalism. But after 1920, the Irish of San Francisco were only religiously Irish, and today even this last vestige of their group identity appears to be vanishing. In a recent commentary, Seamus Breatnac suggested that the crisis in the Irish-American community of San Francisco was not its lack of showing in politics, but its lack of showing at Church on Sunday.[66]

NOTES

1. William Shannon, *The American Irish* (New York: The MacMillan Co., 1963), p. 132.

2. Shannon, *American Irish,* p. 86. For a concise survey of Irish-America consult Lawrence McCaffrey's "Irish-America," *The Wilson Quarterly* (Spring 1985), pp. 78–93.

3. James Walsh, "The Irish in the New America: 'Way Out West," in David Doyle and Owen Dudley Edwards, eds., *America and Ireland 1776–1976* (Westport, Conn.: Greenwood Press, 1980), p. 166.

4. Shannon, *American Irish,* pp. 87–92; Walsh, "Way out West," in Doyle and Edwards, *America and Ireland,* pp. 168–169.

5. *Tenth Census of the United States: Population* (Washington, D.C., 1880), Vol I., p. 902.

6. *Twelfth Census of the United States: Special Report on Occupations* (Washington, D.C., 1904), pp. 720–725; Walsh, "Way Out West," in Doyle and Edwards, *America and Ireland,* p. 169. California's Irish were also successful in the cultivation of the soil, which challenges the commonly held view that Irish immigrants were urbanites. See John Francis Maguire's *The Irish in America* (New York: D & J Sadler & Co., 1868) who made the following observation: "One-fourth of the farms in the state of California is in the hands of Irishmen, and as agriculturalists and stockraisers, the Irish are the leaders in almost every county of the state." Irish attachment to the soil is still evidenced

in contemporary times, *The McGrath Family* (Oxnard: Oxnard Historical Society, 1973).

7. Moses Rischin, "The Classic Ethnics," in James Walsh, ed., *The San Francisco Irish 1850–1876* (San Francisco: The Irish Literary and Historical Society, 1979), p. 5.

8. Rischin, "Classic Ethnics," pp. 5–6; Shannon, *American Irish,* p. 87.

9. William A. Bullough, "Chris Buckley and San Francisco," in Walsh, ed., *The San Francisco Irish,* pp. 27–41; Roger W. Lotchin, "John Francis Neylan," in Walsh, ed., *The San Francisco Irish,* pp. 87–110; John B. McGloin, *San Francisco: The Story of a City* (San Rafael: Presidio Press, 1978), pp. 287–303. The Irish of San Francisco also dominated the city's labor movement from the 1850s to 1920. Dennis Kearney, Frank Roney, Patrick McCarthy, Father Peter Yorke, Michael O'Casey, and Andrew Gallagher make up only a partial list of the city's major labor leaders. Consult the following works: Ira B. Cross, ed., *Frank Roney: An Autobiography* (New York: Arno Press, 1976); Bernard Cronin, *Father Yorke and the Labor Movement in San Francisco 1900–1910* (Washington, D.C.: Catholic University of America, 1943); McGloin, *San Francisco,* pp. 243–261, 279–287; Ira B. Cross, *History of the Labor Movement in San Francisco* (Berkeley, 1935); Robert Knoight, *Industrial Relations in the San Francisco Bay Area 1900–1918* (Berkeley, 1960); Timothy J. Sarbaugh, "Father Yorke and the San Francisco Waterfront, 1901–1916," *The Pacific Historian* (Fall 1981), pp. 29–35.

10. Walsh, "Way Out West," in Doyle and Edwards, eds., *America and Ireland,* p. 175.

11. Bullough, "Chris Buckley," in Walsh, ed., *The San Francisco Irish,* pp. 27–32; James Walsh, "Machine Politics, Reform, and San Francisco," in Walsh, ed., *The San Francisco Irish,* pp. 59–73.

12. Seamus Breatnac, "Should Irish Eyes Be Smiling?," in James Walsh, ed., *The Irish: America's Political Class* (New York: Arno Press, 1976), pp. 28–29.

13. Maguire, *The Irish in America,* pp. 278–279.

14. Hugh Quigley, *The Irish Race in California* (San Francisco, 1878), p. 50; also see Kevin Starr, "Jerry Brown: The Governor as Zen Jesuit," in Walsh, ed., *The San Francisco Irish,* pp. 128–129.

15. Walsh, "The Irish in Early San Francisco," in Walsh, ed., *The San Francisco Irish,* p. 21.

16. Walsh, "Irish in Early San Francisco," pp. 11–12; Walsh, "Way Out West," in Doyle and Edwards, eds., *America and Ireland,* p. 165; R. A. Burchell, *The San Francisco Irish* (Berkeley: University of California, 1980), p. 74. Burchell maintained that the Irish of San Francisco "contained a sizeable number of families to inaugurate a trend that deepened with the passing years."

17. Breatnac, "Should Irish Eyes Be Smiling?," in Walsh, ed., *The Irish,*

pp. 28–29. Perhaps one could argue that these Irish were irresponsible and reckless by leaving the known for the unknown pot of gold, for pipe dreams.

18. McGloin, *San Francisco,* pp. 31–37, 83–95; Robert Mayer, ed., *San Francisco: A Chronological and Documentary History* (New York: Oceana Publications, 1974), pp. 10–30.

19. Walsh, "Way Out West," in Doyle and Edwards, eds., *America and Ireland,* p. 169.

20. *Tenth Census of the United States: Population* (Washington, D.C.), Vol I., pp. 428, 498–499; *Fourteenth Census of the United States: Population* (Washington, D.C.), Vol I., Part I, pp. 118, 123; Walsh, "Way out West," Doyle and Edwards, eds., *America and Ireland,* pp. 166, 171–172; Kevin Starr, "Jerry Brown," in Walsh, ed., *The San Francisco Irish,* pp. 128–129; Burchell, *The San Francisco Irish 1848–1880,* pp. 3, 13, 121. Burchell described the relations between the native stock and the Irish a "cosmopolitan stalemate," and further argued that representatives of the host culture (national) resulted in "tension in accommodation, and in opportunity which was not equal in every respect, but it was not widely dissimilar."

21. *Tenth Census: Population,* p. 416; *Twelfth Census: Population,* pp. 736–739, 800–803, 880–881.

22. *Tenth Census: Population,* p. 416; *Fourteenth Census of the United States Census: Abstract of the Census: Population* (Washington, D.C., 1922), pp. 378–383.

23. Moses Rischin, "Immigration, Migration and Minorities in California: A Reassessment," *Pacific Historical Review,* Vol. 41, no. 1, p. 81.

24. Breatnac, "The Difference Remains," Walsh, ed., *The San Francisco Irish,* pp. 148–149; Walsh, "Way Out West," in Doyle and Edwards, eds., *America and Ireland,* p. 175.

25. Walsh, "Way Out West," in Doyle and Edwards, eds., *America and Ireland,* p. 175.

26. James P. Gaffey, *Citizen of No Mean City: Archbishop Riordan of San Francisco* (New York: Consortium Books, 1976), p. 139.

27. *United States Census of Department of Commerce and Labor: Religious Bodies in 1906* (Washington, D.C., 1910), Vol I., pp. 299–300.

28. Maguire, *Irish in America,* p. 227.

29. For the history of the Catholic Church in California as well as San Francisco, consult Francis J. Weber's works. Francis J. Weber, *Catholic Footprints in California* (California: Hogarth Press, 1970), pp. 48–49, 185–188.

30. Burchell, *The San Francisco Irish,* pp. 89–90.

31. Breatnac, "Irish Eyes," in Walsh, ed., *The Irish,* p. 29.

32. Gaffey, *Citizen of No Mean City,* pp. 178, 212.

33. Gaffey, *Citizen of No Mean City,* pp. 141–175.

34. Gaffey, *Citizen of No Mean City,* pp. 246–256, 259–270.

35. Burchell, *The San Francisco Irish,* pp. 85, 87, 91–92, 95. Burchell discusses the numerous associations centered around the Church and the Irish community and also details the practice of endogamy among Irish Catholics.

36. The only works to touch on the subject lightly are Walsh's *The San Francisco Irish 1850–1976* and Burchell's *The San Francisco Irish 1848–1880.*

37. Burchell, *The San Francisco Irish,* p. 99.

38. Burchell, *The San Francisco Irish,* pp. 109–114. In 1880, the AOH had 10 divisions and 2,000 members. The first Land Reform League in the world was established in California with both its president and secretary Irish born.

39. For an account of Father Yorke's life see James Walsh, *Ethnic Militancy: An Irish Catholic Prototype* (San Francisco: R & E Research Associates, 1975); Joseph Brusher, *Consecrated Thunderbolt* (Hawthorne, N.J.: Wagner Pub., 1973), pp. 71–73.

40. *The Leader* (U.C. Berkeley: Microfilm) 17 March 1906, p. 1; 13 June 1906, p. 5; 20 June 1908, p. 5; 4 July 1908, pp. 1, 8.

41. *The Leader,* 1 December 1906, p. 1; 18 July 1908, p. 1; 22 August 1908, pp. 1, 4; 13 May 1916, pp. 1, 7; 10 June 1916, pp. 1, 5; 22 July 1916, p. 1; 2 September 1916, p. 6; 1 August 1914, pp. 1, 4; 8 August 1914, p. 1.

42. *The Leader,* 26 September 1914, p. 1; 29 September 1918, p. 1; 28 December 1918, p. 4; C. F. Horan to John Byrne, Letter 8 October 1918, John Byrne Collection: Archives of San Jose State University, Box A: Doc. No. A8.

43. *California State Legislature, Journal of the Assembly and Senate,* 34th Session (Sacramento: California State Printing, 1919), Bill No. 21, 25 February 1919, p. 364; Bill No. 18, 14 March 1919, p. 641; 19 March 1919, p. 767; 24 March 1919, p. 904.

44. *The Leader,* 4 January 1919, p. 1; 25 January 1919, pp. 1, 4; 29 March 1919, pp. 1, 4; 5 April 1919, pp. 1–2; 3 May 1919, p. 1; John Power to John Byrne, Letter 28 August 1919, John Byrne Collection, Doc. No. A14aa; Eamon De Valera, *Ireland's Claim to the Government of the United States for Recognition,* Healy Collection, Hoover Institute at Stanford University, 1920. There are many accounts of De Valera's tour of the United States. Most emphasize his tour in the eastern part of the country, while few mention his California visits. See Katherine O'Doherty, *Assignment America: De Valera's Visit to the United States* (New York: De Tanko Pub., 1957); Alan J. Ward, *Ireland and Anglo–American Relations* (Toronto: University of Toronto Press, 1969); Sean Cronin, ed., *The McGarrity Papers* (Ireland: Anvil Books, 1972); Patrick MacCartan, *With De Valera in America* (New York: Brentano, 1932); Francis M. Carroll, *American Opinion and the Irish Question* (New York: St. Martin's Press, 1978); and Timothy J. Sarbaugh, ''Irish Republicanism vs. Pure Americanism:

California's Reactions to Eamon De Valera's Visits,'' *California History* (Summer 1981), pp. 158–172.

45. *Monitor*, 26 July 1919, p. 4.

46. *The Leader*, 27 December 1919, p. 1; 31 January 1920, p. 4; 14 February 1920, p. 4; 28 February 1920, p. 1; 13 March 1920, p. 1.

47. Dispute between De Valera and Cohalan discussed in the following works: Cronin, ed., *McGarrity Papers*, pp.73–101; Carroll, *American Opinion*, pp. 156–160; MacCartan, *De Valera*, pp. 216–17; O'Doherty, *Assignment America*, pp. 16, 161; Charles Tansill, *America and the Fight for Irish Freedom* (New York: Devon-Adair Co., 1957), pp. 30–393.

48. *The Leader*, 20 November 1920, p. 1; 4 December 1920, pp. 1–2; Also see Annual Executive Report of the FOIF 1919–1920, 15-page pamphlet, Fresno 1920, Byrne Collection, Box G: Doc. No. G496.

49. *The Leader*, 28 May 1921, pp. 1, 5; 23 April 1921, pp. 1, 5.

50. Irish–America, in general, was influenced by these events. Lawrence McCaffrey, ''Profile of Irish–America,'' in Doyle and Edwards, eds., *America and Ireland*, pp. 86–89. For Irish republicanism in California from 1920 to present see Timothy J. Sarbaugh, ''Culture, Militancy, and De Valera: Irish Republicanism in Caifornia 1900–1936,'' (M.A. Thesis: San Jose State University, 1980), pp. 113–172.

51. Thomas N. Brown, ''The Origins and Character of Irish–American Nationalism,'' in Lawrence McCaffrey, ed., *Irish Nationalism and the American Contribution* (New York: Arno Press, 1976), pp. 327–358; should also consult the works of David Montgomery for the connection between Irish nationalism and the Irish working class.

52. *The Leader*, 7 March 1923, p. 1. The influence of Ireland, especially upon the immigrant's nationalistic outlook, is thoroughly discussed in Kerby Miller's *Emigrants and Exiles: Ireland and the Irish Exodus to North America* (New York: Oxford, 1985).

53. P. T. Horan to John Byrne, Letter, July 1919, Byrne Collection, Box A: Doc. No. A14.

54. *Monitor*, 26 July 1919, p. 1.

55. *The Leader*, 1 August 1914, p. 1.

56. *The Leader*, 29 April 1916, pp. 1, 4.

57. Michael Funchion, ''Irish Chicago,'' in Peter d'A Jones and Mevin G. Holli, eds., *Ethnic Chicago* (Chicago: Eerdman's Pub., 1980), pp. 20–21.

58. Gaffey, *Citizen of No Mean City*, pp. 180–183.

59. *The Leader*, 30 November 1918, p. 1.

60. In short, this analysis takes into account the influence of the Turner thesis upon Irish America. See JoEllen McNergney Vinyard, *The Irish on the Urban Frontier* (New York: Arno Press, 1976). Although Joseph Scott still needs a biography, sources relating to his life exist. Sister Anita Weyer, ''Joseph Scott:

A Life of Service,'' *Southern California Quarterly* (Sept. 1966) Vol. 48, pp. 241–264; Joseph Scott, ''Joe Scott Story: As Told to Edward Prendergast,'' *Los Angeles Evening Herald* 28 April, 4 June 1952 (Microfilm: Bancroft Library, U.C. Berkeley, 1979); Joseph Scott File (Los Angeles: Los Angeles Tidings Archives).

61. *Dictionary of American Biography* (New York: Scribners, 1962) Vol.7, pp. 521–524; Stephen Birmingham, *Real Lace: America's Irish Rich* (New York: Harper and Row, 1973), pp. 118–129.

62. Maguire, *Irish in America*, p. 280.

63. *Monitor*, 27 May 1916, p. 7.

64. *Sacramento Bee*, 16 July 1919, p. 3.

65. *The Leader*, 14 May 1921, pp. 1, 4.

66. Breatnac, ''Irish Eyes,'' in Walsh, ed., *The Irish*, p. 29.

9   tımothy j. meagheR

conclusıon

It is difficult to generalize from the variety of local patterns in the Irish
American experience revealed in the preceding essays. That is not surprising. The expectation of significant regional variations in Irish-
American history forms one of the hypotheses underlying this book.
Nevertheless, these essays do not simply confirm that hypothesis. The
first important conclusion to be drawn from them is the importance of
probing beneath simple classifications of Irish-American experience by
broad regional categories, in order to investigate the unique traditions
and environments of individual Irish communities. But what of the
principal hypothesis which this collection of essays set out to test: the
turn of the century era as a critical turning point in the history of Irish
Americans? Do the essays substantiate, disprove, or qualify that hypothesis? The evidence is more complicated. The authors of this collection do not agree, for example, on whether the turn of the century, if a
transitional era, was also a time of confusion for Irish Americans. They
also seem to vary in their estimates of the role Irish nationalism played
in the lives of the communities they studied. Nevertheless, some common themes do appear, most notably the emergence of Catholicism as
both the principal force for Irish-American community development
and an enduring focus of Irish-American identity.

Timothy Sarbaugh and Martin Towey address the questions of regional variation most directly. As expected, Sarbaugh found that the
Irish tradition of achievement, optimism, and openness, established in
mid nineteenth century San Francisco, persisted into the late nineteenth
and early twentieth centuries. He attributes the inception of this tradi-

tion and its continuing vitality to the environment of open competition and easy tolerance (of whites at least) which ruled San Francisco from its birth until well into the new century. Those advantageous environmental conditions stemmed, in turn, from the absence of an established WASP elite which could lay prior claims to the city's abundant economic and social rewards, and the later, nearly even, balance among the city's ethnic groups. Irishmen, at least Famine immigrant Irishmen, achieved success far less quickly in Martin Towey's St. Louis than in San Francisco. Nevertheless, the children of the Famine immigrants seemed to move up rapidly, and more important, Towey discovered that Catholic Celts found easy acceptance in St. Louis just as they did in San Francisco. Towey suggests that the causes of this favorable environment lay in St. Louis traditions and the ethnic mix of its population. St. Louis was born a Catholic city; early Irish immigrants confronted no cold, Puritan aristocracy there. Even later as a native stock elite developed, its origins were rooted in the South. These upper class native stock Democrats found Irishmen far more congenial than German Republicans.

Towey's analysis confirms Sarbaugh's contentions on a number of points. Both authors find that the ease of Irish adjustment and degree of Celtic achievement in new world cities was principally contingent upon the nature of local environments. More important, however, they find the roots of favorable environments in St. Louis and San Francisco in the absence of established elites or the sympathy of those elites to the Irish, and the ethnic compositions of the populations of the two cities. Both, then, relegate the vitality of local economies to secondary importance in explaining the degrees of Irish achievement and acceptance. Towey also rightfully rejects a simple geographical determinism which asserts that the further west the Irish traveled, the more favorable the environments they encountered. Instead, he points out the variety of specific historical conditions, not merely geographical location, which shape those congenial environments.

Despite this conclusion, Martin Towey asserts, and Timothy Sarbaugh would readily agree, that the experience of the St. Louis or San Francisco Irish sharply contrasted with that of Celts in Boston. Indeed, both authors use the history of the Boston Irish as a counter example to highlight the great success or quick acceptance achieved by the Irish in St. Louis or San Francisco. It is not clear, however, whether the experience of the Boston Irish, as depicted by Towey or Sarbaugh, accurately represents the history of the Irish even throughout New England, much less the entire East Coast. My own essay on Worcester and Brian Mitchell's on Lowell indicate that the Irish in those medium sized Massachusetts cities did climb the occupational ladder slowly and never achieved integration into the Yankee dominated mainstream—at least not until well into the twentieth century. Nevertheless, it would be a mistake to characterize the experiences of the Irish in Lowell and Worcester in terms of defeat and sullen despair. If Irish occupational progress was slower in Lowell and Worcester than on the West Coast, there was nonetheless substantial progress. More important, Irish relations with their neighbors in these cities, even relations with the Yankees, were far more complicated than a depiction of uninterrupted, suspicious isolation would suggest. Mitchell hints, and I argue more broadly, that Irishmen and Yankees often cooperated in Lowell and Worcester. In the latter city especially, such cooperation in the 1880s and early 1890s nourished fervent hopes among the Irish of reconciling their differences with their Yankee neighbors. Moreover in both cities, unlike Boston, Irish Americans confronted a substantial influx of new immigrants, most of them fellow Catholics. In Lowell this immigration vaulted the Irish into a new intermediate position in the city's hierarchy of groups, but the city's Celts could find no grounds to build lasting bonds with new immigrants like the French Canadians. In Worcester, however, the new immigration provoked the transformation of Irish conceptions of their own identity into a broad religious identification and sparked Irish efforts to forge the new groups into a powerful, multiethnic Catholic coalition.

To argue for sensitivity to local variations in the Irish-American experience is not to overlook the fact that the histories of these individual Irish communities share some common themes. In all of the cities studied (with the possible exception of San Francisco) it appears that Irish upward social mobility and geographical dispersion rapidly accelerated in the turn of the century era. It also seems that Irish populations in all of the cities were increasingly dominated by the American born. Significant changes were also occurring in how Irish Americans conceived of themselves not only in many of these American cities, but in Ireland itself. There is less agreement among the authors on whether those changes were born of crisis and confusion. Almost all, however, recognize the importance of Irish nationalism and the Catholic Church in shaping those self conceptions.

One of the most interesting points made in this collection is Kevin O'Neill's assertion that the people of Ireland also confronted an identity crisis of sorts in the late nineteenth and early twentieth centuries. As O'Neill argues, this Irish identity crisis, like the Irish-American one, was principally a problem for Ireland's upwardly mobile or middle class Irish Catholics. They, like their lace curtain counterparts in America, did not fit the traditional Irish image which mixed lower class, Catholic, and Irish together into a single national identification. Like their American cousins, too, the Irish middle class was alienated from the Protestant and English elites which governed their country. Suspended somewhere between the Irish masses and their Anglo-Saxon rulers, Ireland's lace curtain class struggled mightily to resolve their crisis of identity through the twists and turns of Irish nationalism. As O'Neill details, in Parnell's rise and fall, the Gaelic League, Sinn Fein and finally Patrick Pearse's ideology of revolutionary martyrdom, the Irish middle class searched for a role for themselves which would make sense of their position as respectable and privileged colonials.

It is not clear from the other essays in this collection whether Irish Americans suffered the same *angst* in dealing with their own dilemma of identity, as their middle class cousins did in Ireland. I believe that they did, citing the wild fluctuations of the Worcester Irish in their search for a comfortable conception of themselves in the late nineteenth and early twentieth centuries. In Chicago and Lowell, middle class Irish Americans also seemed to be struggling to reconcile their aspirations for respectability with their allegiances to a foreign religion or their alienation from their native stock neighbors. Dennis Clark, however, discovered no such confusion or ambivalence among Irish-American leaders in Philadelphia during the turn of the century era. Indeed he was struck by the strength of will, savvy, and agility these Irish leaders displayed in easily adapting to the changes occurring both within and outside their community. Timothy Sarbaugh likewise found confident and purposeful Irish Americans in late nineteenth and early twentieth century San Francisco.

Whether Irish Americans were confused or confident, however, may be a less critical point than how they actually grappled with the transformation of their world, and how those efforts to cope with significant change reflected their sense of community and identity. Particularly important to them in this era were the problems of the homeland, Ireland, as it followed its erratic course to national independence. Nationalism figured prominently in virtually all of the Irish-American communities studied in this book. But the history of Irish nationalism in these cities tends to be episodic. As a general rule Irish-American nationalism was strongest in the 1880s and after the First World War. As Sarbaugh suggests, and Dennis Clark and I also imply, this periodization reflects, in part, the rise and fall of nationalism in Ireland itself. Clark, Sarbaugh, and I also indicate that it was in those periods, too, that the goals of Irish nationalism seemed to harmonize best with American ideals. This general periodization is neither universal nor exact, however. In Philadelphia, Worcester, and San Francisco nationalist sentiment also flared up or remained vital in some of the "dead" years of the 1890s or early 1900s. Further, the degree of nationalist militance seemed to vary from city to city as reflected in the Clan Na Gael's popularity in Chicago during the 1880s and Father Yorke's rabid nationalist crusade in San Francisco in the twentieth century. Ultimately then, it appears that the rise and fall of Irish American nationalism and variations in the intensity of its militance must be examined in terms of local conditions.

In almost every city, however, Catholicism rather than Irish nationalism proved to be the most enduring and stable source of cohesion among Irish Americans. Indeed one of the most striking and significant themes to emerge from these essays is the role the Catholic Church played in building up Irish-American communities and defining the identities of their members. In Lowell, Brian Mitchell argues, the remarkable Fathers O'Brien assumed leadership of the Irish community in the 1850s. Over the next half century, they forged an Irish Catholic subsociety and identity distinct from both those of native stock Americans and the new immigrants. The pattern in Chicago, as Ellen Skerrett details, was much the same. There, too, the Church through its extensive network of parishes became the hub of Irish community life as early as 1860. With the decline of Irish nationalism in that city after 1890, the Church's parishes and schools became the principal arbiters of an Irish-American identity that was both Catholic and American. A similar self conception emerged in Worcester in the early twentieth century. There, I argue, Irish Americans finally resolved their dilemmas of identity and role by proclaiming themselves militant Catholic Americans and assuming the leadership of a religiously separate, but multiethnic, new Catholic social group. Though Sarbaugh, Towey, and Clark devote less attention to the Church, its importance in the Irish-

American communities they studied is also evident. Particularly worth noting is Martin Towey's discovery that few of the Irish elite in St. Louis were members of exclusively Irish societies, but a large majority publicly advertised their affiliation with non-ethnic, Catholic organizations or associations.

As noteworthy as the importance of the Catholic Church in these Irish-American communities at the turn of the century was the relative insignificance of the labor movement. Labor seemed to play little or no role in fostering community solidarity or defining a comfortable identity among the Irish Americans examined in these essays. Perhaps the labor movement's absence merely reflects the focus of almost all the authors on the upwardly mobile and ambitious members of their communities. Towey's analysis of the St. Louis Irish elite is a good example. Brian Mitchell also contends that the ability of the O'Briens to capture Lowell's Irish middle class and articulate their aims was an important key to their success. Ellen Skerrett suggests that Chicago's Irish Americans who were most interested in achieving some form of respectability were also most susceptible to the Church's influence. Finally in Worcester, it was the American born and upwardly mobile, as represented by the members of the Knights of Columbus, I believe, who took most readily to the Catholic American identity.

Catholicism's importance and labor's relative insignificance in their essays may, however, spring less from the author's neglect of the Irish-American masses than their efforts to detect the emergence of long term patterns in Irish-American history at the turn of the century. Brian Mitchell and I, in fact, both address the role of labor only to dismiss its importance as a focus of identity in the Irish-American communities of Lowell and Worcester. Moreover, apart from Dennis Clark's concentration on the three Philadelphia Ryans and Martin Towey's collective biographical sketch of the St. Louis Irish elite, almost all of these essays penetrate below episcopal or lay elite leadership to examine their communities at a grass roots level. It is not because of a myopic focus on a single class then, but from the identification of the direction of Irish-American history at the turn of the century that the authors of these essays have stressed Catholicism's importance. Working class allegiances and Irish nationalism spoke to the past of an upwardly mobile and increasingly American born Irish people in the late nineteenth and early twentieth centuries. Catholicism succeeded in speaking to their future. As Brian Mitchell, I, and particularly Ellen Skerrett suggest, the Church did so by permitting, even encouraging, Irish-American yearnings for respectability and patriotic devotion to the new land while providing them with a community and basic beliefs anchored in ancient traditions. In Lowell and Worcester Catholicism also offered a definition of identity and community boundaries which seemed to make sense of the Irish Americans' intermediate social and political positions between the new immigrants and native stock Yankees.

This adaptability of Catholicism may seem surprising, in light of the Church's official decrees of rigid doctrinal orthodoxy in the turn of the century era. Martin Halsey and Robert Curran have already suggested, however, that American Catholics managed to evade conflicts between their American aspirations and Church doctrine by either rationalizing their American experience in terms of conservative Catholic philosophy, or by sealing off the religious and secular sides of their lives into separate compartments. Furthermore, the flexibility of religion and its gradual rise as the principal focus of ethnic identity was not unique to Celtic Americans alone. Indeed, Timothy Smith has argued that religion emerged as the primary definition of identity and force for community development among virtually all American ethnic groups, and for essentially the same reasons as its triumph in Irish-American communities. Rather than tying ethnics to a dead past, religion, Smith notes, provided beliefs and devotion which "were powerful impulses to accommodation and innovation; and helped legitimate the behavior, the perceptions and the structures of association that sustained the process of change."[1]

Celebration of this Irish-American marriage of Catholic fidelity and American patriotism may be carried too far, however. The neat formula reconciling Catholicism's sense of community with American aspirations and loyalties had its defects. The rich folk culture of Ireland, for example, was lost forever, drowned in American mass culture, or abandoned in the pursuit of a "bleached out respectability." More important, even in the turn of the century, it became apparent that the formula could be too easily translated into sterile religion and unthinking patriotism. James Farrell was well aware of the spiritual and intellectual poverty of this Irish-American world. Whatever its drawbacks, on a warm June evening in Chicago in 1916, Patrick Lonigan bequeathed this legacy to his son Studs. It was Studs' world now, for good or ill.

NOTE

1. Robert Curran, *The Shaping of Conservative Catholicism, 1878–1902* (New York: Arno Press, 1978); Martin Halsey, *The Survival of American*

Innocence: Catholicism in an Era of Disillusionment, 1920–1940 (Notre Dame, Ind.: University of Notre Dame Press, 1980); Timothy J. Smith, "Religion and Ethnicity in America," *American Historical Review* 83, no. 5 (December 1985):1157.

BiblioGRaphical essay

There is no single body of historical literature focusing on the Irish in turn of the century America. An understanding of Irish Americans in that period must be gleaned, therefore, from a number of works which touch only briefly or tangentially on the Irish-American experience in those years. These include: historical surveys of Irish Americans; studies of Irish communities devoted largely to the Famine immigration period; and general analyses of social mobility, the family, labor, politics and Catholicism. Only examinations of Irish-American nationalism focus directly on Irishmen as Irishmen rather than the various roles they played in turn of the century American society.

Perhaps the best place to start further investigation of the Irish in the turn of the century era is to begin where this collection began: William Shannon's *The American Irish: A Political and Social Portrait* (New York: McMillan Co., 1963). Shannon's book is written in journalistic style as a series of vignettes and short biographies rather than as a general survey. It is nonetheless chock full of useful and provocative interpretations. Shannon's insight is perhaps best illustrated in the chapter, ''The Changing Image,'' on Irish Americans at the turn of the century, which served as the thematic construct for this collection. Though insightful, neither Shannon's work nor any other history of Irish immigration to America can surpass the breadth and depth of Kerby Miller's *Emigrants and Exiles: Ireland and the Irish Exodus to North America* (New York: Oxford University Press, 1985). Though some might quarrel with Miller's suggestion of the passivity of Irish Catholic immigrants, no other author has examined such a broad array of primary and secondary sources, nor synthesized them better. His discussion of Irish American society in the turn of the century era is particularly provocative and enlightening. Other helpful general histories are Lawrence McCaffrey's *The Irish Diaspora in America* (Bloomington, Ind.: Indiana University Press, 1976) and Carl Wittke's encyclopedic if less interpretive *The Irish in America* (Baton Rouge, La.: Louisiana State University Press, 1956).

The easiest access to the monographic and historical articles on the Irish in the turn of the century era is through Seamus Mettress' *The Irish American Experience: A Guide to the Literature* (Washington, D.C.: University Press of America, 1981) and David Doyle's supplement to Mettress, "The Regional Bibliography of Irish America 1880–1930: A Review and Addendum," *Irish Historical Studies* Vol. XXIII, No. I (May 1983). Doyle's article is worth consulting not only for the valuable additions he has made to Mettress' bibliography, but also for his own stimulating analysis of Irish-American historiography.

Both Mettress and Doyle cite a large number of Irish-American community studies, most of them written within the last twenty years. Unfortunately, as noted in the introduction, almost all of them focus on the history of Irish communities before 1880. Nevertheless, some are not only excellent in their own right but provide information and analysis which are helpful to the study of the Irish in the late nineteenth century. They include: Douglas V. Shaw, *The Making of an Immigrant City: Ethnic and Cultural Conflict in Jersey City, 1850–1877* (New York: Arno Press, 1976); Jo Ellen Vinyard, *The Irish on the Urban Frontier: Detroit, 1850–1880* (New York: Arno Press, 1976); R. A. Burchell, *The San Francisco Irish: 1848–1880* (Berkeley, Calif.: University of California Press, 1980). The few studies of Irish-American communities in the turn of the century era are worth noting for, if they are not numerous, they are nonetheless excellent. Victor Walsh's, " 'Across the Big Wather': Irish Community Life in Pittsburgh, 1850–1885" (Ph.D. dissertation: University of Pittsburgh, 1983) is a good example. Perhaps more than any previous historian of Irish America, Walsh has explored differences in the backgrounds of Irishmen fleeing western Ireland from those emigrating from its eastern counties, and the impact those differences had on the American experiences of the two groups of Irishmen. Margaret Connors Harrigan's excellent dissertation on the Irish in Albany, "Their Own Kind: Family and Community Life in Albany, New York, 1850–1915" (Ph.D. dissertation: Harvard University, 1975) is a highly sophisticated study of Irish family and associational life in that city, and Michael Gordon's thesis on the New York Irish, "Studies in Irish and Irish American Thought and Behavior in Gilded Age New York City" (Ph.D. dissertation: University of Rochester, 1977) is an interesting investigation of the links between Irish culture and American working class protest.

Examinations of Irish-American family life, like analyses of Celtic-American communities, have focused largely on the mid nineteenth century Irish-American experience. There are, however, some important studies of various aspects of Irish-American family life in the turn of the century era. Michael Katz's book, *The People of Hamilton West: Family and Class in a Mid Nineteenth*

Century City (Cambridge: Harvard University Press, 1975) offers some interesting speculations on Irish-American marital practices, as does A. Gibbs Mitchell's dissertation on Irish Americans in Lowell, "Irish Family Patterns in Nineteenth Century Ireland and Lowell, Massachusetts" (Ph.D. dissertation: Boston University, 1976). Tamara Hareven and Maris Vinoskis have explored Irish and native stock fertility rates in Boston in "Marital Fertility, Ethnicity, and Occupation in Urban Families: An Analysis of South Boston and the South End in 1880," *Journal of Social History* Vol. 8 (1975) pp. 69–93, and Hareven and Modell have investigated boarding out among Irishmen and Yankees in the same city in John Modell and Tamara Hareven, "Urbanization and the Malleable Household: An Examination of Boarding and Lodging in American Families," *Journal of Marriage and the Family* Vol. 35 (1973) pp. 467–479. The first full study of Irish American women, Hasia Diner's *Erin's Daughters in America: Irish Immigrant Women in the Nineteenth Century* (Baltimore, Md.: Johns Hopkins University Press, 1983) addresses a long neglected area of Irish American history and is provocative and interesting, but Diner's work is disappointing. It relies too heavily on evidence drawn from native stock observers, overemphasizes the Irish-American woman's disdain for marriage, and underestimates her participation in societies and associations.

Irish Americans have figured in the study of American social mobility from its inception. Stefan Thernstrom's *Poverty and Progress* (Cambridge: Harvard University Press, 1964), which launched the study of American social mobility, concentrated largely on the Irish-American workers of that city. In that work and in his more comprehensive book on social mobility in Boston, *The Other Bostonians: Poverty and Progress in an American Metropolis 1860–1970* (Cambridge: Harvard University Press, 1973), Thernstrom found that the Irish made very slow economic progress. He argued that the ultimate cause of that failure could be found in the Catholic culture of Irish Americans. Clyde and Salley Griffen dispute Thernstrom's contention in their richly detailed study of social mobility in Poughkeepsie, *Natives and Newcomers: The Structure of Opportunity in Mid Nineteenth Century Poughkeepsie, New York* (Cambridge: Harvard University Press, 1976). They attribute the slow pace of the Irish upward climb to the poverty of skills Irishmen inherited from the backward Irish economy. More recently James Henretta's "The Study of Social Mobility: Ideological Assumptions and Conceptual Bias," *Labor History* Vol. 18 (Spring 1977) pp. 165–178, has questioned the value of occupational mobility studies. In particular, he has noted the necessity of measuring success or failure from the perspective of the historical subjects themselves, not by arbitrary standards set by contemporary historians. Both Jay Dolan's *Catholic Revivalism: The American Experience* (Notre Dame, Ind.: University of Notre Dame Press, 1978), and Paul Messbarger's *Fiction with a Parochial Purpose: Social Uses of American Catholic Literature 1884–1900* (Boston: Boston University Press, 1971) offer brief but interesting insights into late nineteenth century Catholic views on social mobility.

The recent books and articles produced by the new labor historians analyze the Irish-American encounter with the industrial economy from a different perspective. These historians are interested in the formation of working class culture and the organization of working class protest. Aside from David Montgomery in his brief essay in David Doyle and James Walsh's collection, almost none of these authors focus exclusively on Irish-American workers. Historians who concentrate on late nineteenth or early twentieth century American labor history, however, can hardly avoid devoting at least some attention to workers of Irish descent. The best of these studies, in terms of their analysis of the Irish-American working class, are: Daniel Walkowitz, *Worker City, Company Town: Iron and Cotton Worker Protest in Troy and Cohoes, New York 1855–1884* (Urbana, Ill.: University of Illinois Press, 1981), Leon Fink, *Workingmen's Democracy: The Knights of Labor and American Politics* (Urbana, Ill.: University of Illinois Press, 1983), and Roy Rosenzweig, *Eight Hours for What We Will: Workers and Leisure in an Industrial City, 1870–1920* (New York: Cambridge University Press, 1983). Walkowitz details the rise and fall of labor protest by the largely Irish iron molders in Troy, New York, and the ethnically diverse cotton workers of nearby Cohoes, New York. He notes how the emergence of an Irish-American middle class and the diversion of Irish energy into the politics of ethnic recognition helped undercut that protest. Leon Fink's analysis of Knights of Labor political movements in the 1880s reveals the intermixture of Irish and working class culture and political interests. Roy Rosenzweig's examination of workers in Worcester, Massachusetts, investigates the working class leisure culture created by Irish Americans and other Worcester workers as an alternative to the recreational patterns and norms which Yankee industrialists tried to impose on them.

Irish Americans in the turn of the century era have figured perhaps even more prominently in historical literature on American partisan and urban politics than in discussions of working class culture and protest. Histories from the ethnocultural school of voting analysis, such as Paul Kleppner's *Cross of Culture: A Social Analysis of Midwestern Politics, 1850–1900* (New York: 1970), for example, treat the Irish as the paradigmatic Democrats of the late nineteenth century. Until recently they also appeared as the archetypal bosses in the boss-reformer dichotomy which characterized most writing on turn of the century, American urban politics. John Buenker, *Urban Liberalism and Progressive Reform* (New York: Charles Scribners and Sons, 1973), and others have demonstrated that the bosses or their representatives were often strong supporters of reform. Other recent studies of urban politics in the late nineteenth or early twentieth century suggest the need for a thorough reexamination of Irish-American political participation, both in terms of their voting behavior—Martin Shefter, "The Electoral Foundations of the Political Machine: New York City, 1884–1897," in Joel Sibley, Alan G. Bogue, and William Flanigan, eds., *The History of American Political Behavior* (Princeton, N.J.: Princeton University Press, 1978) pp. 263–298, Paul Kleppner in Ronald Formisano and Constance Burns, eds., *Boston 1700–1980: The Evolution of Urban Politics* (Westport, Conn.: Greenwood, 1984)—and the roles their leaders played in urban factionalism—David C. Hammack, *Power and Society: Greater New York at the Turn of the Century* (New York: Russell Sage Foundation, 1982) and Geoffrey Blodgett, "Yankee Leadership in a Divided City," in Formisano and Burns, *Boston 1700–1980*.

Perhaps in no arena, not even in urban politics, were the Irish more successful than in the Catholic Church. Biographies of Irish American bishops abound, but perhaps two of the most noteworthy among the recent ones are Robert Curran, *Michael Augustine Corrigan and the Shaping of Conservative Catholicism in America, 1878–1902* (New York: Arno Press, 1978) and James P. Gaffey, *Citizen of No Mean City: Archbishop Patrick Riordan of San Francisco, 1841–1914* (Wilmington, N.C.: Consortium, 1976). Curran's book is especially interesting for its exhaustively detailed analysis of the controversies over Liberal Catholicism at the episcopal level in the 1880s and 1890s. One of the best studies of Irish Americans in the hierarchy, however, especially in the bishops' relations with non-Irish ethnics, is Charles Shannabruch's *Chicago's Catholics: The Evolution of an American Identity* (Notre Dame, Inc.: University of Notre Dame Press, 1981). Mixing social and political history with examination of the policies of Chicago's Irish prelates, Shannabruch recounts the emergence of an American Catholic identity among Chicago's various Catholic nationalities. His book complements well many of the essays in this collection, most notably my own, Ellen Skerrett's, and Brian Mitchell's. Unfortunately the fixation of American Catholic historians on the hierarchy or Rome has meant that the priests and laymen of the Church have been seriously neglected. John Tracy Ellis' collection, *The Catholic Priest in the United States: Historical Investigations* (Collegeville, Minn.: St. John's University Press, 1971), especially Michael V. Gannon's essay, is well worth examination. Lay Catholics, when examined at all, have been studied largely through histories of Catholic societies and fraternal associations. Chronicles of the Irish Catholic Benevolent Union by J. M. Donohoe, *The Irish Catholic Benevolent Union: 1869–1893* (Washington, D.C.: Catholic University Press, 1953) and of the Catholic Total Abstinence Union by Sister Joan Bland, *Hibernian Crusade, The Story of the Catholic Abstinence Union of America* (Washington, D.C.: Catholic University Press, 1951), both done more than thirty years ago, are solidly researched and helpful, if lacking in interpretive analysis. On the other hand, Christopher

Kauffman's recent history of the Knights of Columbus, *Faith and Fraternalism: The History of the Knights of Columbus, 1882–1982* (New York: Scribners, 1982), is both meaty and insightful.

No aspect of Irish-American history at the turn of the century, not even their roles in the Church and politics, seems to have roused more scholarly interest than Irish-American nationalism. Nevertheless, there are still some significant gaps in the historical literature on Celtic-American nationalism. The best work has been done on the Irish-American nationalist crusade of the 1880s. Thomas Brown's classic interpretive monograph, *Irish American Nationalism, 1870–1890* (Philadelphia: J. B. Lippincott, 1966) and Eric Foner's excellent article, "Class, Ethnicity and Radicalism in the Gilded Age: The Land League and Irish America," *Marxist Perspectives* Vol. I No. 2 (Summer 1978) pp. 6–55, remain the best analyses of the Irish-American response to the Land League crisis and Parnell's Home Rule agitation. Michael Funchion's book, *Chicago's Irish Nationalists* (New York: Arno Press, 1976) and Victor Walsh's essay, "A Fanatic Heart: The Cause of Irish American Nationalism in Pittsburgh during the Gilded Age," *Journal of Social History* Vol. 15 (Winter 1981) pp. 187–203, however, are excellent analyses of Irish-American nationalism in local settings. The literature on Irish-American nationalism during and after World War I is more extensive. The best of these works are Alan Ward's *Ireland and Anglo American Relations 1899–1921* (Toronto: University of Toronto, 1969) and Patrick J. Buckley's *The New York Irish: Their View of American Foreign Policy, 1914–1921* (New York: Arno Press, 1976). On the whole, the literature focusing on the later period in nationalist history lacks the interpretive insight of the studies done on Irish-American efforts to free the homeland in the 1880s. Particularly disappointing is their failure to link the evolution of the nationalist movement to broader social and political trends in Irish-American life in the same way that Brown and Foner did for the earlier period. Perhaps an even more significant deficiency in the historiography of turn of the century Irish-American nationalism is the lack of virtually any significant examination of Irish-American nationalist sentiment in the 1890s and the early 1900s. Only parts of books such as the first chapter of Ward's *Ireland and Anglo-American Relations* provide much information on this period.

index

Act of Union, 104, 126
American Association for the Recognition of the Irish Republic (AARIR), 169, 170
American Catholic identity, 2, 14, 83, 86, 87, 101, 120, 123, 131, 136-137, 155-156, 185-187
American Federation of Labor (AF of L), 15, 63. *See also* Unions; Working class solidarity
American Protective Association, 62, 81, 85, 142-143, 166
Ancient Order of Hibernians, 86, 103, 122, 130, 154-157, 167, 171
Anglicization, 47
Anti-Catholic Nativism, 5, 6, 14, 55, 65, 85, 117, 120, 165, 166. *See also* American Protective Association; Know Nothings
Asian-Americans, 164, 165

"Big Cinch," 152
Blacks, 2, 135, 140, 142, 144
Boston, 4-6, 17, 140, 145, 153, 157, 161-163, 182
Boston Associates, 53, 54
Bridge Street (Lowell, Massachusetts), 65-67

Brown, Thomas N., 11, 127, 170
Burchell, R. A., 167
Butt, Issac, 37-38, 40

Catholic Church, 14, 16, 183, 185-187; in Chicago, 117-118, 120-124, 136; in Ireland, 32-33, 39, 45-47; in Lowell, 59, 64-68; in Philadelphia, 97-99; in San Francisco, 161, 165-167, 171, 174; in Worcester, 86-88. *See also* American Catholic identity; Catholic identity; Catholic schools; Parishes
Catholic Ghetto, 14, 86-88
Catholic identity, 14, 28, 83, 87-88, 117-120, 134, 136-137, 154-157, 166-167, 174, 183, 185-187
Catholic Liberalism, 14, 18, 84-85, 166
Catholic Schools, 65, 87, 98-99, 118, 130-134
Chicago, 1, 2, 17, 19, 57, 104, 184-186; Catholic church in, 117-118, 120-124, 136; Catholic identity in, 119-120; Irish politics in, 124-126; nationalism in, 126-128; residential mobility in,

Chicago (*continued*)
134-137; social mobility in,
118-119, 133
Chicago Fire, 118, 131
Chicago Normal, 131, 132
Chicago *Tribune,* 117, 125-126, 129
Chinese, 142, 164
Christian Brothers, 130-131
Civil War in America, 4, 55, 84,
94, 144, 151
Clan Na Gael, 86, 103-105, 109,
115 n.27, 122, 127, 129, 167,
184. *See also* Nationalism
Clare, County of, 27, 28
Clark, Dennis, 64, 184, 186
Cohalan, Daniel, 108
Cohan, George M., 10, 12
"Combine," 152
Community and communal values:
in Chicago, 121-122, 124; in
Ireland, 35; in Lowell, 56; in
Philadelphia, 93, 96
Community studies, 3, 4
Construction work, 54, 77, 94, 95,
125
Contractors, 1, 94, 95, 125
Corrigan, Michael, 14, 18, 19, 98
Cronin, Patrick, 128, 129, 136
Cullerton, Edward "Foxy," 124,
126, 133
Curran, Robert E., 187

Davitt, Michael, 11, 34, 40, 41,
102, 127
De La Salle Institute, 130-132
Democratic party, 7, 16-17, 55, 62,
84-85, 106, 124-125, 127, 136,
151-152. *See also* Irish in Amer-
ica, in politics
Depression of 1893, 63, 85
De Valera, Eamon, 169-170
Devoy, John, 39, 103, 104, 108

Dillon, John, 102-103
Doheny, Edward, 169, 172
Donovan, John J., 61, 62
Dorney, Maurice, 128, 131
Doyle, David N., 5, 8-9, 113
Dublin, Ireland, 42, 47
Duggan, James, 120, 126
Dunne, Edward, 108, 125, 128
"Dynamite Campaign," 127, 128

"Easter Rebellion." *See* Irish Rebellion of 1916
Englewood in Chicago, 130-131

Famine, the Great Irish, 3, 29, 40,
94, 117
Famine Migration, 6, 54, 64, 117,
141-142, 182
Farrell, James T., 134, 187
Fenian Brotherhood, 99, 122,
126-127, 167
Foner, Eric, 11, 12, 115 n.36
Ford, Patrick, 12, 39
French: compared to the Irish in
Ireland, 42; in St. Louis, 140,
142
French Canadians, 17, 19, 183; in
Lowell, 55-57, 59, 62-63, 66, 71
n.43; in Worcester, 76, 80-81,
86-87, 183
Friends of Irish Freedom (FOIF),
167-168
Funchion, Michael 127, 133

Gaelic Athletic Association (GAA),
86, 168
Gaelic League, 47-48, 86, 167-168,
184
Geographical variations in Irish
American experience, 5-6, 9, 16,
18, 181-183; Chicago, 119;
Lowell, 59; St. Louis, 140, 157;

San Francisco, 161-164, 173-174. *See also* Boston

George, Henry, 12, 15

Germans, 9, 18-19, 164; in Chicago, 121, 123, 124, 126, 129, 130; in Philadelphia, 98; in St. Louis, 139, 141-142, 144-147, 151, 153-157; in San Francisco, 164

Gibbons, James, 14, 18-19, 98, 167

Gladstone, William E., 38, 41, 45, 101

Glazer, Nathan, 2, 4

Greeks: in Lowell, 56, 60, 63

"Hamline controversy," 125, 126

Handlin, Oscar, 4, 140

Hanna, Edward J., 165, 171

Harrigan, Edward and Anthony Hart, 5, 10

Haymarket Square riot, 128, 129

Hibernian Society, 66, 68

Holy Family parish (Chicago), 121-122, 125-126

Home Rule movement: in Chicago, 126-127; in Ireland, 38, 40-41, 44; in Lowell, 59; in Philadelphia, 101-106; in St. Louis, 153; in San Francisco, 168; in Worcester, 84

Horowitz, Donald, 5

Hyde, Douglas, 47, 168

Identity, Irish group definitions of, 2, 5, 184-187; in Chicago, 119, 121, 123, 129-130, 134; in Ireland, 28, 33, 43; in Worcester, 83-88. *See also* American Catholic identity; Catholic identity

Ireland, 2-3, 7, 10-13, 15, 59, 77, 82, 88, 102-113, 124, 126-128, 135, 168-173; Catholic Church in, 32, 33, 39, 45-47; community in, 34-36; Gaelic League in, 47-48; Home Rule in, 38-42, 44; Irish Republican Brotherhood in, 38-39; Land League in, 37, 38-42; land system in, 29-37; landless laborers in, 29-32, 35; marriage and family in, 30-34; middle class in, 37, 42-48; Parnell, Charles Stuart and, 27, 39, 41, 44-45; Parnell, the fall of, 44-46, 49; Pearse, Patrick and, 48-49; Sinn Fein in, 47; "Strong" farmer, 30-32; women in, 36-37

Ireland, John, 14, 18-19, 126, 166

"Irish Crowd," 141, 145

Irish in America: and Catholic Church, 14, 16, 59, 64-68, 86-88, 97-99, 117-118, 120-124, 136; and other ethnic groups, 7, 16-18, 55-56, 61-63, 97, 141-145, 176 n.10; and nationalism in Ireland, 3, 11, 12, 38, 59, 84, 86, 88, 99-112, 126-130, 153-155, 167-173; in politics, 3, 15, 17, 55, 61-62, 84-85, 95, 106, 124-126, 136, 150-153, 162; social mobility, 2-3, 8-10, 60, 77, 79-80, 96, 118-119, 133, 145-147, 162-163, 171, 183; women, 36, 54, 60, 147

Irish National League, 101, 102, 111, 127, 138

Irish Parliamentary Party, 37, 41-42, 45-47, 50, 99, 103-106, 128, 154

Irish Rebellion of 1916, 3, 12, 29, 49, 105-106, 160

Irish Republican Brotherhood (IRB), 37-40, 46, 49-50, 127

Irish Republican nationalism, 161, 167, 171

Italians, 2, 19, 77, 86-87, 97-98, 164

Jesuits, 121, 130
Jews, 9, 60, 71 n.43, 98
Joyce, James, 27, 45

Knights of Columbus, 13-14, 185;
   in St. Louis, 154, 156-157; in
   Worcester, 87
Knights of Father Mathew, 154,
   156, 157
Knights of Labor, 15, 128
Know Nothings, 55, 65, 70 n.14,
   142-143

Land League: in Chicago, 125; in
   Ireland, 37, 39-40, 42, 50; in
   Philadelphia, 99, 101, 111; in San
   Francisco, 167; in Worcester, 84.
   See also Nationalism
Leader (San Francisco), 167,
   169-170
Leadership, 93, 110, 112
Light, Dale, 94, 102
Lithuanians, 4, 12, 19, 77, 86, 87,
   97
Lonigan, Patrick, 1-2, 134, 187
Lonigan, William "Studs," 1, 134,
   187
Lowell, Massachusetts, 183-186;
   Catholic Church in, 59, 64-68;
   Irish politics in, 55, 61-62; na-
   tionalism in, 59; residential mobil-
   ity, 57-58; social mobility, 59-61;
   working class solidarity, 63-64,
   68

McCaffrey, Lawrence, 5
McGarritty, Joseph, 105, 106, 108
Machine politics, 7, 68, 124, 127,
   163, 174
McQuaid, Bernard, 14, 18, 19
Maguire, John F., 163, 165
Marriage and family patterns, 10,
   30, 33, 83

Mayo, County of, 39, 40
Merrimack River, 56, 66
Messenger (Worcester), 82, 87, 88
Middle class Irish: in America, 8, 9,
   11, 14, 184; in Chicago, 118,
   131-135; in Ireland, 37, 42-48,
   184; in Lowell, 55, 60-62, 67-68;
   in Philadelphia, 97, 101, 104; in
   St. Louis, 145-147, 156-157. See
   also Respectability
Miller, Kerby, 13
Mitchell, Brian, 183, 186
Monitor (San Francisco), 166,
   169-170, 172
Moynihan, Daniel P., 2, 4
Mundelein, George, 120, 132

Nationalism, 3, 11, 12, 183; in Chi-
   cago, 126-128; in Ireland, 38; in
   Lowell, 59; in Philadelphia,
   99-112; in St. Louis, 153-155; in
   San Francisco, 165, 167-173; in
   Worcester, 84, 86, 88. See also
   Clan Na Gael; Home Rule; Irish
   Republican Brotherhood; Land
   League; Parnell; Postwar
   nationalism
New England, 5, 17, 119, 183
"New Immigrants," 3, 9, 17, 18
New York City, 9, 16, 17, 162,
   163, 172
Noonan, Edward A., 152, 156

O'Brien, John, 64, 65
O'Brien, Timothy, 64-65, 67
O'Brien, William, 102-103
O'Brien, William P., 66-67
"O'Brien Dynasty," 64, 65, 67,
   185
Occupational Status, 7, 8; in Chi-
   cago, 118-119, 131, 133; in
   Ireland, 43; in Lowell, 54, 55,
   60; in Philadelphia, 96; in St.

Louis, 141, 145-147; in San Francisco, 162, 171; in Worcester, 79-80. *See also* Social Mobility; Middle class

O'Connell, Daniel, 38, 97, 120

O'Connor, John F., 79-81

Onahan, William J., 117, 125

O'Neill, Kevin, 183-184

Oratory, 97, 99, 109, 111

O'Shea, William, 44, 102, 130

Overstoltz, Henry, 151-152

Parishes: in Chicago, 118, 121-123, 130, 134-137, 137 n.3, 137 n.6; in Lowell, 54, 63-68; in Philadelphia, 98; in Worcester, 87

Parnell, Charles Stuart, 27, 39, 41, 44-45, 84, 85, 98, 101, 102, 128-130, 184. *See also* Home Rule; Nationalism

Parnell, the fall of, 44-46, 49, 102, 130, 136, 184

Pearse, Patrick, 48-49, 105, 170, 184

Peasant proprietorship, 39, 41

Phelan, James, 162, 172-173

Philadelphia, 16, 162, 163, 184, 186; Catholic church in, 97-99; contractors, 94-95; nationalism in, 99-112

Poles, 2, 3, 19, 56, 60, 66, 77, 80, 87, 97, 121, 126, 130

Postwar Irish American nationalism, 12, 88, 107-110, 168-171

Powers, John "Johnny," 124-125, 133

Redmond, John, 103-106, 111, 154

Republican party, 62, 82, 84-85, 124, 144, 136, 151-152

Residential mobility, 57-58, 81, 119, 134-137, 147, 150

Respectability, the Irish search for, 11, 184; in Chicago, 126, 128-129, 136; in Ireland, 44, 46; in Lowell, 65, 68, 70 n.13; in Philadelphia, 101, 104; in San Francisco, 170, 174. *See also* Middle class Irish

Riordan, Patrick, 165-167

Ryan, James J., 94-96, 112

Ryan, John P., 97-98, 112

Ryan, Michael J., 99-113

St. Elizabeth's parish (Chicago), 122

St. Elizabeth's School (Chicago), 131-132

St. James' School (Chicago), 131-132

St. Louis, 97, 105, 181-182, 186; Catholic identity in, 154-157; Irish politics in, 150-153; nationalism in, 153-155; residential mobility, 147, 150; social acceptance, 153-156; social mobility, 145-147, 148-149

St. Michael's parish (Lowell), 65-67

St. Patrick's Day, 83, 155

St. Patrick's parish (Lowell), 54, 57, 64-66

St. Vincent de Paul Society, 124, 141

San Francisco, 5, 105, 140, 145, 153, 157, 181-185; Catholic church in, 161, 165-167, 171, 174; Irish politics in, 162-163; nationalism in, 165, 167-173; social mobility, 162-164, 171

Sarbaugh, Timothy, 181-182, 184, 185

Scott, Joseph, 169, 172-173

Shannon, William, 2-3, 6-7, 9, 19, 58-59, 79, 93, 161

Sinn Fein, 47, 111, 153, 154, 168, 184

Sisters of Mercy, 130, 131
Skerret, Ellen, 185, 186
Skilled Blue Collar workers, 61, 72
 n.48, 76, 80, 94, 133, 145
Smith, Timothy, 187
Social Mobility, 2-3, 8-10, 183; in
 Chicago, 118-119, 130-133; in
 Lowell, 60; in Philadelphia, 94,
 96; in St. Louis, 145-147; in San
 Francisco, 162, 171; in Worces-
 ter, 77, 79-80
Sullivan, Alexander, 127, 131
Survivance, 56, 63
Swedes, 76, 79-80, 123

Temperance, 9, 84, 118, 125, 154,
 156
Tenant Farmer, 29, 34, 128
Textiles, 53-54, 59-61, 76, 93
Towey, Martin, 181-182, 185-186

Ulster, 75, 105, 109
Unions, 15, 63-64, 72 n.57, 97,
 128-129, 176 n.9, 186
United Irish League, 99, 103-106,
 111

Vatican, 14, 85
Versailles Peace Conference, 108,
 109, 171

Walsh, James, 5, 9, 140, 164-165
Walsh, Julius, 152, 156
Washington Park, 134-136
Whig party, 55, 151
White Anglo Saxon Protestants, or
 "Yankees," 16-18, 182-183; in
 Chicago, 123; in Lowell, 54, 56,
 60, 67, 70 n.70; in St. Louis,
 140, 142-143, 145, 151; in San
 Francisco, 164, 176 n.10; in
 Worcester, 75-76, 78-79, 82-84
White Collar worker, 61, 79-81, 94,
 132-133, 146-147, 162
Wilson, Woodrow, 12, 108-109
Worcester, Massachusetts, 183-184,
 186; Catholic Church in, 86-88;
 Catholic Liberalism in, 84-85;
 Irish politics in, 84-85; na-
 tionalism in, 84, 86, 88; residen-
 tial mobility, 81; social mobility,
 77, 79-80
Working class consciousness or solidarity, 8, 12-15, 186; in Chicago,
 118, 128-129; in Lowell, 63, 68;
 in Philadelphia, 98; in Worcester,
 85
World War I, 2, 12, 29, 88,
 104-105, 108, 168

Yeats, W. B., 27, 46
Yorke, Peter Christopher, 166-170,
 173
Young, Ella F., 132

aвоυt the contributors

DENNIS J. CLARK is executive director of the Samuel A. Fels Fund in Philadelphia. He has written extensively on the Irish in America, including *The Irish in Philadelphia: Ten Generations of Urban Experience, The Irish Relations: Trials of an Immigrant Tradition,* and a host of articles and essays.

TIMOTHY J. MEAGHER is Assistant Archivist at the Archives of the Archdiocese of Boston. He formerly taught at Worcester Polytechnic Institute in Worcester, Massachusetts. His articles on Irish Americans have appeared in *The New England Quarterly* and *The Journal of Social History.*

BRIAN C. MITCHELL is a program officer at the National Endowment for the Humanities. He has written a number of articles on the Irish in Lowell and on Lowell history. His book, *The Paddy Camps: The Meaning of Community among the Irish of Lowell, Massachusetts, 1821– 1861* will appear in 1986.

KEVIN O'NEILL is an Associate Professor of History at Boston College and co-director of the college's Irish Studies Program. He has recently published a book, *Family and Farm in Pre Famine Ireland: The Parish of Killishandra,* on demographic and economic change in early nineteenth century Ireland.

TIMOTHY SARBAUGH is a doctoral candidate in history at Loyola University of Chicago. His articles on Irish-American nationalism have appeared in *California History* and *The Pacific Historian.*

ELLEN SKERRETT has served as the research coordinator of a two-volume history of Chicago's Catholic parishes, Harry C. Koenig, ed., *History of the Parishes of the Archdiocese of Chicago.* She has written articles and essays for *Chicago History,* among other journals. Her essay "The Catholic Dimension" will appear in Lawrence McCaffrey, ed., *The Chicago Irish* in 1986, as will her book with Dominic A. Pazga, *Chicago: City of Neighborhoods.*

MARTIN G. TOWEY is Professor of History and Director of Archives and Oral History Center at Saint Louis University. He formerly served on the faculty of the University of Missouri. His principal research interests involve the social, cultural, and intellectual history of the Midwest, with emphasis on the St. Louis region. He has written numerous articles on these areas. He is author of *Historic Architecture of Gasconade County, Missouri* and *Democracy in Art: The W.P.A. People's Art Center in St. Louis.*